SERFS UP;

FINANCE, FEUDALISM & FASCISM:

*Ruminations on the Political Economy of Our Time
while there is Still Time*

Gregory A Daneke

PREFACE

The America political economy is deeply dysfunctional. In particular, its globally networked Money & Banking systems, once pivotal to our prosperity, have become wildly and willfully parasitic. Capping a half-century of radical transformation (corresponding to the mere span of my adult life) our political and financial institutions evolved into a ponderous Ponzi (pyramid) scheme. It requires greater debt merely to service the interest on past debts. Once the greatest creditor nation, we swiftly transformed ourselves to the greatest debtor. We also dismantled and shipped offshore the lion share of the greatest industrial base the world has ever known. Meanwhile middle class wages stagnated while the incomes of the top 5% skyrocketed, as rent-seeking sought to replace growth delimited by resource and environmental constraints. This curious political economy was the result institutional evolution specifically designed to pander to depredation. A once "inclusive" economy became an "extractive" one, on par with any other benighted "banana republic". While often precipitated by the unpredictable perils of empire, much of this transformation proceeded from a conscious policy agenda shaped by a small cult of economists, media moguls, and ultra-rich ideologues that insinuated themselves into the global financial elite. This ideological agenda may not be the prime source for all our difficulties, yet the destructive power of these ideas has been immense. The programs and policies they promoted have contributed significantly to the displacement of democratic capitalism with fascistic feudalism.

The growth of this cancerous political economy, while widespread, can be confronted and contained. Revitalization and extension of constitutional safeguards are the first steps, but ultimately radically enhanced institutions must be introduced derived from increased socioecological understanding such as those emerging from research into the evolution complex adaptive systems. Failure to confront these predators intellectually as well as politically will only intensify catastrophic financial and resource collapse. These observations may appear strident and opinionated to say the least. Yet, they reluctantly arrived after a career spent in leading research universities, punctuated by episodes of significant public service and corporate consulting. Moreover, they were refined via numerous discussions with a wide range of experts in the fields of banking, finance, and government.

Many mentors, colleagues and friends have influenced my thinking over the years but more than a few might not support my conclusions. Thus, I recognize them, yet absolve them all of any responsibility. They are: Paul Adler, Kenneth Arrow, Brian Arthur, Elizabeth Brake, Donald Campbell, Heather Campbell, Deborah Daneke, Wilda Dick, Kevin Dooley, Edwin Epstein, Nicholas Georgescu-Roegen, Edward (Ned) Gramlich, Evelyn Grant, Adam Holbrook, John Holland, Erich Jantsch, Steve Light, James March, Walter Mead, Mancur Olson, Elinor (Lin) Ostrom, Melinda Rhoades, Alexander Sager, Frederick Thompson, Ilan Vertinsky, and Aaron Wildavsky.

CHAPTER 1: THE GREAT DISPOSESSION

Money, money changes everything. We think we know what we're doin. That don't mean a thing. It's all in past now. Money changes everything. _____ **Cyndi Lauper**

[The behavior of the rentier state] embodies a break in the work-reward causation ... rewards of income and wealth for the rentier do not come as the result of work but rather are the result of chance or situation. _____ **Douglas Yates**

Those who build walls are their own prisoners. I'm going to go fulfill my proper function in the social organism. I'm going to go unbuild walls. _____ **Shevek (Ursula Le Guin)**

Every gun that is made, every warship launched, every rocket fired signifies, in the final sense, a theft from those who hunger and are not fed, those who cold and are not clothed. This world of arms is not spending money alone. It is spending the sweat of its laborers, the genius of its scientists, and the hopes of its children.
_____ **Dwight Eisenhower**

[B]usiness and financial monopoly, speculation, reckless banking, class antagonism, sectionalism, war profiteering. They had begun to consider the government of the United States as a mere appendage to their own affairs. And we know now that Government by organized money is just as dangerous as Government by organized mob. _____ **Eleanor Roosevelt**

Whenever I taught a course in Business & Society (especially to engineers), I would start them off with the wonderful science fiction book by the late, great, Ursula Le Guin, The Dispossessed: An Ambiguous Utopia (1974). This brilliant social commentary, disguised as science fiction, was a handy device for stimulating discussion of basic societal organization without the distortion of familiar national references. It tells the story of Shevek, a brilliant young physicist raised on an anarchist planet run by voluntary syndicates (Anarres), who journeys to an Earth-like planet (Urras). His path-breaking work has exhausted the meager scientific resources of his hard-squabble planet, so he accepts an invitation from scientists on Urras to pursue his "General Temporal Theory" (like relativity). His theorizing is of little practical utility on tiny Anarres. While technically free to work on it as he wishes, he struggles with the social pressures to contribute to his society, as well as his forbidden desire for individual recognition.

Urras has several nations, with bi-polar empires, one authoritarian and communist (Thu) the other vaguely democratic and capitalist, yet with extreme social divisions and undercurrents of authoritarianism (A-Io). A-Io has a hierarchical and patriarchal society, reminiscent of Edwardian England (e.g., Downton Abbey). One of his new colleagues (who hold high status and have beautiful trophy wives) confides that his father was a butler, but there is little additional evidence of social mobility. Shevek's ancestors were once citizens of A-Io, but were driven into exile, led by their sainted female leader, Odo. They flee to a nearly barren rock of a planet. Odo and the other founders invent a new language for Anarres with NO personal pronouns, as well as organize a society where all forms of possession, including coupling, are discouraged. Gender equality is complete, and children are raised in common.

While they have a tiny amount of trade with their former homeland, Shevek is the first human cargo. Unbeknownst to the guileless Shevek, he was brought to Urras because his ideas might have military applications. Tall and woolly he is like a sasquatch on Urras (where even the women shave their heads), and his fumbling and bumbling adventures range from a sexual misunderstanding to near assassination (when his speech to a dissident gathering is broken-up by the militarized police). Among other things, he concludes that despite their market economy (e.g., three competing mail services) his hosts are possessed by their possessions. In his intense disgust for Urras, he loses sight of the ambiguities back on Anarres. For example, how his science syndicate conspired to both stifle and then steal credit for his work, or how his playwright friend is destroyed for his critical dramatizations.

My students would have lively discussions about the limits of both cooperation and competition, and which planet they would prefer and why. Despite admiring the "mutual aid" and equality of Anarres, they were routinely put off by the austere conditions. The vast majority choose Urras because it is lush, green and abundant. It seldom occurred to them that realistically many, if not most, of them would be domestic servants on Urras. They merely assumed that they would be among the tiny elite despite the limited upward mobility. Delusions of grandeur are particularly common among business students, and it is not always a bad thing. A few of my female students chose Anarres, where women were completely equal to the men, but most either ignored the facts (like their male counterparts) or latched onto the Fascinating Womanhood (Andelin, 1963) style speech of one of the trophy wives that explained how they use their womanly wiles to clandestinely control their husbands.

I retired from teaching just before such discussions would be discouraged in many US classrooms, and/or require multiple "trigger-warnings". Professors are now expected to issue warnings when some portions of their classroom discussion might upset increasing fragile student sensibilities. Students are invited to simply get up and walk out. Rather than accept the increased work of providing alternative learning experiences many professors just engage in self-censorship to the level over kill. In sum the post-modern university is seldom a place where young minds are directly confronted with unsettling facts, ideas, and learned opinions. In my informed opinion, this violates a core element of a university's reason-for-being, but then I am probably a relic of a bygone era. I have to admit that the new peer-to-peer and collaborative learning are an improvement upon my simple Socratic methods; nonetheless, I worry a great deal about the emerging content restrictions.

DISPOSSESSION BY ACCUMULATION

Despite declining classroom confrontations, college students are becoming painfully aware of their economic alienation when on average they graduate 45,000 dollars in debt (with many much higher), which cannot be reduced in bankruptcy. I could not get a credit card until I was 25 and had completed my Ph.D., and now banks hand them out like candy to 17 and 18 year olds on freshman orientation day. College debts are especially burdensome for those who cannot find employment in their fields of study. My discussions with "Occupy" members in various cities suggest that they have a number of uncommon insights into their new serfdom. But much like medicine only a century ago, they have great diagnostics, but very few treatments. Wall Street has at least given them a rallying point for their resistance (albeit futile thus far).

When I attended the University of California, it was still virtually tuition-free, until Governor Ronald Reagan gradually increased certain "fees". It is noteworthy that elites had lobbied vociferously against the opening up higher education to the uppity unwashed masses in the era just before I was born. Many had even fought against educational opportunities (beyond trade schools) being extended to returning WWII vets via the "GI Bill of Rights". But much of academia found that the lower classes enhanced their environments, and when I was ready for college, the door was wide open. Monstrous tuition increases have now priced so many from my socioeconomic status out of a college education altogether, or offer the prospect of paying off debts for many years to come. The lack of affordable higher education is merely a small portion of the Great Dispossession, where gradually other basic rights are reserved for the privileged few.

Essentially, we have now turned our full array of imperial exploitation, which Distinguished CUNY Geographer, David Harvey (2003) characterized as "dispossession by accumulation", in upon ourselves. The modern pattern of unproductive accumulation harkens back to "primitive accumulation" (see, Glassman, 2006), where, through conquest and coercion, kings and emperors displaced community ownership and parceled these lands and their inhabitants (serfs) onto various lesser lords to secure their vassalage. Serfdom was not officially abolished in some parts of Europe until the middle of the 19th century, and serfs and peasant farmers routinely suffered devastating famines into the early 20th century. In our time unproductive accumulation manifests itself through a number of destructive instrumentalities that find their origins in the systems of Money & Banking. The hallmark of our present epoch of neofeudal dispossession is hyper-financialization, yet it is not mutually exclusive from other devices such as crisis creation, expropriation, labor exploitation, environmental degradation, and militarization, as well as continued "neoliberal colonization"(e.g., privatization and resource capture).

Neoliberalism (see, Read, 2009) is such a very confusing concept, particularly since it has little to do with contemporary liberalism and its practice does not match its theory nor its theory match historical formulations. Rajesh Venugopal (2015), International Development Professor at the London School of Economics is so critical of its ubiquity that he contends it has lost nearly all of its meaning. While I do not share his condemnation of most neoliberalism studies, I have chosen the term

NEOFEUDALISM. I realize it is more polemical, but I believe it more accurately depicts the character and consequences of this ideological movement. Its new landed gentry are corporate CEOs, who on average earn 400 times the average wage in their firms (up from 20 times in the 1960s), bankers, and hedge fund managers. The top 25 hedge fund managers earned on average nearly a billion dollars apiece in recent years. That is billion with a B. This means that these hedgehogs receive about as much as all of the civil engineers, or two and half times as much as all the kindergarten teachers in America. These new Robber Barons join the ultra-rich & infamous and their offspring as well as new tech monopolists in a mega rentier society.

THE RENTIER SOCIETY

Perhaps it will be useful for me to clarify what I mean by rent and rent-seeking at this early juncture. Generally speaking, RENT is an increase in wealth without reciprocal societal benefits. Classical economists (e.g., Smith, Ricardo, Mill, etc.) viewed rent as a major problem. For them, it was mostly "unearned" and largely unproductive, as well as the result of inheritance and/or crude accumulation. Many modern mainstream economists maintain that there NO such thing as unearned wealth, ergo no rents nor rentiers. Even contrived monopoly rents are often explained away as "natural". As the grand wizard of Chicago School economists, Milton Freeman asserted, "there is no such thing as a free lunch". But he was mistaken. Oligarchic rentiers are eating the lunch of the masses every day, and NOT just in the "transition economies". Peter Mihalyi and Ivan Szelényi (2017) maintain that rent-seeking is still a humongous problem for all the economies, and that understanding of rentier behavior is extremely useful in unraveling "the mechanisms of corruption". Plus they point out that an appreciation of the dynamics of unearned wealth is vital in making "a critical distinction between inequalities arising from profits and wages and inequalities arising from rents". They identify three types of rent-seeking found in all modern economies:

1. *Market capture by political elites;*
2. *State capture by oligarchs; and,*

3. *Capture of oligarchs by autocratic rulers through selective criminalization and the redistribution of their wealth to the loyal new rich (p13).*

When mainstream, especially so-called "Public Choice", economists (discussed below) speak of rent-seeking, it is mostly type 1 (by politicians and bureaucrats) that concerns them. I am concerned with all three, and especially the latter two (by oligarchs and autocrats). Plus, the corporate versus government dichotomy is largely counterfeit since our new feudal political economy is pretty much run by and for the 1%. Rentiers, as John Stuart Mill defined, are those who "make money in their sleep". In recent years the preponderance of rent-seeking has shifted from the landed gentry to bankers & financiers, and rent takes the form of interest on debt. Like the lords of old, the new rentiers add little to production, especially when they can use financial games (with the aid of central bankers) to increase the value and on their existing assets and protect reckless speculation. Meanwhile, politicians and bureaucrats are merely courtiers to these neofeudal lords, routinely cutting taxes on their ill-gotten gains. In our winner-takes-all society, concentrated wealth has never claimed so much while contributing so little. Massive rent extraction is also the hallmark of economic stagnation. The FIRE industry (Finance, Insurance, and Real Estate) has joined other heavily subsidized industries (Oil, Defense, Big Pharma, and Information Tech.), as a gleaming jewel in the crony-capitalist crown. Beyond the FIRE firms, our leading companies (in terms of capitalization) include a search engine, a social network, an online sales retailer, a video distributor turned content provider, a cell phone designer & manufacturer, a car sharing network, and an electric car company that has yet to turn a profit (yet has higher valuation than any of the big 3 automakers). Generally speaking, these new technology-based, paper tigers employ relatively few people, exploit the commonwealth, and manipulate consumers. Given several decades of stagnant wages for the masses, the average consumer can barely afford the various toys and diversions that continually pop up on their PC's and phones without becoming slaves to debts, and their burdens expand via the alchemy of COMPOUND INTEREST and fees. The emerging engine of an even more rent-extracting economy is the capture of information. Consumer, as well as industrial information is mined, stolen, stored, and reprocessed into new commodities, and systems that further reduce opportunities in the real economy. Individuals spend an inordinate amount of time daily engaged in social networks that are becoming decidedly anti-social (e.g. promoting disinformation and easily captured by troll armies). It is a subtle, yet viciously atomizing and parasitic economy.

THE GREAT FINANCIALIZATION FIXATION

So how did our economy get so far up its own bum? FINANCIALIZATION is the primary reason. Gerald Epstein (2005) explains: "financialization means the increasing role of financial motives, financial markets, financial actors, and financial institutions in the operation of the domestic and international economies (p.3)". Greta Krippner (2005) further defines it as a "pattern of accumulation in which profit making occurs increasingly through financial channels rather than through trade and commodity production (p.174)". The essence of financialization, according to the late/great pillar of British economic sociology, Ronald Dore (2007), is "the increasingly strident assertion of the property rights of owners as transcending all other forms of social accountability for business (p. 1098)".

Financialization has made banking the tail that wags the economic dog. Banking profits alone have gone from 5% to 25% of GDP. Fundamental flaws at the heart of our Money & Banking systems are hugely amplified through the machinations of Central Banking (the Federal Reserve in the US). These banking cartels, greatly aided and abetted, but officially independent from the state, have given themselves a perpetual motion money machine, that generates wealth literally out of thin air, without the risks of innovation, production, employment, or competing in global markets (aside from money markets). This auto-aggrandizement by the MASTURBATORS OF THE UNIVERSE paralyzes and displaces the "real economy" with a monstrously mounting debt overhang. Their agenda quickly converges on the reductio ad-absurdum when the economy cannot grow enough to service the debt. Like bloodletting in pre-modern medicine, draconian austerity and added dispossession (e.g., selling off the commons, the infrastructure, or other elements of the public patrimony) are prescribed as a cure for declining growth. All-the-while that debt is exploding, its marginal productivity dramatically declining. In the 1960s a dollar of debt would buy you almost 70 cents increased GDP

(Gross Domestic Product), over the last few decades it has fallen nearer to a dime. Thus, GDP (supposedly all goods and services) has become less indicative of the real economy. Ultimately, financialization is a giant ZERO SUM GAME, feeding the fake by stealing from the real.

The modern devices of financialization have exploded along with advanced computational and communication capabilities. We now have instantaneous worldwide capital mobility, rapid (as well as rabid) rehypothecation (multiple repledging of collateral), as well as virtually unlimited leverage. Hence the present epoch is unparalleled in scale & scope. However, episodes of runaway financialization are a relatively routine in history of economics. An era of financialization usually accompanies periods of boom and bust (once known as "Panics" or severe recessions). Occasionally recessions become sufficiently prolonged to call them depressions. As the old joke goes, it is a recession when your neighbor is out of work; it is depression when you're out of work. But, depressions introduce deeper difficulties, such as deflationary spirals (see, Fischer, 1933). Despite their relative frequency, the actual dynamics of major economic downturns never quite made it into macroeconomic policy discussions (see, Krugman, 2018). The reasons for this myopia are complex, for now, suffice it to say that much of it stems from the fact that the models used do not include the main culprits, i.e., Money & Banking. I know it seems inconceivable but these central factors, as well as other key socio-political machinations, really are exogenous (outside) the models we use for macroeconomic policymaking. To the extent that such items are accounted for at all, it is as outside "exogenous shocks" upon the system. It is also worth pointing out that capture of economics by neofeudal forces also succeeded in making macroeconomics one dimensional as well as blurring the traditional distinction between micro and macro (see, Stiglitz, 2018). In sum, our economics is a vast Potemkin village (a facade over a rotting system).

CONFESSIONS OF A FORREST GUMP

The general theme of dispossession dynamics has been a part of my thinking for many years, but the pressures of "publish or perish" often forced me into paths of narrow orthodoxy, albeit mostly critical of the prevailing methodologies. My epiphany was less a jolt from the saddle on the "Road to Damascus" than the delayed awareness of proverbial "frog in the boiling water." Gradually I realized that the insular scope and methods of economic inquiry were completely imperious to change, given their ideological and institutional hi-jacking. Yes, I was more than a bit slow on the uptake. I have often thought I must be some sort of Forrest Gump figure, so near to the intellectual vortex and policy corruption that I could not see the forest (or the Gump) for the trees. If you who have not seen the modern classic Forrest Gump (Academy Award winning film of 1994, starring Tom Hanks), it is still on TV on a fairly regular basis and you really should consider it required viewing. Gump is a loveable, dim-witted fellow who unknowingly interacts with all of the major events of his era (from Elvis to George Wallace, and from JFK to Viet Nam, Watergate, the AIDs crisis, and Apple Inc.).

In my high school civics class, we debated Eisenhower's famed Farewell Speech (regarding the rise of the Military Industrial Complex) yet like most Americans, I did not appreciate how much things had already eroded. A few of my high school classmates lost their lives in Viet Nam (I gave up my student deferment, took my changes with the lottery, and got a high number); yet, very few of us understood what that war was really about even as we joined in protests against it. At UC Santa Barbara I attended some of the last public lectures by the likes of Rexford Tugwell and Maynard Hutchins, but discounted their warnings regarding the decay of democratic institutions. I worked on National Energy Policy Review during the "Gas Line Summer of 79" and witnessed the power of oil lobbyists as well as their military and banker friends first hand, but still did not fully comprehend the level of corruption. I saw Jimmy Carter (the last honest president of the United States) being victimized by ultra-dirty tricks (particularly the hostage hold) so sinister they would've made Trump blush. I was outraged, but could not imagine that this was business as usual in American politics. I am still pretty much dumbfounded by my willful ignorance.

I studied and taught policy making (both corporate and public) for nearly a half century within primarily a rationalistic framework and hence as mostly an abstract exercise. When on those fairly rare but significant occasions I engaged with the real world, I would dismiss my frustrations with the maxim that "power could only handle the truth in small doses" and/or if it substantially confirmed their biases. Yet despite a relatively synoptic vantage point on the evolution of our political economy (from production to consumption and from consumption to destruction), I really did not start to connect the dots until some point following terrorist attacks of September, 11, 2001. Sure, I knew our government was corrupt, but I did NOT appreciate what extremes that corruption might take. I wanted to believe that only a few elements of our economy were manipulated by the elite forces, and I resisted the reality of such a brutal kleptocracy. Furthermore I failed to grasp that our financial apparatus was one huge Ponzi (pyramid) scheme (as Bernie Madoff tried to tell us). Academia is not labeled "Ivory Tower" for nothing. Situational awareness is disproportionally and inversely related to one's level of effort. My periodic dipping of my toe in the real muck of national and corporate policy did not necessarily alleviate my intellectual delusions. Plus all-the-while I thought I was battling theoretical elements within certain applied branches of my discipline (energy & environment and science & technology) it had not yet dawned on me that ideology was the real problem. Only reluctantly did it register that all-encompassing war of ideas had already been completely lost well before my puny, yet miraculous career, had even began. I had been muddling (occasionally blithering) around with my own set of ideological blinders firmly attached.

My blue collar upbringing (in an era of extraordinary upward mobility), mild autism, and a curious cognitive dissonance combined to manifest a more profound level of Gumpism when it came to elites. For someone who actually read the classic elite theorists (Pareto, Mosca, Michels) as well as C. Wright Mills (1956) and William Domhoff (1967), my inability to recognize their overwhelming importance is puzzling even to me. It is noteworthy that scholars from difference disciplines view elites differently: political scientists see pluralism and competition, sociologists see collusion and conspiracy, and economists don't see a damn thing. My own strange aversion to elites went well beyond my training in economics, however. In my case, it is as if I chose to discount something I disliked to the point of questioning its very existence. In America of course, elites invest a good deal of time and resources to maintain the mystery of their existence and their level of power. Yet, my disconnection was something different and bordered on pure stupidity. The mythology of the meritocracy was so engrained into my being that I simply ignored the oligarchy all around me. So profound was my stupor and/or subconscious allegiance to my class that I rejected out of hand attempts to recruit into so-called "secret societies". My uncle on the mother's side was a VP & Tax Controller at Mobile Oil and a 33rd + degree Mason. He offered to sponsor me, but I did not see the relevance. During my brief marriage, my father-in-law was the Assistant Surgeon General and a Bohemian. He once suggested that he would take me to the Grove, and I responded with something absurdly stupid like "why would I want to hang out with a bunch of rich old men". One of my deans, was a member of Reagan's kitchen cabinet, led the S&L Resolution, and later became the FDIC Chair. He got me on a national policy taskforce (on productivity and innovation), but I swiftly resigned when I realized we were just there to white wash the White House. I naively thought we could "speak truth to power", rather we were expected to help coronate the new neofeudalism (to which I was still pretty much oblivious, at the time). Oh to have remained in my blissful ignorance. I was such a bewildered Boy Scout back then. Despite the many that do good works, the basic idea of secret societies still gives me the creeps. When it comes to the political machinations of wealth, it is as the evil emperor told Luke Skywalker as he nearly killed him with his hand lightning, "only now do you understand...the power of the Dark Side".

MONEY CHANGERS CHANGE EVERYTHING

Financial manipulations have played a major role in most social upheaval and evolution (as well as devolution) since the inception of Money & Banking systems. However, the scale and scope of the financialization nowadays dwarfs previous epochs by a long shot. Financialization presently permeates every nook and cranny of human relations. In the best of times, it merely steals a bit from the future and energizes the present, yet in current debt driven epoch, financialization strip mines all potential value from the present as well as the future in order to create the illusion economic growth.

When an economy becomes addicted to engineered wealth it fundamentally alters all human relationships. In particular, it debases the basic philosophy of business enterprise (see, Daneke & Sager, 2015), where bogus economic theories (e.g. "shareholder primacy") produce myriad dysfunctional management practices. Firms become mere receptacles of debt, and financial management tools are specifically designed to disguise the more demented dimensions. Consider how the Carillion (huge UK construction firm) collapse exposed a loop hole in supply chain financing systems (called "reverse factoring"). It allows firms to hide mountains of debt (500 million pounds in this case) in "trade payable" accounts.

Current money and credit systems in general facilitate a level raping and pillaging that make the sack of Rome look like a day at the beach. Corporate executives are heavily incentivized to not only screw their workers, customers and other community stakeholders, but also to undermine their own shareholders. Long lost economist and chronicler of the rentier class, Thorstein Veblen (1904) contended that this "predatory impulse" and the propensity for strategic "economic sabotage" has always been embedded in business, but was often kept in check by the "engineering mentality" (pride of workmanship, etc.) However, in our era where large numbers of actual engineering students are majoring in "financial engineering" and taking jobs running stochastic programs (which detect arbitrage opportunities in piles of data) for hedge funds, the desire to build things and employ people may have also fallen by the wayside. Nevertheless it was not until the real economy had tanked and "corporate raiders", like perennial presidential hopeful Mitt Romney, were still trying to pass themselves off as "job creators" did it dawn on most of us that Wall Street and Main Street have very different agendas. And, government obviously favors the former. In the first omnibus spending bill of the Trump era, Congress rewarded the job destroyers by effectively doubling their levels of leverage. Mitt's former firm, Bain Capital, recently sent another established enterprise, iHeartMedia (once called Clear Channel, the biggest radio broadcaster in the nation), to the dust bin of history with 20 billion in debts. As cereal entrepreneur turned scholar, Suren Dutia (2012) points out "private equity" (PE) is often completely antithetical to entrepreneurship.

In Josh Kosman's (2009) excellent chronicle of various "leveraged buyouts" he illustrates how they often led to labor off shoring, asset stripping (including raiding pension funds) debt overloading, and bankruptcies. PE now stands for PIRATE EQUITY, when, with very little initial investment, the use of clever financial tricks (such as "junk bonds"), and the aid of the big banks and lax government rules, a group of "vulture capitalists" can essentially buy a firm with its own assets. Then they sell off and/or offshore big chunks, abrogate its liabilities and labor contracts, pay themselves huge fees, and walk away leaving the gutted shell for the creditors to fight over. Consider how Ceberus (sounds like an STD) Capital bushwhacked the old meister of the new bushmaster (a favorite of school shooters), Remington Inc. (with 2 billion in debts). It is as if I bought your home, and when you went to pay off the loan you were told that I took out additional loans in your name, as well as took your kids college fund. Except your personal bankruptcy options are much more tightly circumscribed. For example, when Toy-R-Us went bankrupt, it was still allowed to pay executive bonuses. Moreover, since 2006 many private equity funds have barely produced average S&P returns for investors, yet have extracted nearly a half trillion in fees according to Oxford professor, Ludovic Phalippou (2017).

This ravaging of the real economy by mostly unregulated raiders, while serious, pales in comparison to the activities of fully sanctioned Central Bankers (e.g. the Federal Reserve). Only in the wake of our on-going financial crisis, did the massive siege engines of the new medieval economy (e.g., trillions in "quantitative easing" following hundreds of billions in direct bail outs) begin to come into view. As the saying goes, "when the tide goes out can you see who swimming in the buff". The naked political power of financial elites (another terra-incognita where mainstream economists are concerned) was full frontal. Suspect private gains were overwhelmed by the surreptitious socialization of loses. Financial interests were rewarded twice for their mammoth mismanagement of risk. The fake economy recovered for the moment through the infusion of more liquidity, as well as NOT having to pay for it many sins. The real economy, however, continues to stagnate. Meanwhile, our corrupt regulatory agencies proceeded to promote a feudal pattern of privilege. Despite mounting evidence of widespread criminal fraud, it became obvious that not even a single one of our new financial overlords was ever going to take the perp walk. Pulitzer Prize winning journalist, Jesse Eisinger, (2017) refers to the US Department of Justice, as "The Chickenshit Club" in this regard. The revolving door between the financial service industries and regulatory agencies has always spun like a top, yet in recent years the number of general purpose administrators who came directly from Wall Street has grown exponentially. Across the globe a significant number of high level and chief executives come from financial services (including foreign branches of Wall Street firms, as well as the various Central Banks and international banking organizations). Bankers literally rule the world in a way not seen since the time of the Medici.

The overdeveloped world now mirrors various underdeveloped nations in their level of unadulterated corruption. The term kleptocracy (the rule of thieves) once reserved for criminal tin pot tyrants of tiny beleaguered nations now applies to our own only slightly more subtle criminality. What was once relatively clandestine is now brazen. The US, for example, has the best government money can buy. Fordham Law Professor, Zephyr Teachout (2014) in her detailed, yet lively, history of government corruption in America explains much of what was once completely outlawed (e.g., lobbying was illegal) is now new normal, and our current campaign finance laws allow what would have clearly be considered bribes just a generation ago. The Trump Presidency with its outrageous commercial conflicts, nepotism, and deep oligarchic connections is on a pace to make all past corruptions combined seem like child's play (note, Cole, 2018). Yet from my perspective the flood of money into politics, and the general corruption of political figures is not as insidious as the way in which "dark money" was used to corrupt the intellectual enterprise. Jane Mayer (2016) in her history of the "Radical Right", buttresses her analysis of politics for purchase, with a detailed discussion of how multi-millionaires/billionaires (e.g., Koch Brothers, the Mercers, the Adelsons and other royal families), and various corporate founda-tions also undermined legitimate academic inquiry into the political economy via their funding of un-think tanks and university programs. Not satisfied with their virtual control of economic departments and business schools, they also funded programs in schools of government and law. The "Law and Economics" movement and the so called Federalist Society (whose members include all the conservatives presently serving on the Supreme court) have been especially effective in raising up an entire generation of legal scholars, lawyers, and judges dedicated to obliterating any remaining New Deal constraints upon corporate power (especially in the areas of labor relations and antitrust), while also placing presidents above the law. What is so sinister about this political weaponization of academic theory and practice is the hypocrisy of extolling anarchic anti-government (as well as anti-social) themes on behalf of industrial and banking interests so well attached to the public teat. Ultimately, the state is much more a "creature of the money" than money is a creature the state (see, Beggs, 2017).

TRIGGER WARNING

It should be clear by now that this is a bit of a diatribe. It is based upon evidence and experience, but is still more than a tad polemical, to say the least. I am obviously quite opinionated. However, I do NOT support the prevailing intellectual nihilism that all opinions are created equal, or that what you heard on Fox News (or NPR for that matter) is as good as careful research and reflection. I undertook a massive amount of research for this book (including dozens of informal interviews with powerful individuals and concerned citizens) to understand for myself what the hell was going on. Plus, I sought to reduce the confusion that resulted from several journeys through the belly of beast. The more I dug, the deeper some of my convictions became; however, I also modified my beliefs and opinions substantially. I expect that some of the observations and interpretations will upset you. If not then it you are already more jaded that I. In that case, I hope I can still give you a glimmer of hope. Either way, you have been forewarned.

It has always been a bit curious to me that a certain subliminal set of the Marques of Queensbury Rules of intellectual fisticuffs existed in the social sciences (perhaps even superliminal in economics) where questioning motives is completely beyond the pale. What makes this exceedingly puzzling is that historically when inconvenient ideas arose they were often shot down by way of unmitigated character assassinations, or accusations of impure ideological motives. But, only on the part of the transgressor to the status quo mind you. For Veblen it was the accusation of womanizing, because he treated women as equals. For Soddy it was the claim of anti-Semitism, resulting from his work being embraced by the "alt right" of his time (between the wars England had its own burgeoning black shirts). This particular attack on the character of a scholar is especially damming today, yet it is often preemptively and erroneously invoked whenever the banking system is scrutinized. One can only hope that banking is now sufficiently diverse and secular that one might be able question particular practices without being dismissed with the handy non-sequitur of harboring ethnic or religious hostility.

Another interesting all-purpose adhominen that concerns me most is the assertion that inconvenient facts are mere conspiracy theories. So when did human collusion only become possible in the minds of a handful of foil-hatted kooks? It is as if elites never existed, or even if they do they never get together in places like Davos, Jackson Hole, or Bilderberg. One need not deal with the message if the messenger is swiftly shot or labeled a conspiracy theorist. Many Americans act as if they believe that all court intrigue and skullduggery is relegated to the ancient past or the present TV fictions. During my childhood we still routinely changed leaders through bodily as well as character assassination (including close calls for Ford, Reagan, and the Pope). Yet, most still hold tight to the "lone wolf theory of history" where alienated and unaffiliated individuals (or 19 wayward Saudis) act without any design or sanction from those in power. I am not here to tell you who killed JFK or J.R. Ewing for that matter. Believe it or not, I am NOT interested in conspiracy theories. I would like to know what really happened to Building 7 at the World Trade Center (the third and smaller tower that collapsed completely into its own footprint, despite NOT being struck by a plane), but I accept that I probably never will. Plus, a part of me really hopes that if the conspiracy theories are true, Americans never wake up to the possibility that a particular administration could allow thousands of them be killed to support a geopolitical agenda. And that is all I will say about 9/11. Moving forward my slight brushes with the shadowy underbelly of power brokers, plotters, and agent provocateurs will be tangential at best. I am primarily interested in exploring how and for whom our political economy actually works. As luck would have it, most of its maneuverings are increasingly occurring in plain sight. However, if merely opening one's eyes involves exposing certain protracted ideological projects and their policy machinations, then so be it. While I will strive not to pull any punches, I hope to not grind any axes to excess; well maybe just a bit of excess.

Since this could be my last book, I cannot resist giving poetic license to my existential angst. For example, I explore why most bankers are wankers and why sustainable energy systems will not displace our addiction to oil anytime soon. I also touch on why much of the stuff done in name of defense is actually a financial process that makes us and the planet less safe as well as much more indebted. Furthermore, I broach how the complete collapse of our civilization and/or totalitarianism are very real possibilities. I assert that, contrary to the reigning theories of economics, history and cultural evolution really do matter; a great deal in fact. Overall I seek to illuminate how scientifically faulty formulations and feudalistic influences might greatly diminish the human prospect, particularly when they are deeply embedded in critical institutions and policy processes. But, fear not, it is not all doom and gloom. There is some good news to mention as well, such as the fact that humans are much more cooperative and compassionate creatures than our institutions currently allow us to exhibit on a regular basis. Moreover, institutions can be redesigned to promote rather than impede our better angels.

HORIZONS FULL OF LIMITS

When it comes to institutional redesign, it is essential that it begin fairly soon to avoid the various dead ends looming on our current course. By way of simplification and summary I present them as "peaks". The concept of peak does not necessarily imply the end of the road, but merely the downward slope. In case of non-renewable natural resources, the peak if merely the half-way point in the exhaustion of supply. However, it is well to note that since the global population continues to explode, exhaustion proceeds at an exponential rather than arithmatic pace. It took all of human history for us to reach a population of 3 billion in the 1950s, but only roughly the next 60 years to double that number, and if growth continues at the current rate it could double again well before the end of this century. Respected Cornel University resource ecologist, David Pimentel (2011), however, suggests that widespread starvation may prevent us from reaching this target. Uncontrolled climate change will dramatically reduce agricultural productivity worldwide. Without a couple more earth like planets to plunder, economic growth itself becomes problematic.

While I was studying resource economics in the early 1970s an alternative view was causing quite a stir. It was an exercise in "systems dynamics" (e.g., Forrester, 1971), models which look at webs of interactions with careful attention to feedback loops. The

Limits to Growth (Meadows, et. al, 1972) was immediately dismissed by economists maintaining that there are NO LIMITS (markets will simply produce higher prices and spur technological substitutes). "The Limits" had obvious limits (it was not calibrated for precise predictions); however, at the time I wondered how economists could be so obtuse. I did not realize that EXPONENTIAL GROWTH, even if fake, is beating heart of our debt driven financial system, and it is this phantom wealth machine as much as resource constraints that provide our greatest peril at present. Obviously these factors are not mutually exclusive, and the necessity of greater debt generation contributes to all sorts of environmental degradation, malinvestment, and global militarization. Perhaps a peek at the following peaks might begin to frame of this unfortunate synergy:

1. Declining supplies of cheap energy required to fuel the sprawling, auto-addicted cities, or to drive new waves of industrial expansion globally, amid a mounting climate catastrophe (peak carbon);
2. Hyper-leveraged credit and default systems, mark to magic accounting, and massive transfers of debt from private to the public institutions, amid astronomical levels sovereign liability (peak debt);
3. Over capacity and widespread redundancy amid accelerating automation and the rise of precarious employment systems (peak work);
4. Proliferation of weapons of mass extinction and the financialization of conflict amid the engineering of perpetual warfare and widespread militarization of society (peak war);
5. Imperial overreach and decline signaling hegemonic transition to non-democratic states amid the widespread rise of authoritarian leadership (peak democracy); and,
6. Over-reliance upon mythical beliefs systems and pseudo scientism amid widespread corruption, inequality, and a general restoration of medieval oligarchic arrangements (peak ideology).

If these do not seem damn daunting, then you need to check your meds. Nonetheless, it is not too late to address them. These factors while difficult to ameliorate, are not completely intractable. So grab a hearty beverage, turn off the cell, find a comfy chair, and BUCKLE UP.

CHAPTER 2: THE RISE OF NEOFEUDAL ECONOMICS

Most libertarians are worried about government but not worried
about business. I think we need to be worrying about business in
exactly the same way we are worrying about government.
_____ **John Perry Barlow**

Vassals of an outdated ideology unrelated to the real world, they
can, when questioned on this issue, only mumble neoliberal
mantras that have delivered the world economic stagnation, rising
inequality and global environmental crisis.
_____ **Richard Flanagan**

One of the profound effects of economics in our day is that the
people with the money and the power have embraced the guilt-free,
external-less, everything-will-turn-out-okay-in-the-end
philosophy of economics in order to justify their own evil works.
And the economists, for the most part, have sucked up to that
money. _____ **Jane Smiley**

Everything reminds Milton Friedman of the money supply.
Everything reminds me of sex, but I try to keep it out of my papers.
_____ **Robert Solow**

The institution of a leisure class has emerged gradually during the
transition from primitive savagery to barbarism; or more precisely,
during the transition from a peaceable to a consistently warlike
habit of life. _____ **Thorstein Veblen**

 One might think that economics would have much to tell us
about the mess we're in. Au contraire, economics in the modern era
has been expressly designed to sweep all the inconvenient reality
under the rug. The dust mound has grown immensely, and still
there are few shovels in sight. While I only had a tea spoon, it was
all this grungy stuff that interested me most, and until recently I
couldn't understand why it interested so few of my economist
colleagues. Being cursed with these predilections, I tended to
gravitate toward the nearly extinct Institutional or Evolutionary
Economists as they offered insights on par with those found in my
in philosophy, political science, and other social science courses. I
once had an aged Austrian professor of political philosophy who
had studied with members of the Vienna Circle, barely escaped the
Nazis, and came to California after a long career at Princeton. He
was quite a character, and I can still hear him railing in a debate

with Herbert Marcuse that "were it not for America we would both be lampshades". He admonished that if I really wanted to learn political economy I would need to go study in Europe. But since I did not have sufficient funds to make it much further than Oxnard (40 miles south), I had to content myself with the dusty volumes I could find in the libraries at UCSB and UCLA (via the free express bus that connected the campuses). His other lasting effect upon me came by way of his somewhat self-serving theory about contributions in the social sciences. In essence, he asserted that given their mathematical and mental energy demands, physical scientists must make their contribution before turning 30, or not at all. While in the social sciences path breaking insights come much later in life because one must master several disparate disciplines. Plus, youthful scholars simply did not know enough about all the hidden connections in a complex world. Advanced computational tools might now have removed a bit of age restrictions in the so-called "hard sciences". But, given the insular nature of academic departments, the second part remains more valid than ever. Moreover, as I rapidly converge on old age myself, I appreciate his theory all the more. Yet, I no longer delude myself that I will ever be appreciated, especially among economists, for any earth-shaking discoveries. Nevertheless, at least I am finally starting to understand our political economy.

A CULT DISGUISED AS A SCIENCE

It took me quite some time to figure out that despite it mathematical prowess, policy power, and other elements of stolen status economics is actually the least scientific of all the social sciences. It is noteworthy, that their Nobel Prize is a fake; it is actually the Swedish Central Bank prize in honor of Alfred Nobel, and some of his family continues to protest the misuse of his name, and its award at the same time as the authentic scientific prizes. Mainstream economics, of the sort which dominate most US universities, government agencies, as well as most private enterprises, is generally speaking quite methodologically myopic. Yet what really makes matters worse is that it has been captured by powerful ideologues. This group was bent on fashioning elaborate myths to camouflage their neofeudalistic agenda. In short, economics is a cult disguised as a science. Its methods are deductive from dogma, rather than inductive from observations. It is mostly formal in its use of math, and in rare cases of experimental findings, they are not easily replicated. Economic behavior is actually often so culturally bound that if it were a real science it would focus on institutional evolution and use ethnographic (such as anthropology) as well as social psychological approaches. Unfortunately, economics is an extremely insular and static discipline where history, politics, and power matter NOT. The classical study of political economy had been pretty much purged from many American universities (especially in California) back during the McCarthy Era (see, McCumber, 2016).

Economics, from the Greek "affairs of the household", is far worse than poor science it is brainwashing on a planetary scale. Economics, given its self-anointed prestige, is used to promote a neofeudal societal agenda and has actually altered our culture and engendered social devolution. Those Greeks who coined the phrase must be rolling over in their graves at the fact that this trivial element of commerce has become the queen of the social sciences. For them politics was the architectonic science, as it was the porthole to the soul. Hence Plato in The Republic spoke of the tripartite state mirroring the tripartite soul (what for Freud became the "id, ego, and superego"). Economics has been for the last several decades primarily an ideological project, specifically designed to not only maintain the status quo ante, but to refashion human existent into a new feudal order.

Mainstream economics has had various guises, so bear with me moment and I will attempt to provide a score card. The prevailing scope and methods of modern economics is referred to as Neoclassical Economic Theory as it blends classical naturalistic philosophy (e.g., Malthus) with mathematical methods (e.g., marginal utility theory, see Jevons, 1862). Simple enough, but hang on, this is where it gets confusing. The ideological project which grew out of neoclassical economics is called neoliberalism, as it invokes classical liberal philosophy (e.g., Smith, Locke, and Mill) regarding the minimalist state, as well as the inviolate market. But, it is mostly a canard since it requires powerful states to sanction, fund, and enforce with violence its various prerogatives. While having little to do with modern liberalism, various portions of its policy agenda were adopted by conservatives and liberals alike. Plus, neoliberalism, like its alter ego globalization, has become a pejorative term, and thus those who support these projects rarely refer to themselves as such. Sorry, are you completely confused? In order to cut to the chase and call a spade a spade, I prefer to associate the ideological project that captured mainstream economics with its most basic embedded and onerous objective, the restoration of bastardized version of feudal society. Thus, I substitute neofeudalism for neoliberalism.

One final point of confusion, business schools also led the way in sweeping aside the old or original institutionalism (also called "Evolutionary Economics", see Veblen, 1898; also note Hodgson, 2007) by constructing a complete sham called "neo-institutionalism"(e.g., "transaction cost economics" see, Oliver Williamson,1985), which actually has little to do with institutions aside from those that promote corporate agglomeration. The REAL institutional economics deals with "enculturation, empiricism, evolution, and systemic processes" (see, Mayhew, 2018) and not merely legal and regal conventions. Nonetheless, Williamson did receive a fake Nobel for helping to obscure the role of institutions and evolution in economics. Meanwhile the only trace of Veblen in the current business curriculum is the "Veblen effect" (the ostentatious pricing of luxury items) in marketing studies.

PESKY PELERINS AND THE GRAND APOLOGIA

Academic economics actually began as a branch of applied ethics in departments of philosophy and theology. Adam Smith held the Chair in Moral Philosophy at Glasgow. He was a product of the Scottish Enlightenment, and derived his economic ideas from a foundation of social observations, including an attempt to understand things like altruism and reciprocity (which he called "mutual sympathy"). Smith offered a detailed (amazing for his time) psychological as well as ethical explanation in the first of his two volume treatise, The Theory of the Moral Sentiments (1759) upon which he built his Inquiry into the Nature and Causes of the Wealth of Nations (1776, a good year). It is also noteworthy that when he spoke of "free markets" he meant free from monopolies and cartels, such as the British East India Company (EIC). Unfortunately the actual theories of Adam Smith have been selectively extracted and shamelessly modified over the years. As a result, he now serves as the deceptive patron saint for "market fundamentalism" (see, Kennedy, 2005: Hühn & Dierksmeier, 2016).

When I first went to Washington in the 1970s they sold ties at the American Enterprise Institute with Smith's cameo doting them, and the new converts would scuff them up with light sand paper from a pack of matches to create the illusion of natural beard wear at the knot. At the time I thought that this is emblematic of the political forgery by a small tangent to economics, and that it would soon be exposed and expunged. Obviously I was totally wrong. Significant portions of the intellectual history of economics is what were expunged instead, and Adam Smith's fate befell most of the famed classical economists. Inconvenient ethical and political concerns have been carefully and completely ignored, leaving only a handful of naturalistic notions enabling the fake scientism of neoclassical economics. Some of the more troubling scholars (e.g., Frederick Soddy) were merely erased completely. Like lipstick on a pig, merely adding mathematics (especially with formulas stolen whole cloth form 19th century Newtonian physics texts, see, Mirowski, 1991) does not a science make. In fact it directly led to exclusion of all the moral and political reasoning that had made classical economics so enlightening. No wonder they call it the "dismal science" when all the truly interesting stuff was carefully extracted from academic economics. Despite being waist deep in the policy muck, they went to great links to maintain their fake neutrality and fraudulent scientific status. Thus many mainstream economists merely pretend to ignore all of that messy social reality that actually informs the human condition. By the midpoint of the century this vacuum was gradually being filled with an insidious ancient ideology infused deep into the nervous system of the discipline, where it remained hidden and thus beyond analysis. What better way to hide your ill-founded dogma and associated policy agenda than deep within an enterprise which claims to be completely devoid of such items. Furthermore, what began as short-hand (or "stylized") caricature to aid mathematical deductions (i.e., "homo-economicus" or economic man) became an apology for predation and outright sociopathy. Not only did they toss away all the compelling cultural and socio-psychological dough when they cut out their little cookie man, they spread on a thick icing of greed and a pile of narcissistic candy sprinkles. Economics became the anti-social social science.

Many of the most prestigious economics departments and what became business schools have been handsomely funded by wealthy bankers and industrialists before the turn of the 20th century; and economic scholars gradually learned on which side their bread was buttered. But the pace of ideological capture quickened following WWII. A small band of economists, conservative pundits, and wealthy sponsors (including displaced nobles) met at a hotel in the small Swiss village of Mont Pelerin in 1947 to revive their ideological project and thereby rid the western world of the remnants of New Deal progressivism. The secretive Mont Pelerin Society (MPS), or Pelerins for short, would spearhead a guerilla insurgency via a number of well-funded foundations (e.g., Heritage Foundation), research centers (e.g., Center for Study of Public Choice), and think tanks/lobbying organizations (e.g., American Enterprise Institute). They surreptitiously built the foundation of a powerful and malignant ideology as well as fortifying the pretense of an unparalleled science. Behind a smoke screen of free market mythology they promoted the devolution of society and the restoration of the financial aristocracy.

Having salted the fields of intellectual discourse with their elite funded think tanks, and capturing prestigious departments and editorial boards, during the previous decades, the Pelerins and their acolytes were strategically placed to exploit the induced chaos to come. By the 1980s they had completely captured the halls of power via Ronald Reagan and Margaret Thatcher. Recall how she gleefully exclaimed that "there is no such thing as society" and TINA ("there is no alternative"). Economics which was mostly "voodoo" (as Bush senior called it) was presented as natural law. Meanwhile, the underlying agenda of "socialism for the rich and free enterprise for poor" became so popular with Republicans and Democrats alike that is was given the label of the "Washington Consensus". Soon the "New Democrats" and "New Labour" joined their conservative colleagues in furthering the neofeudal agenda.

Concurrently the Pelerins were buttressing the pillars of globalism and the larger neoliberal financial project. Noted economic historian, Phillip Mirowski (2012) refers to them as the "Neoliberal Thought Collective", and highlights their inordinate political power, as well as their hypocrisy. Over a dozen of its members (and fellow travelers) have received their knockoff Nobel since the inception of the economics prize in 1968: including their founding president, Friedrich von Hayek and his successor Milton Friedman. Hayek might well be much sore amazed to see how his Road to Serfdom (1944) was paved and lighted by his fellow

Pelerins. Hayek's plea for competing currencies was completely ignored. Plus his well-known warnings regarding the totalitarian dangers of central planning neglected to notice that such planning is regularly carried-out on an even grander scale by global bankers, oil executives, and arms merchants (note, Daneke, 1984).

Our present epoch has been romanticized as merely another "Gilded Age" with new technological "Robber Barons" (Stanford students once wanted to use the phrase for their sports teams, but powerful alums swiftly put on the kibosh). It should be pointed out that at least Leland Stanford Sr. and his ilk built things and employed people, unlike the current generation who mostly extract rents (more like the original Raubitter, who charged tolls on those who sailed past their castles on vital European rivers). Scholars of American Gilded Ages, such and Henry George (note, 1879; 1897) and Thorstein Veblen (via several books, but best known for 1899); would have clearly have seen latent feudalism at work in all the present day rent-seeking. Veblen, for example, suggested that institutional evolution from the "primitive savagery" to "predatory barbarism" to "quasi-peaceable barbarism" was less a progression than a continuum, with digression a prominent possibility. With the "predatory instinct" being generously rewarded by public policy, the potential for even greater barbarism is ever-present. Veblen took note that the vast majority of human history was spent in noble savagery (i.e., hunter-gatherers), and pretty much viewed it as a halcyon era of relative equality and cooperation. This stands in stark contrast to the Hobbesian (Hobbes, 1651) "state-of-nature" myth (maintained by most economists), where life was "nasty, brutish and short". Interesting enough, Veblen's view has been increasingly reconfirmed by the archeological evidence. Yale's Sterling Professor of Political Science (and leading expert on agrarian and "non-state" economies), James C. Scott (2017), has complied much of this evidence in his book, Going Against the Grain: a Deep History of the Earliest States. Drawing upon his earlier work on anarchism and "resistance to dominance", he explains how husbandry and agriculture evolved from a fail-safe strategy of nomadic peoples into a focal point for state-based taxation, enabling ancient elites to pay armies and feed slaves, as well as maintain themselves in the lap of luxury. The rise of agrarian state was the point when life became "brutish and short" for the hunter gatherers. Like Veblen, Scott would probably subscribe to Rousseau's more lyrical tale of the origination of civil society, where a fool meets a rogue who convinces him that road he is on and the once idyllic commons it crosses now belongs to him and thus he must become his serf. Our own descent into serfdom is more subtle, yet no less felonious. In sum, our recast economics is not only an apology for predation it is an active agent in the disintegration of societal processes.

THE END OF POLITICAL ECONOMY

When I first studied economics in the late 1960s the grip of neofeudal ideology was just beginning to tighten. When I confided to one of my professors that I wanted to pursue a Ph.D. in political economy, he told me that it really no longer existed as a field of study in economics, and that I would have to pursue a degree in political science. Besides, he added, that the term had become a euphemism for Marxism, and that I would never have an academic career were I to venture there. Based on his admonition I chose to abandon my original plan of pursuing a Ph.D. at UC Riverside (near where I grew up, and where I had already sat in a couple of extremely stimulating courses, during the summers), as it still had a fairly robust cadre of "radical political (although not necessarily Marxists) economists". So radical, however, that years later their department was literally divided in two (with the mainstream group getting most of the students and resources). I settled upon UC Santa Barbara where I received a teaching fellowship and where I could cobble together a graduate program between its excellent political science (with several Ivy League professors, still in their prime, who had escaped colder climes) and economics departments (with leading energy and environmental specialists). Plus, it also still had a number the legendary figures hanging around at the Center for Study of Democratic Institutions.

Early in my doctoral studies, however, I came to realize that political economy really was dead. Every time I found the term mentioned in the context of modern economics, it had been turned on its head. For example, The Journal of Political Economy that Veblen helped found and managed at the University of Chicago was then only publishing articles applying narrow economic models to explain political behavior rather than explorations of how politics impacts the economy as Veblen had intended. Essentially, mainstream economics had unceremoniously banished politics, as well as most societal processes, in their pursuit of shabby scientism. If accounted for at all it was as exogenous variables (outside of their tidy models) and/or excluded via "ceteris paribus" (all things being equal). That is it merely assumed that on average these external factors would cancel each other out. In short all the inconvenient social and political factors were effectively neutralized and made irrelevant. Meanwhile the ideology of the Pelerins was seeping into the illogical cracks left by this methodological sleigh-of-hand. While pushing neo-anarchist ideas at the micro-level, the macro agenda sought the supranational ruling imperatives of the so-called "globalists" (see, Slobodian, 2018).

By the time I took up my first post-Ph.D. teaching position at Virginia Tech in 1975, the Pelerins were already well dug in. Their Center the Study of Public Choice (CPC) was a relatively unassuming enterprise and occupied a modest old house on a duck pond at the edge of the campus that had once been university president's home. Its local libertarian luminaries included Gordon Tullock and James Buchanan, who would become the recipients of massive amounts of largesse from conservative oligarchs (and other anti-democratic ideologues see, MacLean, 2017) as well as fake Nobel for Buchanan. Their particular branch of the ideological project held that all public officials were merely seeking rents and inherently hostile to the market. My own views on the bizarre alpha & omega status of the market were shaped by the likes of Karl Polanyi (best known for his 1944 classic) and at the time I also had a bit of faith in public service in the "public interest" (and still do, but far less blindly so). Most of the folks at the CPC had never read Polanyi's meticulous historical analysis of the evolution of the market concept, but dismissed him out of hand for questioning their deity. Even Adam Smith seemed to know that the notion of unbridled markets is mostly a canard, and when they do function well it is the result of judicious societal sanctions. It is worth repeating that when Smith and the other classical economists invoked free markets they generally meant freedom from the influence of corporate combines, banking interests, and the power of the landed aristocracy.

Little did I appreciate at the time that the types of debates we had in Blacksburg had already been settled in favor of the Pelerins well laid (and paid) plans in most graduate economics and business programs across the country. When Milton Friedman came to campus to visit his son David (a physicist turned economist), deliver the graduation address, and hold court at the Center, I thought here is guy who just loves being outrageous; but, he can't really believe this junk. After all, he actually told the graduating class that they should close all the places like their alma mater and just have competition between private universities. I could not imagine at the time that neofeudalism hidden under a pile warmed-over libertarian ideas were already poised to assert an elephantine influence in the halls of power. It is noteworthy perhaps, that David went on to become a professor of law at Santa Clara (and a leading figure among "anarcho-capitalists"), and his son Patri was the founder of the "Seasteading" (sovereign floating islands) movement. Milt's progeny and other minions abide.

Under the guidance of the Pelerins and their intellectual offspring the libertarian conceit was extended to further promote the policies of dispossession. The bait and switch of extolling "free markets" (which to them mean NO government interference) while delivering oligarchs and cartels proved a potent propaganda device. Each time monopolies constrained innovation and retarded economic growth compliant politicians from across the spectrum would call for additional deregulation and end up facilitating more restraint of trade. This ideological three-card monty allowed neofeudalism to quickly morph into new solutions for the crises it created; all-the-while, further squandering vital resources and discrediting the public sphere. As Jeff Madrick (2014) explains, this process of gaining policy support to some horribly unfounded ideas (ranging from the invisible hand to the efficient markets hypothesis and Say's Law to the universal value of globalization) meant that even when their laissez-faire policies failed, it only served to reinforce the deceitful dogma.

THE DISPLACED PROPHETS OF PREDATORY ECONOMICS

Prior to the economic crisis that began early in this millennium (and is not over yet), the typical economist had never read nor perhaps even heard of those economists who sought to explain past and prevent future depressions (e.g., Henry George, Thorstein Veblen, Frederick Soddy, and Hyman Minsky). Their insights into critical dynamics are still completely ignored because the mainstream economics largely maintains the mythology that such crushing crises are now virtually impossible. Moreover, even if crises do arise they contend that can be quickly ameliorated by Central Bank interventions. Since mainstream economists fail to recognize the role of power and politics, they could never admit that crises are a predictable byproduct of prevailing political economy. In other words, the basic incongruities of Capitalism (see, George, 1878; Veblen, 1899; Soddy, 1925; 1934; and, Schumpeter, 1934) are rarely broached, and inherent instabilities (see: Minsky, 1992) that produce the next crisis are simply papered over (both literally and figuratively) by banking interests (note Soddy, 1934).

Henry George is one of my personal favorites, close behind Thorstein Veblen (my all-time hero). George inspired the likes of John Dewey by explaining how the socialization of land was vital to a democratic society (see, England, 2018). George is the Tom Sawyer of economists, a quintessential American character. Born near Philadelphia in 1839 to a large family, he was forced drop out of school for work at an early age. He was a completely self-taught economist (by reading widely and corresponding with leading figures, including John Stuart Mill). Despite his lack of formal training he was interviewed for a professorship at UC Berkeley. His opus (1879), Progress and Poverty: An Inquiry into the Cause of Industrial Depressions and of Increase of Want with Increase of Wealth: The Remedy, was a best seller in his lifetime and should be required reading for anyone who wants to call them self an economist. But of course, very few have even heard of him. He went to sea as a cabin boy at age 15, and witnessed object poverty in India and worker discontent in the form a mutiny at sea. Having failed as a gold miner in British Columbia, he returned to San Francisco to become a printer/journalist, an advisor to California governor Henry Haight (who had campaigned against monopoly), and founding editor of San Francisco's Daily Evening Post. He relates his own Paul on the road to Damascus story, while riding horseback high in the Oakland hills. He asks a passing teamster what land was going for below, and he points off to a distant location and tells him "a fellow over there is selling for 1000 an acre" (a fortune at the time). It was then he had his epiphany that rising inequality amid economic progress was driven in large portion by land speculation, which in turn fuel boom and bust cycles. The arrival of publicly financed Union Pacific Railroad had granted a huge windfall to speculators and absentee landlords. He came to believe that a progressive land tax, by removing incentives for rentiers, was the answer to most economics problems. He would say, "I do not want to seize their property, I just want to tax away their rent". His single land tax movement caught on across the globe, particularly in Britain. Mason Gaffney of UC Riverside (see, Gaffney, et al. 1994) maintains it also launched a counterrevolution in the form of elites funding anti-Georgist economics departments at major universities. Had George not succumb to pneumonia, he might have beaten back the Tweed Gang. In the 1897 NYC mayoral race, he ran on the United Labor Party ticket. His ideas are still popular among a small handful of Ecological (see, Czech, 2009) and even Public Choice (Borcherding, 1998) economists, but virtually unknown to most of the current generation of mainstream economists. Meanwhile of course, land wealth concentration has intensified. Of the roughly 4 billion acres of inhabitable land on the planet, less than 20% is owned by its inhabitants.

One name that has become better known of late is Hyman Minsky. He is another of my favorites for his unassuming boldness. Plus, his observations are particularly essential to this discussion. Drawing upon Keynes and Irving Fisher among others, Minsky (1987, 1992) observed that financial systems are driven mostly by greed and fear toward greater and greater instability. In his book, Can It Happen Again (1987), the "it" being another Great Depression, he offers an emphatic yes. In fact, he explains that our financial systems are pretty much designed to make it happen. In his "instability hypothesis" (1992), he begins by calling to question the mainstream monetarist theories, by suggesting that he "takes banking seriously as a profit seeking activity (p. 7)". His service as Director of the Mark Twain Bank in St Louis (while a professor at Washington University) gave him a distinct feel for the underlying incongruities of banking, and his major professor (Joseph Schumpeter) gave him a an appreciation for the internal dynamics and contradictions of Capitalism. Minsky maintains that instabilities do NOT necessarily come from "external shocks"; rather they are engendered within the financial system itself. Inevitably credit waves are pushed to the "Ponzi stage" where investors can meet neither principle nor interest from cash flow and rollovers. They must either conduct a fire sale of assets (triggering panics) or borrow more at higher interest, just to pay existing interest. Schumpeter (1934) had observed that waves of economic development are nearly always followed by a second wave of unproductive credit expansion, in which asset values must be inflated to meet the interest requirements. This not only promotes bubbles and crashes, but slows growth. Ultimately the fake economy enabled by advances in the art of "money for nothing" displaces and destroys productive activity, expands inequalities, and leaves us with a slow simmering depression.

Very little of the dispossession of the last few decades could have been accomplished without the ideological subterfuge of mainstream economics. Ancient kings held power through religious dogma, and by laboriously tracing their lineage to the Gods themselves. The propaganda of these ancient potentates, however, is not a patch on modern academic economics. What better way to provide an impregnable shield for power and privilege than to disguise your dubious doctrines as scientific discoveries and characterizing these devious distribution devices as natural processes.

The US's much overstated victory in the cold war was held up as irrefutable evidence for the intellectual as well as practical inevitability of this contrived cult. But just while they were taking their victory laps on behalf mythical free markets, western civilization was in dire need of alternative energy investments (wind, solar, fuel cells, etc.) and if all the cost of carbon and conflict were not hidden it might have happened. The joke of the era was "how many economists does it take to change a light bulb? None, the market will take care of it".

It was a cruel joke indeed that those who had benefited so mightily from the public largesse (e.g., virtually free access to public lands, weak regulations, and huge tax breaks, as well as direct infrastructure and other subsidies) regarded themselves as paragons of the natural market processes. Just as land was lumped into capital, labor relations were given over to certain ill-founded naturalistic notions, such as the infamous "lump of labor fallacy" (the idea that the amount of work is somehow fixed). This ludicrous idea was used to undermine employment regulations on the one hand and encourage early retirements on the other. Recently it has resurfaced to disparage immigration and promote protectionism. Meanwhile, hard won health, safety, and labor rights as well as environmental protections have been dismantled in the name of "regulatory reform" (see, Daneke & Lemak, 1985) and the welfare state bludgeoned as well. In essence, the "social contract" has thus been shredded in the name of a counterfeit science. It is as if economics and associated business practices had conjured an alternative cosmology in which the sun rotated around the earth and somehow shinned more powerfully upon the Masturbators of the Universe.

Legendary classical economist, David Ricardo (1817) maintained that the principle problem of political economy is the strategic readjustment (via spending and taxation) of the distribution of wealth between land, labor, and capital (rent, wages, and profit). The grand deceit of the neofeudalists is that these adjustments occur automatically (via the marginal productivity distribution myth), without power or politics. Assuming that the original distribution is sacrosanct, everyone magically gets exactly what they deserve. For them the distribution of wealth is a matter of "natural law" (as in, Bates-Clark, 1908). Yet back in the real world forces have been continuously manipulated, especially of late, so that virtually all increases in wealth accrue to capital (which for them includes rent). One major manipulation has been the active suppression of labor's bargaining power. And, special tax treatment of capital gains goes without saying. Moreover, astronomic asset inflation, hyper-leveraged debt accumulation, governmental backstopping, and financialization generally have facilitated massive amounts of phantom wealth for the rentier class. While ignored as arcane theory, the monoculture of monetarism and the melding of micro and macroeconomics have also contributed greatly to the distributional dilemma. In short, the Pelerin paradigm is complete repudiation of the economics enterprise.

CHAPTER 3: RESISTENCE IS FUTILE, MOSTLY

In economics, it takes a theory to kill a theory; facts can only dent the theorist's hide. _____ **Paul Samuelson**

No society can surely be flourishing and happy, of which the far greater part of the members are poor and miserable....How selfish soever man may be supposed, there are evidently some principles in his nature, which interest him in the fortune of others, and render their happiness necessary to him. _____ **Adam Smith**

Economists got away from really questioning how the world works, how decisions actually got made. If something doesn't conform to neoclassical models ... people are not somehow behaving themselves properly. _____ **Brian Arthur**

The market... represents only the surface of society...There is no probing into the depths of things, into natural and social facts that lie behind them. In a sense, the market is the institutionalization of individualism and non-responsibility. _____ **E. F. Schumacher**

Our thesis is that the idea of a self-adjusting market implied a stark utopia. Such an institution could not exist for any length of time without annihilating the human and natural substance of society; it would have physically destroyed man and transformed his surroundings into a wilderness. _____ **Karl Polanyi**

Many of us didn't get the memo or failed to master the secret hand shake. So we decided to waste our careers trying to get economics to live up to claims of scientific integrity or at least abandon its apology for privilege. To say we were foolhardy would be an understatement. We failed to notice that the epistemology (how they know what they know) of economics was specifically designed to undermine reform. Control of the top journals, promotion committees, and political appointments, greatly amplify narrow professional self-selection and arrogance. Max Plank once said that science progresses one funeral at a time. But the Pelerins have proven self-replicating, and not just biologically (e.g., the Friedman clan). In fact even more radical and reprehensible notions are now filtering into economics from blogosphere and from Far Right donors. Those of us who thought better science would make a difference did not realize we were dealing with a well-funded cult, bent on obfuscation (note, Smith, 2010). While not an exhaustive list, the delusional sub-disciplines and tangents included: afore mentioned institutional or evolutionary economics (note, Hodgson 2015; Mayhew, 2018), ecological economics (e.g., Daly, 1999), military conversion & peace studies (e.g., Dumas, 1986; Melman, 1988; Beer, 2001), political/human ecology & economic geography (see, Gare, 2002; Peet et. al. 2011), and complex adaptive systems (see, Daneke, 1999; Arthur, 2014). Meanwhile, beleagued bands of business ethicists (see, Freeman, 1991) and critical management scholars (mostly in Europe, see, Alvesson & Willmott, 2012) have also fought valiantly, yet futilely. None of us remotely managed to significantly alter mainstream economic thinking or appreciably slow the neofeudal juggernaut.

Leaving Virginia Tech for DC during the Carter years, I was deluded enough to think that we were actually redressing some of the many market imperfections and information asymmetries in national energy policy (e.g., battling cartels). Ronald Reagan swiftly destroyed this pipe dream, when his first act was tearing down the solar collectors from the White House. Returning to the ivory tower at the University of Michigan (a hot bed of what is now called "complexity theory") I again fell into my stupor of believing that by better capturing certain critical nonlinear dynamics policies might ultimately improve. Meanwhile, mainstream economists continued to maintain that nonlinearities were totality irrelevant, so they were. During my next brush with reality (serving on a White House Taskforce), I was reminded that when it comes to conflicts between truth and power, never betwixt will meet. I was still stunned that serious academics were providing cover for ideas that they knew to be bogus. The task force was assembled to provide credibility for the erroneous conclusion that productivity decline (which was really not declining at the time) was a result of union featherbedding and environmental over-regulation. Why was I so surprised that so many economists held engrained biases that colored their research so dramatically? Just dumb I guess. Even when I began notice the vast and extremely lucrative opportunities for economists emerging in finance and banking (and other rentier rewarding policy venues); the widespread nature of economic prostitution still escaped me. The titanic turnstile to the Federal Reserve, World Bank, International Monetary Fund, and the Bank of International Settlements, is immensely ruminative for academic economists who are willing to toe the line.

BURGEONING BUNDLES OF BLACK SHEEP

This does not necessarily imply that there are no honest intellectual brokers among economists. Many earnest scholars hammer away at the prevailing orthodoxy from relatively obscurity and a few even have stellar careers (e.g., Joe Stiglitz, Dani Rodrik, etc.). Moreover in Europe, many prestigious universities still maintain pockets of heterodoxy in contrast to the overwhelming monoculture of big US universities, especially as business programs became the vast cash cows. But even in the ancient educational centers "orthodoxy" often means the neoclassical economics paradigm and it associated ideological pachyderm. Several years back a small handful of economics students in France and England sought to address "the elephant in the room". These cheeky kids launched an open challenge to their orthodox professors, originally calling their movement "Post-autistic Economics". Realizing their insensitivity they quickly re-named themselves "Real World Economics". A good choice, in light of recent psychological studies that show that many highly functioning autistics (i.e., Asperger Syndrome), like myself, have too much rather than too little empathy. One of their patron saints, a brilliant Aussie and follower of Minsky, Steve Keen (2001) has demonstrated that many "heterodox" economists are hardly lacking in mathematical rigor, while also overcoming the rigor mortis of the orthodox. Moreover, the Santa Fe Institute (bastion of state-of-art tools) has brought together the likes of Sam Bowles (see. Bowles & Gintis, 2013) and leading macroeconomics theorist and University College London Professor, Dame Wendy Carlin (note, Carlin & Soskice, 2015) among many others to develop a new undergraduate economics curriculum called the CORE Project. However, I wonder if current crises will await the gradual arrival of these CORE thinkers near the halls of power (a generation or two from now) and how their policy ideas will fair in an epoch of increasing myth and mysticism. I applaud these efforts, nonetheless, and accept that ideas in "good currency" (both literally and figuratively) could change things in the blink of an eye. Meanwhile the orthodox abide, and the lion share of academic and policy-making posts still go to hardcore neofeudal economists.

The good news is that there are small bundles of black sheep, mostly hanging out in the back waters of academia. However, their ranks are growing and their influence is beginning to be felt. Rarer yet are those who directly slaughter one of the sacred cows. For example, there are a number of brave souls associated with something called Modern Monetary Theory (MMT, see, Kelton, 2001; Mitchell, et.al. 2016, and for an excellent lay introduction see Rojer, 2014). Harkening back to the Chartalists of a previous century, their "modern" element refers to the advent of universal "fiat" money (backed by nothing, aside from a huge military), which began in earnest in the 1970s. Moreover, they maintain that money machinations have been misused to serve certain "narrow interests" and to exacerbate inequality and instability. MMTeasers seek the demystification of money (starting with exposing the mainstream origination myth regarding the replacement of barter). They also reveal how political manipulations transfer the vast benefits of money management to societal elites. For example:

> Money scarcity is basically a political decision, as with Congress's imposition of an arbitrary limit, the debt ceiling, on the amount of money that the federal government borrows. It's largely motivated by those who would like to keep wealth concentrated in the hands of a few, who can personally benefit from the metaphorical printing press via government spending or direct access to the Fed (Rojer, 2014, p. 6).

MMT scholars focus on how hidden monetary processes might be redirected to serve wider societal interests. They present a number of policy perspectives that are only possible if one admits how money systems actually work (or fail to work). Generally speaking they maintain that the so called BOND MARKET is an elaborate neofeudal charade (a hugely expensive and ineffective method of maintaining interest rate targets and generating bank fees), when targeted fiscal policy would generate greater social utility at lower costs (for a simple explanation, note Winningham, 2018). They also support programs for generating real "full employment" without runaway inflation (e.g., "Job Guarantees" see, Wray, 2009). As one might expect they have been savagely attacked by mainstream scholars as well as political hacks for their attempts to endogenize money (put it back into macroeconomic policy models). Judiciously engineered ignorance regarding the role of money is prerequisite of neofeudalism. Architect turned economist J. D. Alt (2017) refers this situation as "monetary mental illness", and suggests that it is pure pandering to "the fat cats".

Questioning how the money works has long been the "third rail" (that which carries the deadly levels of electricity) for economists. Wayward Belgian Central Banker, Bernard Lietaer (2013), recounts how his MIT classmate, Paul Krugman, once warned him "you can never touch the money system". The MMT assumption that governments can merely re-assert power over their money is the only fly in the ointment that I can detect. But there also a danger that global exchanges would exact their pound of flesh from US dollar (further eroding its privileged status). As I will elaborate later, elite forces use the Central Banks (which are governmental in name only) to control most of the planet's money and generate galactic levels of fake wealth for themselves. These private entities are the sovereigns of the sovereigns, and the mega-bankers and their mainstream minions vigorously enforce Krugman's admonition as well as maintaining the myth that money is some sort of naturally evolved process that beyond the scope of government policy. It remains highly problematic that financial sovereignty can be returned to the people or that money might be managed in such a way as to better serve the public interest. But recognizing the possibility, even if small, might be worth further exploration.

Another powerful tangent to the prevailing orthodoxy is INEQUALTY research, and it is beginning to emerge in some of the more prestigious academic institutions. The topic has been virtually taboo in mainstream economics circles for decades (during which inequality as well as iniquity skyrocketed). Economists, generally, avoid all issues related to the distribution of wealth like the plague. Paul Krugman (2014) quotes influential Pelerin, Robert Lucas (of rational expectations fame), as follows: "Of the tendencies that are harmful to sound economics, the most seductive, and in my opinion the most poisonous, is to focus on questions of distribution (p. 1)". A small handful of scholars, ignored these edicts, and until very recently toiled away on the topic in relative obscurity. For example there is Sir Anthony (Tony) Atkinson of Oxford, who gave us the "Atkinson Index" (a concrete measure of distributional problems). His Economics of Inequality (1983) is a modern classic. But few economists have read it. A couple of young scholars, Thomas Piketty of the London School of Economics (LSE) and Emmanuel

Saez of UC Berkeley have worked with Atkinson and have recently rekindled interest among others. The French born, Piketty caused quite a stir (albeit short-lived) with the publication of his opus, Capital in the Twenty-First Century (2014; also note his comments on the political predicament, 2018). His weighty tome became a surprising best seller among mostly non-economists. In the past to the extent that economists spoke of inequality at all, they focused on trivial differences such as a college education versus high school, and so on (i.e., differences that pretty much addressed themselves). Piketty placed his laser focus upon the top 1 percent, and illustrates, with an abundance of historical data, how the concentration of wealth in fewer and fewer hands is a direct result of public policy choices (especially taxation). He also demonstrates how capital creation often outstrips economic growth, and when real growth slows wealth concentrations intensify. Plus, he explores how upward mobility is declining and that dynastic (inherited wealth) is on the rise. Finally he also documents how "trickle down" is clearly a myth. The greatest American fortunes are now about 1 million times larger than the average annual household income. The wealthy are now about 20 times richer than they were only 25 years ago. Now 80% of working Americans live from paycheck to paycheck, and nearly as many have less than 1000 dollars in reserve for an emergency. Inequality research chronicles this dispossession by design.

In case it is not obvious, I admit that I admire most of these unorthodox scholars and not just because they are the underdogs. I have to wonder, however, if the planet and our democracy will wait the decades needed for a truly scientific economics to take hold and guide policy. I am especially apprehensive when places like Silicon Valley are building a new aristocracy based in ancient ideologies. I fear it may all be too little too late. Besides mainstream economics appears to be able to adapt and thus absorb methodological advances without modifying its underlying ideology. Denying one has an ideology is helpful in promoting the collective unconsciousness. Consider how they were able to embrace "behavioralism", especially in finance (see, Just, 2013) and yet remain ideologically unscathed. Even the complex systems approach (discussed at length below), which is so clearly antithetical to neoclassical/neoliberal economics, has been graphed onto mainstream studies, in such a way as to barely distract from the underlying ideological project. It might also be the case that the opiate of ideology has become so acculturated that reality no longer matters. While we have lost our faith in many America's institutions, we still cling tightly to myths such as "rugged individualism" and "national exceptualism". These deeply rooted dogmas have become cultural imperatives and are so well blended with mainstream economic snake oil that certain elements will remain regardless. An ecological approach to economics, embracing the tools and concepts COMPLEX SYSTEMS (look to Daneke, 1999), is essential to unraveling these processes and products of long standing enculturation.

THE COMPLEXITY CONUNDRUM

Early in the development of economics along the lines as complex systems, the Santa Fe Institute held a conference bringing together leading physicists and economists (see, Anderson, et.al, 1988). The physicists there kept asking the economists, "You don't really believe that stuff do you" (e.g., General Equilibrium)? When I was first introduced to complex systems by UC Berkeley business researcher Erich Jantsch (see, 1975: 1980), I felt it was the "fulcrum in the void" that vindicated many earlier systems formulations (such as, Churchman, 1982). Moreover, I believed that complexity science could reconcile social learning and adaptation with the prevailing imperatives of autonomy and rationality, via what I came to call "systemic choices". While still deeply in Forrest Gump mode, I could never quite understand why these types of insights were not sweeping through economics, especially in light of the work being done at Michigan. Of course, back then in the early 1980s, I was still mostly oblivious to the ideological capture of economics, writ large. Plus, I had no idea of the lengths to which the Pelerins and their disciples would go to maintain their neofeudal policy agenda and how interwoven it was with methodological restrictions. Moreover colleagues would say, "why would I want to bother with simulations of realistically diverse agents when my simple, super-rational, single agent model takes me to nearly the same place, most of the time"? I would say nearly and mostly don't cut it, and your results are tautological (true by definition). Plus, I would add that if it really ends up in approximately the same place, then that just goes to show how smart interacting semi-rational agents might be, which usually got chuckle.

It is critical to point out, that while complex systems theory shares a number of antecedents with earlier systems and cybernetic explorations, it actually by-passes much of their perceived ideological inadequacies. Systems thinking in general grew out of the excellent work by various engineers and diverse (including social) scientists during WWII under the rubric of Operations Research (OR). Early successful application in business and industry mostly drew upon the mechanical or closed systems (where no energy is exchanged across borders) perspective. Social systems, however, are clearly open or living systems. Early complexity science focused on certain persistent nonlinear problems in fields such as fluid and aero dynamics, as well as population biology (predator/prey dynamics). Complexity science did not religiously adhere to artificial distinctions, and thus began to find wider applications (see, Prigogine, 1980) across the sciences. Curious processes, such as "dissipative structures", "qualitative state change", and "self-organization (spontaneous emergence)" and other heretofore puzzling dynamic processes could now be explored, especially given advances in computational and informational methods (e.g., cellular automata and neural networks, as well as game theory, see, Daneke, 1999). Gradually these combined breakthroughs were being appreciated by a new generation of social scientists (working with biologists and computer scientists) such as the ones I encountered at the University of Michigan and the DOE Labs. With the help of famed physicists from places like Cal Tech and various social scientists from Michigan, Stanford and U Mass., these groups were gathered in places like the Santa Fe Institute for the Study of Complexity, and the rest is history. Except that the Santa Fe Express has yet to fully leave the station. Ideological controversies and residual anti-systems thinking still throw a pall over the enterprise. Assuming that this continued antagonism stems from earnest concerns, such as the oppressiveness of old top-down systems models (as opposed to pecuniary fanaticism), critics should chill out. Complex Systems Models are BOTTOM-UP. Epstein and Axtell (1996) explain the basis of what is now called "agent-based modeling" as follows:

> [W]e give agents rules of behavior and spin the system forward in time and see what macroscopic social structures emerge...we part company with certain members of the individualist camp insofar as we believe that the collective structure , or institutions that emerge have feedback effects

in the agent population, altering the behavior of
individuals (p. 16-17).

Overall, complexity science renders a completely different set of perspectives from those of neoclassical/neoliberal economics. First of all complex systems reverse, yet revitalize "methodological individualism". Economists say that the individual is their unit of analysis, but not real individuals, only the mythical economic man (who must behave the way the model says he should). By direct contrast, complexity models greatly broaden our perspective, by slightly shifting the unit of analysis to sets of interactions between diversely motivated individuals and their institutions. In this way, agents are free to surprise us, and they often do. What complexity reveals is that human agency is actually a systemic process. Moreover, complexity supports a participatory imperative, and in a fundamental way they are more DEMOCRATIC. Distinguished mathematician and social theorist, John Casti (1994) observes that many economic inquiries assume "simple systems", where only a small number of firms or few decision makers dictate the outcomes. He cites political dictatorships, privately owned corporations and the Catholic Church, with their patterns of low interaction between the lines of command and a centralized authority. Complex systems, on the other hand, assume a "diffusion of authority", even if they have a central leader. As Casti explains:

> *...in actuality the power is spread over a decentralized*
> *structure. Actions of a number of units then combine to*
> *generate the actual system behavior. Typical examples of*
> *these kinds of systems include democratic governments,*
> *labor unions and universities. Such systems tend to be*
> *somewhat more resilient and stable than centralized*
> *structures because they are more forgiving of mistakes by*
> *any one decision-maker and are more able to absorb*
> *unexpected environmental fluctuations (p. 272).*

In other words, complex systems mirror the actual ecology of human agency, where the "wisdom of crowds" can enhance resiliency and improve the performance of individual responsibilities and societal structures (note: Brush, et. al., 2018).

Another unique systemic feature that is central to the ecological approach is the process of EMERGENCE where interactions produce novel properties and behavioral patterns, and where "the whole is greater than the sum of its parts". "Emergence" is inherent byproduct of turbulence and this element that is another key point of departure from mainstream economics. Complexity economics pioneer, Brian Arthur (2013) explains that complexity emphasizes non-equilibrium, while neoclassical economics remains mired in the quest for non-existent equilibrium. He elaborates as follows:

> *Where equilibrium economics emphasizes order, determinacy, deduction, and stasis, complexity economics emphasizes contingency, indeterminacy, sense-making, and openness to change...This view, in other words, gives us a world closer to that of political economy than to neoclassical theory, a world that is organic, evolutionary, and historically-contingent (pp. 1-2).*

In short, non-equilibrium is how the economy works, particularly in light of recurring financial crises. As Arthur maintains, most of the important stuff is NOT about "allocative efficiency thought markets", it is about "formation". Formation involves:

> *...how an economy emerges in the first place, and grows and changes structurally over time. This is represented by ideas about innovation, economic development, structural change, and the role of history, institutions, and governance in the economy... (p.17).*

Ergo, complexity economics, according to Arthur, should be used to restore "the grand tradition of political economy".

TOWARDS AN ECOLOGY OF INSTITUTIONS

I have chosen to call this revitalized approach to political economy, INSTITUTIONAL ECOLOGY (see, Daneke, 1999). Like the old institutional (or evolutionary) economics, it draws heavily from other more authentic social sciences (e.g., psychology, anthropology, geography, history and political science) as well as the biology and the humanities. While not exhaustive, it would at least include the following ingredients:

1. Institutions Matter (norms, culture, individual & social traits, and political power influence the course of the economy);

2. Systemic Choices Count (cooperation, altruism, fairness, and reciprocation as well as pecuniary motivations shape individual choices);
3. History is Vital (path dependency, lock-in, and adaptive & exaptive recombinations shape progress);
4. Emergence is Key (perpetual novelty, and whole greater than the sum of its parts);
5. Nonlinearity is the Nexus (feedback driven distortions, chaotic cascades, and non-equilibrium dynamics, produce unintended consequences); and,
6. Evolution is Integral (individuals and societies co-evolve via agency as well as inexorable forces and produce constant change, mostly glacial, but periodically revolutionary).

I must admit when it comes to economics I no longer harbor the delusion that this approach will become the new "normal science" (via: Kuhn, 1962) any time soon. Since mainstream economics is NOT a science (with inductive theory building and replicable experiments (or much validation for that matter), it is even more recalcitrant than Kuhn characterized, especially given its neofeudal motivations. At this point I would merely assert that Madame Thatcher was dead wrong. There are viable alternatives, as well as more scientifically valid, and socially constructive policy pathways, but I suspect it I will be long dead before they become the new economics orthodoxy.

Studies which use complexity science tools and concepts are, nonetheless, making inroads. Heather Campbell of the Claremont Graduate University and her colleagues (Campbell et. al. 2015) did path-breaking work using agent-based modeling (ABM) to address heretofore intractable issues such as "environmental justice" in their study of sustainable cities. The Legendary, Giovanna Dosi and his colleagues (Dosi et. al., 2016) used ABMs to explore the impact of labor market reforms on unemployment and income inequalities. Dominik Hartmann and his colleagues (Hartmann, et. al., 2017) delved into a broader set of institutional issues that link economic complexity to income inequality. Bertotti & Modnanese (2016) did much the same for differing tax regimes and tax evasion strategies. Michael Schlaile and his colleagues in Stuttgart (Schlaile, et. al. 2018) point out how ABM can be used to revitalize evolutionary economics and facilitate "responsible innovation". Los Alamos scholar and physicist, turned financial advisor, Dorn Farmer, among others have argued that complexity models should be used to redesign financial regulations, with a focus on reducing the persistence of fraud (see, Ruhl, 2016; and Witzling, 2016). Anthropologist, Ron Wallace (2017) maintains that crises that have reoccurred regularly over the 400 year history of western Capitalism could be better predicted using ABMs and Boolean Networks. This of course this assumes that crisis avoidance rather than creation is the objective. In sum, a complex systems approach to economic institutions would not only unravel the mountains of "systemic risk" in global banking networks (note, May, et. al. 2007; and, Haldane & May, 2010) it would, if given the chance, lay bare the fatuous and fetid underbelly of prevailing economic policies.

For these and other obvious reasons mainstream economics tends to ignore most complexity research, unless it can be easily misinterpreted to support the status quo. The most likely scenario is that complexity concepts and methods will continue creeping into fields such as risk management and critical business studies, as well as various real social sciences (see, Byrne and Callaghan, 2013). In economics however, it is likely to merely continue to generate many a bizarre bastard with the ubiquitous broodmares of neoclassic mythology. All-the-while neofeudal ideology will continue on its merry way, and certain especially sacred realms will remain unassailable.

CHAPTER 4: BANKERS HAVE ALWAYS BEEN WANKERS

Permit me to issue and control the money of a nation, and I care not who makes its laws. _____ **Mayer Amschel Rothschild**

The most hated sort, and with the greatest reason, is usury, which makes a gain out of money itself, and not from the natural object of it. For money was intended to be used in exchange, but not to increase at interest. And this term interest, which means the birth of money from money, is applied to the breeding of money.... Wherefore of the modes of getting wealth, this is the most unnatural. _____ **Aristotle**

History records that the money changers have used every form of abuse, intrigue, deceit, and violent means possible to maintain their control over governments by controlling money and its issuance. _____ **James Madison**

The death of Lincoln was a disaster for all Christendom....I Fear that the foreign bankers with their craftiness and tortuous tricks will entirely control the exuberant riches of American and use it to systematically corrupt civilization. _____ **Otto von Bismarck**

[Banking is] the privilege of taking the golden eggs laid by somebody else's goose....The development of our financial oligarchy followed, in this respect, lines with which the history of political despotism has familiarized us; usurpation, proceeding by gradual encroachment rather than by violent acts; subtle and often long-concealed concentration of distinct functions. _____ **Louis Brandeis**

Well perhaps not all bankers are always wankers, but certainly many. Furthermore, even if they are not complete villains, they are a far cry from the neutrally competent, god like mediators assumed by prevailing monetary models. Given their institutionalization of auto-aggrandizement, not to mention their parasitism, calling them wankers is spot on (even mild). As a basic enterprise banking has always been more than a bit dodgy. For much of human history banking was in fairly ill-repute, given religious and civil prohibitions such as the charging of interest (usury). More corrupting yet is the "fractional reserve" provision which allows banks to loan out or invest themselves much more money than they ever have on deposit. Reserves are mythically maintained at 10%, but banks routinely engage in labyrinthine machinations that reduces this percentage substantially. Leverage on deposits is small in comparison to hugely multi-leveraged investment instruments they often carry on their books. The institutions designed to shore-up these fundamental flaws and prevent bank runs are themselves a source of myth and monstrous instability. With the backstop of central banks, banking as an enterprise has made an art out of pulling money out their bum (see; McLeay, et.al. 2014). Keep in mind that loans are assets to banks and these assets are used as collateral on further loans. Moreover, collateral can be repledged (rehypothicated) many times over (e.g., 100 X 1 at the City of London) that these loans on loans on loans become ethereal, yet generating bank fees at every turn. Imagine if you could get away with counterfeiting by just scribbling on a piece of paper (or computer screen), and those scribbles would magically become legal tender. During the colonial period one enterprising New Jersey business man built a factory to manufacture wampum (the intricate beaded belts held to be precious by indigenous peoples). These counterfeits were used to purchase furs and even lands from the tribes. Banks are still manufacturing their own version of wampum today, and we are legally bound to use it for the payment of taxes and accept it in exchange for things that we deem precious.

Other magical financial creations such as DERIVATIVES (that derive their value from another asset or transaction) have raised the level of leverage and fake wealth to galactic proportions (as in many times the GDP of the planet). Derivatives can be purchased with tiny installments, allowing special investors (whales) to control infinitely more potential wealth, trusting the banks to cover their asses as well as over leveraged assets. Since the ascendancy of Central Banks, which are actually private cartels rather than government agencies, banking is both more sacred, as in "too big to fail or jail" (TBTFOJ), and more profane. How can a self-proclaimed free market economy have entities that are not allowed to fail, or a nation that believes in the "rule of law" which exempts bankers? Having governments and central bankers willing to backstop a reckless banking industry has, when combined with elaborate levering devices, led to nearly civilization ending risk miscalculations. Insane asset inflation amid misguided nuclear missiles of speculation (and out and out fraud) became the norms when the risks are mostly born by the tax payers.

THE WIZARDS OF WANK

As Goldman Sachs CEO, Lloyd Blankfein, stated the big investment banks are "doing God's work". They must be, since we treat them like gods. I suspect perhaps he was pulling our leg, but I assume he is earnest when he asserts the magisterial importance of "market making". Goldman, however, seems equally interested with making mayhem. When we heard Congressional testimony back in 2008, we too wanted to know why Goldman clearly damaged so many of its own investors (selling mortgaged back securities that were specifically structured to fail). However, this demonstrates a lack of understanding of what an investment bank does. They have clients and they have customers, and they are in the business of finding customers for whatever "crap" they and clients want to sell. Goldman has a long history of infamy, dating back to its founding by German born, Marcus Goldman in 1869. Particularly egregious were a type of mutual fund (actually Ponzi schemes) it ran during the roaring 20s that cost 42,000 investors their life savings. It precipitated the Penn Central Bank disaster with its faulty (or defaulty) short-term paper in the 1970s. Goldman also helped Greece hide its debts (so they could join and then become the basket case of the European Union) and they drove Jefferson County, Alabama, among other places, into bankruptcy with bond swaps. Matt Taibbi (2010) chronicled Goldman's role in both creating several vast bubbles and exploiting their bursting. He summed up their work as a "great vampire squid wrapped around the face of humanity, relentlessly jamming it blood funnel into anything that smells like money". As he explains:

> The bank's unprecedented reach and power have enabled it to turn all of America into a giant pump-and-dump scam, manipulating whole economic sectors for years at a time.... All that money that you're losing, it's going somewhere, and in both a literal and a figurative sense, Goldman Sachs is where it's going: The bank is a huge, highly sophisticated engine for converting the useful, deployed wealth of society into the least useful, most wasteful and insoluble substance on Earth....(p.1).

All the while, Goldman was allowed to maintain its virtually un-regulated status as a pure investment bank. However, when crises hit it was converted (literally overnight) to commercial bank status to insure it access to the Federal Reserve's Discount Window, and the US taxpayers. It helps to have friends and former or future employees in high places. Recall that the Treasury Secretary at the time was Hank Paulson (former Goldman CEO). In fact, 5 of the last 6 US Secretaries of the Treasury once worked at Goldman, and alumni of this one bank also occupy an inordinate number of high ranking government positions across the globe. Trump has set a new record bringing 8 Goldmanites in through the revolving door and in overriding new banking rules. Even when it failed a portion of its 2018 "stress test" Goldman was allowed to divert another 5 billion from reserves to special investors. When Steve Bannon was leaving the Trump White House, he exclaimed "we are now ruled by the Goldman Sachs Regency".

While unprecedented in political power, Goldman Sachs is hardly alone in dirty dealing. Most of the major banks have joined in the hall of shame. Consider the bank that still holds the name of infamous Robber Baron, J. P. Morgan, and now J.P. Morgan-Chase (JPMC). It is pretty much in a dead heat with Goldman. Their rap sheet of historical crimes and collusions would fill volumes, and their direct role the on-going financial crises is indisputable. Yet, recently, they added additional frauds to the payment of fines for past frauds. Only an industry that had completely captured their regulators would be so bold as to settle claims for wholesale mortgage fraud, with mortgages they no longer owned (see, Dayen, 2017). That's right; JPMC was using mortgage relief to settle most of its "hand slap" settlement from 2013. The only problem is that it already sold most of the properties for which it was now claiming a 4 billion dollar credit toward approximately 5 billion in fines. Moreover, it had already been paid default claims on many of the properties. This level of outrageous audacity boggles the mind, but it is standard operating procedure among those who know they are special elite class unto themselves.

Simply stated, banking is a highly "criminogenic ecosystem". They began with a basic swindle and have been pushing the boundaries of legality and engaging in political corruption for centuries. As Bill Black, former S&L (Savings & Loans, or "thrifts") prosecutor turned reformist economics professor, suggests in the title of his excellent book on "accounting control fraud", The Best Way to Rob a Bank is to Own One (2005). Back in the 1980s the S&L Crisis was a microcosm of banking in general. After massive deregulation, the S&Ls became a graduate school for scoundrels (including arms and drug dealers, see: Pizzo, et. al., 1989), and widespread "looting" ultimately cost the US tax payers nearly a half trillion dollars. Today, paying regular fines for violations of securities laws is part of the basic banking business model, and hardly puts a dent in their profits. US authorities have collected 150 billion in fines resulting from the financial crisis of 2008 as well as sending 324 individuals to prison briefly. But not a single one of those individuals was an executive with a major bank. Banking institutions are vital to the functioning of any economy, yet they have also facilitated much of the malinvestment and mayhem in human history.

A VERY BRIEF HISTORY OF BANKING

Banking is nearly as old as civilization itself. Activities that we might recognize as primitive banking arose in Persia and Mesopotamia between the 4th and 3rd millennia BC. But banking really got cranking with the rise of large scale agriculture. Some of the earliest bankers were intimately involved in the growth, storage and transport of food and fodder, yet banking quickly proceeded from the basics of seeds, animals and equipment to financing the irrigation and transportation networks as well as other indirect control of the commodities. Seasonality and other risk factors (from war to weather) made agriculture and husbandry rich sources of financial creativity. Meanwhile of course the nexus of creativity was mostly focused upon the disposition of credit, amid persistent religious as well as social strictures.

While greatly oversimplified the history of banking can be summarized as a series of battles over the management of money, debt, and interest. In the ancient world emperors and kings were center stage, and the gradual evolution from gifting to grifting revolved around the payment of debts and taxes. In the early Middle Ages the church, which was also a political/military power, struggled to contain the banks via usury laws, but by the mid to late the middle ages, banking dynasties gained their own political power and by the late middle ages kings were subservient to the banks that funded their various wars. In the modern era democratic governments, especially in the US, have struggled mightily with occasional victories over the unbridled power of the banks.

Ultimately, however, it is usually the banks that have prevailed, by asserting their monopoly over the finance of nations.

The word bank refers a table, such as those that Jesus overturned on the steps of the Temple in Jerusalem. In the ancient world, Temples were the centers of community and commerce, and hence also the primary location for the changing of money. The early institutions of Money & Banking flourished along with production agriculture in places like the "Fertile Crescent" (between modern day Iraq, Kuwait, and Syria). In his brilliant anthropological study, Debt: The First 5000 Years, David Graeber (2011) explains that banking grew out of book keeping and the individuation of debt. The code of Hammurabi (1754 BC) included sections on the recording of interest bearing debt. Graeber maintains that maintenance of "inescapable debt", the pillar of modern banking, was an essential violation of basic human relationships that served us quite well for thousands of years. Before debt there was reciprocal gifting (see also: Mauss, 1954) in which all members of the community were mutually indebted. Contrary to prevailing origination myth, Money & Banking did NOT emerge from barter, rather it was the institutionalization of debt. Debts were a convenient source of indentured servants, and a poor indebted farmer could have his entire family indentured. However every seven years, debts would be canceled by the Law of Jubilee, and the first word for freedom, "amargi" (Sumerian for a return to mother) would be granted. As Cambridge historian, Moses Finley (1973) in his renowned classics lectures (The Ancient Economy) points out that such social safety valves were vital. Since all revolutionary movements of the ancient world were about the cancellation of debt and/or the redistribution of land.

During the middle ages prohibitions replaced pardons. And, Priests and pontiffs stepped into the breach in the battle over banking. Of course, USURY (the charging of interest on loans) was the focal point. The level of interest was often capped by law in the ancient world, but during the so-called Dark Ages any level became a nearly mortal sin. Dante assigned usurers to the "seventh circle of hell". The direct charging of interest on loans was prohibited by most of the major religions for centuries and still prohibited in certain sects of Islam to this day (of course bank fees are allowed). Occasionally these religious prohibitions were often given the force of law, as with Emperor Charlemagne in 800 AD. Punishments in the hereafter issued from pulpit, however, were only matched by episodic legal enforcements. Moreover, hell fire insurance as well as get out jail free cards could be purchased with a few well painted frescoes in a chapel or two. As with modern Islamic banking, usury work-a-rounds became increasing inventive along with the increasing trade and commerce. But these efforts were often secondary to those undertaken to increase the political power of banking.

One strategy saw banks evolving directly out of religious orders. The Knights Templar, a Catholic military order, founded one of the first major banks in Europe in 1100, with funds they acquired providing protection and financial services to pilgrims journeying to the Holy Land. The Templars were famous for making loans to purchase fortifications of their own design and construction across Europe, as well as the funding of armies and wars. Phillip IV of France was so deeply in debt to the order, that he decided to spread misinformation about their various satanic iniquities and organized a sneak attack on many of their cloisters simultaneously in 1307. These carefully coordinated attacks (giving rise to Friday the 13th superstitions) allowed Philip to seize their wealth and torture priests into well scripted confessions. Other powerful banking dynasties absorbed the extremely lucrative war arbitrage market along with their control of commodities.

The growing power of the banks is best expressed in the excellent (Golden Globe winning) dramatization of the story of Henry VIII and Anne Boleyn, Wolf Hall (2015). Henry's world wise, first minister, Thomas Cromwell, explains:

> No ruler in the history of the world has ever been able to afford a war. They're not affordable things. No prince ever says, this is my budget, so this is the kind of war I can have....

> The world is not run from where he [Henry] thinks. Not from border fortresses, not even from Whitehall. The world is run from Antwerp, from Florence, from places he has never imagined; from Lisbon, from where the ships with sails of silk drift west and are burned up in the sun. Not from the castle walls, but from counting houses, not by the call of the bugle, but by the click of the abacus, not by the grate and click of the mechanism of the gun but by the

*scrape of the pen on the page of the promissory note that
pays for the gun and the gunsmith and the powder and
shot.*

THE DUKES OF MORAL HAZARD

In modern times, the banks overcame the dual threats of
usury and debt forgiveness (except for themselves), and their
misplaced military mission was magnified by permanent warfare
(both cold and hot). Meanwhile their political power grew to
unimaginable levels. Tightly regulated bankruptcy laws and
astronomical interest allowances, not to mention ever burgeoning
military budgets, have made obscuring risk and extending debt the
raison d'état of the modern age. Hidden governmental underwriting
and convoluted risk concealment has magnified what economists
call "moral hazard" (tacit or actual insurance that inspires reckless
risk taking). And, the TBTFOJ banks are the dukes of moral hazard.
With the tax payer as insurer of last resort, risk is effectively
separated from reward. While large scale debt forgiveness was
pretty much lost to antiquity, restructuring, reorganizations, and
bankruptcy (from the ancient practice literally breaking the tables),
have become a major portion of the modern business tool kit. Nobel
laureate (and Yellen hubby) George Akerlof and Paul Romer (1993)
refer to it as "looting" (particularly when tax payers take a bath
along with workers and creditors) and they contend it is a
ubiquitous profit mechanism. Firms routinely use bankruptcy to
jettison their pesky pension obligations. President Trump has a
history of regularly stiffing his creditors via bankruptcies. Of
course, entire countries can default on their debts periodically, and
wholesale restructuring is occasionally undertaken (e.g., Mexico
bailout of 1982), especially when it benefits the banks. Plus, after
the disastrous reparations following WWI, we have the rather
rarified example of continental war debts being forgiven along with
the Marshall Plan following WWII. Banks were not completely
uncompensated, however. Mega reset bottoms remain mostly
among the pages of the Old Testament, however.

Modern bankruptcy laws were enacted on a rather ad hoc
basis to smooth over economic crises. Moreover, they were often
reversed when abuse inevitably resulted. Economic crises during
the 1690s (including plague, and the wreck of the much of the

merchant fleet in a storm) inspired the British parliament to enact the Queen Anne laws in 1706 to allow partial repayments and prevent the bulk of the merchant class from being taken off to debtor's prison. Following the collapse of land speculations, the first official US bankruptcy law was passed 1800, and repealed in 1803 in response widespread fraud. The Panic of 1837 brought a second bankruptcy law in 1841 (repealed in 1843). Economic upheaval following the civil war prompted more bankruptcy provisions in 1867. They lasted up until repealed in 1879, after infamous railroad speculator Jay Cook's mighty Philadelphia banking combine itself declared bankruptcy and caused the Panic 1873 (which lasted to 1877). In the Great Depression, bankruptcy Acts of 1933 and 1934 withstood a Supreme Court challenge (Local Loan v. Hunt, 1934) when justices decided that certain individuals and firms deserved a "fresh start". Provision for greater latitude in corporate reorganizations was provided by the Chandler Act 1938. Following the economic chaos of the 1970s the Chandler Act was extended to individuals and embellished for corporations in the Bankruptcy Reform Act of 1978.

With the movement of neofeudalism from the think tanks to the halls of power beginning in the 1970s, bankruptcy laws were more tightly tailored to banking as well as corporate interests. In 1982 the Supreme Court stepped in to curtail the power of bankruptcy courts, yet via 1984 amendments reorganizations proceeded at a rapid pace. However, these measures were more effectively intermingled with the creative finance during this era of merger mania via modifications of antitrust enforcement. Integration on several fronts continued with Bill Clinton's comprehensive bankruptcy reforms of 1994, which among other things created a National Bankruptcy Review Commission. By the time George W. Bush signed the Bankruptcy Abuse Prevention and Consumer Protection Act (a misnomer if ever there was one) in 2005, debt forgiveness was exclusively reserved for certain neofeudal lords. For example, things like student loans (now pushing well past 1.5 trillion dollars) will forever burden the new debt serfs.

Meanwhile of course, usury really had become relegated to distant past. Occasionally legislatures step in to cap credit card interest below 20% (e.g., Card Act of 2009), but overall with fees and penalties the sky really is the limit. The very last man to serve time in the stocks in colonial New England had been found guilty of usury (having charged slightly over 1%). With the beginning of the new nation, most states adopted the national cap of 6%, but compounding and fees varied greatly. Banking deregulation in the run up to the Great Depression saw many state usury laws abolished altogether. In 1916, the Uniform Small Loan Law allowed interest to rise to 33%. From the end of WWII till the 1980s, a cap of 36% held across the US, but Veteran Administration Loans were frozen at 6%, and mortgages could be assumed by non-vets. Beginning in the 1980s the US Congress passed a series of laws that over-ruled state restrictions and allowed home mortgage loans to become highly creative (e.g., adjustable rate, interest only, and the infamous "sub-prime" loans). In 2006 Congress reinstated a 36% cap, but only for active military families. Despite the passage of Dodd-Frank, with its Consumer Protection Bureau (2010), predatory lending prevails. Today "payday" or "car title" loan shops (with indirect links to global financial institutions) can effectively charge more than 500%. Old school, knee capping, loan sharks can barely compete.

THE EVOLUTION OF CENTRAL WANKING

Legalized loan sharking, while egregious, is still junior league wanking, when compared to colossal wealth and power made available to global elites through the provision of central banking, especially when it includes control of the money supply. Through these institutions we have given bankers the ultimate power to direct the finance of nations, influence the ebb and flow of vital global commodities (e.g., oil) and even provoke wars. As Lord Actor would say, so much absolute power will "corrupt absolutely". Our own Faustian bargain with central banks made us the most powerful empire the world ever has known. But now it is sustained by a Mount Everest of debts, and it means serfdom for the multitude. As our hegemonic power wanes our new feudal lords become increasing parasitic. To our credit perhaps we fought the power of banking for most of our history, albeit without much success.

As a product in perpetuity of Britain, the US inherited their Central Banking system, whether we wanted it or not. While not the first Central Bank, the Bank of England (BOE) is certainly the big kahuna. Initially established as a joint stock company, it was designed to allow private subscribers to loan directly to the cash strapped governments (engaged in perpetual wars). In the beginning it was no more the Bank of England (BOE) than Bank of America is the bank of America. However, like most Central Banks, it gradually became "the bank of the bankers". With its official Royal Charter in 1694, it gained the privilege of issuing bank notes, and eventually their notes would become the national currency, but only after running battles with "bullionists", "Chartalists", and even some "mercantilists" over the next couple of centuries. It was not granted its monopoly over the currency until 1844, and was not actually a government entity until taken over by the Attlee government in 1946. In keeping with the rise of the new neofeudalism (via Thatcher) it was gradually granted increasing autonomy in the 1980s and given operational independence once again by Gordon Brown's government in 1997.

American misadventures with Central Banking were not nearly so gentlemanly. The American Revolution was as much a fight against British banking as anything else. According to Ben Franklin, the major issue was the right of the colonies to have their own coinage, with taxation a distant second. Popular history conveys the tale of taxes on things like tea. It is humorous that members of current Tea Party (an Astroturf creation of powerful elites) are oblivious to the fact that the original tea rebellion was against a private trade cartel. Plus, the notorious British East India Trading Company (EIC) was interwoven with the lords of Threadneedle Street. More comical yet, is Broadway's history destroying portrayal of "Hamilton". In the real world, he was a rabid neofeudalist, who blackmailed the Congress by threatening a military takeover. His creation of the First National Bank was a device for paying war debts with interest to profiteers and buttressing financial elites with indirect ties to the BOE. Jefferson's vision of maintaining an agrarian utopia may have been misplaced, yet his assertions that Central Banking was a pathway back to feudalism resonates to this day. The US National Bank patterned after its mother bank (the BOE) and was given most of the powers Hamilton prescribed in 1791. The new federal government was required to purchase 20% of the shares and could appoint 20% of the board, so obviously control rested firmly in private hands, and no pretense to the "public interest" was initially attempted. It was essentially a bank to bully (and occasionally bankrupt) the various the state-chartered banks and terrorize farmers. So heavy handed was its self-interest, that Congress voted to NOT renew its charter 1811.

The obscure War of 1812 (where the British briefly invaded and burned parts of the US capital and Canadian borders were reconfirmed) has been credited to this interruption of British banking in America. Somehow however, the war was explained via the other minor disputes such as issue of "impressed seaman" a practice by the Britain navy of stopping US ships on the high seas and relieving them of a few of their English born crew members (immortalized in Melville's Billy Bud). The bank cartel quickly regrouped and restored most of their privileges, but did not get the US Congress to charter a 2nd National Bank in 1816. This second bank was needed to backstop the risks of large scale infrastructure investments (such as the Erie Canal which also began that year).

Corruption and scandal made the 2nd National Bank worse than the first. Two attempts were made to have it declared unconstitutional. Seen as a pillar of the new aristocracy, the bank became the target of populist President Andrew Jackson. He was a general, land speculator, and legislator, and was as unrelenting in his "Bank War" as he was in his genocide of indigenous peoples (even those tribes that were more "civilized" than the whites who sought their lands). He fought to withdraw government funds from the "devil bank", and return the country to metal coinage. Benefiting from a boom period during which the value of land, cotton, and especially slaves had rose precipitously, Jackson paid off the national debt in 1835. He survived an assassination attempt by an iterant house painter, once employed by one of his senatorial opponents. When a bill to re-charter the national bank arrived on his desk he vetoed it, ending the 2ndCentral Bank in 1836. The Bank of England immediately raised interest rates and its US associate banks stopped exchanging paper for species, initiating the Panic 1837 and a deep recession that lasted until the mid-1840s (during which nearly half the banks in the US failed). The anti-bank movement more or less prevailed, and President Van Buren initiated the era of the "Independent Treasury" (independent from the banks, not the government) in 1846.

The Civil War, Reconstruction, and westward expansion provided so many lucrative debt opportunities that bankers seemed somewhat satisfied with the loose knit confederation in national banking during the ensuing period. During the war of course, Lincoln had openly defied the banks and their heavy interest charges by printing his own "Green Backs" (interest free). But his plans for further interest fee financing of reconstruction died with him. A couple of additional acts during this era attempted to strengthen the power of the US Treasury Department (e.g., establishing the Office of the Comptroller of the Currency) to coordinate the free-for-all. Panics and cascading small bank failures proceeded at fairly regular intervals, and gradually pressure built up for another national bank.

FED BY "THE FED"AND OTHER FICTIONS

Apparently the third time was the charm, however, the establishment of the Federal Reserve required a level of skullduggery not seen outside to the pages of a John Le Carre' novel. In 1907 a massive Panic (also called the "Banker's Panic", or the "Rich Man's Panic") began. Following Teddy Roosevelt's "trust busting" and a failed attempt by investors to corner the copper market, New York bankers dramatically withdrew liquidity and the contagion quickly spread. At one point the crisis was so dire that Roosevelt was forced to hold his nose and allow huge Steel merger that clearly violated the Sherman Anti-trust Act. Moreover, he was also forced to ignore the biggest trust of all, the mysterious "Money Trust", whose existence was publicly identified in the Pujo Commission Report in 1913. This tiny congressional commission assembled to provide a post-mortem of the Panic of 1907, contended that a small cabal of international bankers controlled the lion share of US industry. Officers of J.P. Morgan alone sat on the boards 112 companies (with a combined capitalization of 22.5 billion, back when the entire New York Stock Exchange was only 26.5 billion). Oddly enough the rationale given for a new Central Bank was to curb the power of the Money Trust. Propaganda claimed that the bankers opposed another Central Bank. "Don't throw me in that there briar patch" cried Brer Rabbit. Only a few brave souls (e.g., Brandeis, 1914) pointed out that this might be as greatest con game of all time. All the while, bankers and senators met in secret to fashion another central bank. Morgan's private train would whisk them away in the middle of the night to his secluded estate at Jekyll Island, Georgia. The Act establishing the Federal Reserve (not much more a government agency than the

Federal Express) went for a vote on Dec. 23, 1913, after several members of Congress had already left for the holidays. With the final ratification of the 16th Amendment or the Income Tax (sold with the promise that it would only tax the rich) that same year, the banks now had all they needed to build their perpetual motion money machine. More lies by Woodrow Wilson regarding additional measures to police new banking system were only surpassed by his forgotten campaign promise to keep the US out of WWI. The big banks had already been financing weapons and war bonds for both sides. The "war to end all wars" was about as successful as the bank to end all banking crises. Even grading on the curve the performance of "the Fed" has been a D+ at best. While Panics may have become less regular, its overall role in inflating bubbles and facilitating violent crashes is undeniable. It is the great engine of dispossession for the masses. Even former Fed Governor and Hoover Fellow at Stanford, Kevin Warsh, referred to Fed policies as "reverse Robin Hood" in a 2014 talk at the Brooking Institution.

Irish born, French banker/economist, Richard Cantillon (1755/2010), who acquired great wealth via John Law's Mississippi Bubble, observed that monetary policy (especially by central banks) inherently redistributes wealth upward. Despite praise for his work from Adam Smith to Stanley Jevons, the "Cantillon Effect" is virtually unknown outside of small circles of unorthodox economists. The Federal Reserve's wild credit expansion is a paradigm of this process. The Fed was specifically designed to safeguard the interest of extreme wealth. The first significant test for the Fed came quickly at the end of its coming out party, the "Roaring 20s". Ultra-easy credit (and a 62% increase in the money supply) had fueled insane speculation. From 1929-1933 the Federal Reserve radically contracted the money supply by 33%, which turned a stock market crash into the Great Depression. Half of the US banks failed, but some big banks flourished. Franklin Roosevelt (FDR) referred to them as the "banksters", and they called him "an enemy to his class". FDR sanctioned investigations (e.g., the Pecora Commission) and prosecutions of bank executives, as well as pushing for significant reforms. Dreading more radical reforms, and not satisfied with merely funding fascism in Europe, a group of industrialists and financiers hatched a plan for a US coup (note, Denton, 2012). Known as the "business plot" it was foiled when their choice to lead the attack on the White House, Marine Corps

General, Smedley Butler (a two time recipient of the Medal of Honor), reported it to Congress (who proceeded to cover it up).

FDR was able to channel widespread public anger with the banks into significant institutional reforms, and their power subsided over the next few decades. Acts enabling Federal government to regulate securities came in rapid succession (in 1933 and 1934), the later establishing the Securities and Exchange Commission. The most effective residual banking reform to come out of the New Deal was the GLASS-STEAGALL ACT (of 1933), which erected a fire wall between investment and commercial banking. Moreover, the Central Bank's autonomy was loosely circumscribed by Treasury Department until 1951, when an "accord" again granted it complete independence. Of course, Federal Reserve Notes were still the coin of the realm, as well as the global reserve currency via the Bretton Woods Agreements following WWII. John F. Kennedy briefly threatened to have the US Treasury reintroduce an interest free, hard currency (silver certificates), via Executive Order, 11110 on June 4, 1963. But both he and his plans were short-lived.

BUBBLICIOUS ECONOMICS

The absolute power of the Fed has been gradually restored in the late 1960s. Even after Nixon unilaterally abandoned Bretton-Woods, replacing the Gold-backed dollar with the secretly devised "Petro Dollar" (see; Clark, 2005), its status as the Central Bank among Central Banks was only enhanced. The Fed was credited with "whipping inflation" via the draconian interest rate hikes of the "Volker Bear". Moreover, their power grew as they seemed to be addressing cycles of stagnation. Yet in reality it merely substituted financial growth for actual growth. It is noteworthy that for the Fed, inflation is mostly about wages and only the wages of us peasants (as executive remuneration was moved into stock options). Moreover, vital items for the average Jane, like food, fuel, and housing are not in their index. Hence the Fed's remarkable ability to inflate various asset markets (feeding the rich) has increased in ferocity. Fed Chair (1987-2006) Alan Greenspan (a disciple of libertarian novelist Ayn Rand) kept interest rates in the sub-basement and rapidly moved the economy from one massive bubble to another (e.g., dot-com to housing), all the while keeping the increasingly insignificant metrics of inflation low. Among stock traders this era was known as the "Greenspan Put". Meanwhile since the repeal of Glass-Steagall in 1999, Fed regulated banks were given carte blanche to join in this speculative free for all. Everybody wanted to get into the act. Industrial firms like GM became their own banks, and banks developed their own hedge funds and other "Shadow Banking" links to allow ludicrous levels of leveraging. GM no longer cared about building cars, except as platform for building car loans. GM also got into home loans repackaging them as financial instruments. It was its banking activities not its lack of car sales that drove it into chapter 11 and government bailouts.

Of course these mega bubbles ended badly. In fact they ended so badly that now the ending itself has become a bubble. Since 2008 the US has been in a slow motion depression. As with the Great Depression, DEBT DEFATION (see: Fisher, 1933) was an actual danger. Only this time things really were different. The US entered the 1930s with an intact industrial base, an abundant oil supply, and budget surplus. After the housing crash of 2007, even near zero rates could not produce the required inflation. Ergo the Fed undertook even more legerdemain in the form of "quantitative easing" replacing private debt with public debt. Like a neutron bomb (that kills the people but leave the infrastructure in place), they saved the banks but destroyed the nation (and the anger is still being exploited by demagogues).

Back in the olden days when I studied macroeconomics, monetary policy was merely one tool (amid trade, fiscal, and manpower policy). One of my professors said "it would be a very dark day if we ever had to monetize the debt". Well this darkness still engulfs us, and the Ponzi scheme of adding more debt at interest to pay the interest on past debts has nearly reached the reductio ad absurdum point. The mere fact that extraordinary temporary emergency measures, like near zero interest rates (ZIRP), have become a permanent fixture should be unsettling. Plus, the free money addicted stock market (where firms load up with debt to finance stock buy backs) shudders at a quarter of a point increase or the mere suggestion that the Fed might start to whittle down it bulbous balance sheet. All of this should suggest the Federal Reserve is as more cause than it is cure. At present we are all caught-up in a global banking tornado, and "we're not in Kansas anymore Toto".

For the most part, nearly all of the world's Central Banks are reading from the same play book. So much so that a significant portion of the Global GDP is completely smoke and mirrors. Economists contend that the recession ended June of 2009, yet Central Banks were still purchasing private debt to the tune 200 billion a month in September of 2017. In the bad old days before fuel injection and electronic fuel pumps, one needed to prime the carburetor if they ran out gas. So the state of our economies is like having to have someone sitting on the front fender of our old jalopy with the hood and air cleaner off, continuously priming from a bucket, and splashing gasoline all over the engine and into the road as we're traveling at increasing speed. Instead of nationalizing the banks, we have been nationalizing entire economies. Except that Central Banks are not really the government, are they? The European Central Bank's (ECB) balance sheet is 35% of GDP, and the Bank of Japan (BOJ) is 70%. Moreover, the BOJ owns the lion share of the Nikki (60% of the ETFs alone). The ECB owns nearly 10% of the corporate bond market, as well as much of the European sovereign debt. The Bank of England alone owns over 30% of UK sovereign debt, and brit-exodus will probably demand more direct purchases and market manipulations. Keep in mind that all this purchasing is done with money that literally comes out of thin air (replacing private IOUs as well as public IOUs, with poorer performing treasury IOUs). This creates and incredible drag upon these economies and it passes beaucoup debt and a stagnant economy onto the next generation. In short, Central Banks are merely keeping the corpse of the much of the global economy on display. Even the anemic GDP growth is basically bogus, and all the cheap capital engenders overcapacity and huge misallocations in existing assets, while starving innovation.

We have scores of zombie industrial firms and retailers, joining the ranks of our zombie banks and zombie government programs, giving new meaning to the "zombie apocalypse". Meanwhile banks remain incentivized behave like hedge funds (that used to limit membership to millionaires who could afford the risks). I interviewed a former employee of the Bank of International Settlements (the global bank of banks) in Switzerland and he confided (off the record) that "banking has always been a magic show, and most economists feel obliged to not reveal how the tricks are done." With accelerating deregulation and arrival of new quantitative techniques the magic show became a three ring circus.

CHAPTER 5: FINANCE UBER ALLES

Finance, like time, devours its own children.
_____ **Honore de Balzac**

A lot of people forget that having debt you can't pay back really sucks. Debt is not just a credit instrument, it is an instrument of political and economic control. _____ **Matt Stoller**

The ruling passion of the age is to convert wealth into debt in order to derive a permanent future income from it, to convert wealth that perishes into debt that endures, debt that does not rot, costs nothing to maintain, and brings in perennial interest.
_____ **Frederick Soddy**

The powers of financial capitalism had another far-reaching aim, nothing less than to create a world system of financial control in private hands able to dominate the political system of each country and the economy of the world as a whole. This system was to be controlled in a feudalist fashion by the Central Banks of the world acting in concert. _____ **Carrol Quigley**

There is a simple rule here, a rule of legislation, a rule of business, a rule of life: beyond a certain point, complexity is fraud. You can apply that rule to left-wing social programs, but you can also apply that rule to credit derivatives, hedge funds, and all the rest of it.
_____ **P. J. O'Rourke**

In the last few decades the stranglehold of finance has become increasingly unquestioned and continuously buttressed with bailouts, relaxed regulations and the abandonment of criminal enforcements by democrats and republicans (labor and tory) alike. "Bubba" and the "Half-Black Prince" (Clinton and the Obama) were especially helpful in this regard. The Bush Presidents, as one might expect gave away the store, especially when it came to war profiteering and "W" did more to destroy the American economy and democracy than King George III. The Bush dynasty comes from a long line of arms merchants and grave robbers (e.g., Geronimo's skull), including Senator Prescott Bush, (namesake of current political aspirant, Jeb's son, George P.) whose bank continued to finance Hitler even after the US entered WWII. George W. set the bar of financial disaster very high, but Trump could easily surpass even him, given the number of Wall Street moguls in his administration and his assault upon the very weak Dodd-Frank financial reforms; so much for populism.

The political power and negative economic impacts of Money & Banking are not new, it has ebbed and flowed for centuries; yet, the complete ascendancy of finance is of more recent vintage. The super-villain status of finance tended to coincide with a number of theoretical developments, influenced by its attachments to faulty neoclassical methods and neofeudal ideology. Rice Distinguished Professor of Business, Edward E. Williams (2011) traces the academic evolution of finance from mundane "descriptive and taxonomic" discipline dealing with the "practical phenomena (stocks, bonds, and credit arrangements)" to theoretical misadventures driven by unfounded economic assumptions and ill-suited mathematical tools. He further observes how this tainting of finance with arcane tools and concepts and their pursuit of a mythical "optimal capital structure" (a perfect balance of debt and equity) were quickly adopted in the real world and directly led to a number of practical debacles, including "the collapse of 2008". He describes how "theoretical constructs of questionable value" (e.g. the Efficient Markets Hypothesis, see, Fama, 1970) "replaced practical wisdom". Williams explains,

> ...why finance went from being a useful, albeit not all knowing, discipline to a state where its pronouncements presently are not only unuseful but can be absolutely harmful. Essentially, finance morphed into a branch of 'economic science' (p. 5).

Ultimately academic finance would become "a façade that fooled practitioners" and played a major role converting a productive economy into haven for rent-seeking. Opportunities for legitimate profits, from building a better mouse trap (or better mouse for that matter), can slip away or merely be over-looked, when wealth without production balloons.

The unprecedented turbulence in world events during the 1970s and 1980s scattered the dots and obscured the connections of global institutions. It was a complete macroeconomic tsunami, when seemingly random events came in rapid succession: the "Nixon Shock" (leaving Bretton Woods and the Gold Standard unilaterally and virtually overnight), the loss of the Viet Nam War, the opening of China for world trade and investment, Watergate, two major Oil Shocks, Stagflation (giving way to double digit inflation), the Hostage Crisis, the Iran-contra Scandal, the Savings & Loan Crisis, and Black Monday (the largest one day global stock market crash in history) as well as the Scandinavian banking crisis.

THE "HIT MEN" COME HOME

While these increasingly curious events mirrored those of past macrocycles and imperial misadventures, the sheer scale and scope of underlying financial change was breathtaking to say the least. When Ronald Reagan took office the US was the world largest creditor nation and when he left the largest debtor. His "supply-side" economics had tripled the debt. Moreover, the world's greatest industrial economy was literally dismantled, carted off, and/or converted to a so-called "service economy" in a mere decade, during the 1980s. For the alchemists of consumption without production it was merely a matter of finance, with household as well as government debt rising astronomically. The imposition by central bankers of "financial repression", discouraged savers and inspired corporate raiders, executives, and government officials to merely pile on more debt. Meanwhile, antitrust enforcement became exceedingly lax as mergers and acquisitions soared, and monopoly (or monopsony) power grew (see, Stucke & Ezrachi, 2017).

In the 1990s global crises proceeded pell-mell and the pace of financialization quickened. Like dominoes falling, countries and regions were brought to the brink of financial collapse by IMF and World Bank "Hit Men" (see, Perkins, 2004), with debt restructuring and forced austerity insuring that much of a country's patrimony would be transferred to multinational corporations. Gradually the rape, pillage and pandering to kleptocrats expanded its focus from the underdeveloped to cannibalizing overdeveloped nations as well. The 1990s began with a recession in the US, and by the end of the 90s, induced economic crises occurred in India, several Asian countries, Mexico, as well as culminating with the collapse of the Soviet Union, and the Russian financial default.

Meanwhile back in the United States, North American Free Trade Agreement (NAFTA) was finally fully baked and Glass-Steagall was repealed and replaced by the Gramm-Leach-Bliley Financial Services Modernization Act of 1999, and signed into law by William Jefferson Clinton. Alan Greenspan would say of Clinton (a Democrat) that "he was the best republican president I even worked with". With his inauguration address, Clinton signaled Wall Street that they had nothing to fear by invoking his favorite Georgetown Professor, Carroll Quigley. It makes little difference whether his great opus, Tragedy and Hope (1966), a detailed history of the Anglo-American banking cabal, is dismissed by some as conspiracy theory, if the President believes it. Bubba and his band of banking bandits have provided fodder for entirely new conspiracy theories. However in all fairness, Glass-Steagall was already on its last legs. Like the separation of church and state, the law that separated commercial and investment banking had been undermined for decades. Glass, himself, attempted to repeal it while the ink was still wet in 1935. Since the 1960s the fire wall was assaulted from all sides, with bankers jumping over and tunneling under at every opportunity. Even before repeal, Citi Bank was allowed to illegally acquire Salomon Smith-Barney.

By the time the dot-com bubble violently burst and the various accounting frauds came to light in the early 2000s, a new generation of financial engineers had taken the wheel and were smashing down on the accelerator. In 2001 China was admitted to full status in the World Trade Organization (WTO, and it was already far too late for US manufacturing jobs (see, Autor, et. al., 2013). A whole new set of tricks where fashioned to keep capital flowing into the US. With the help of the Federal Reserve, global hot money and speculation was merely moved from one bubble to the next. I recall giving a talk to the Canadian Bar Association in early 2006 about the implications the Sarbanes-Oxley Act (affectionately known as SOX). These rules focused primarily upon accounting firms, but also placed corporate executives on notice. I told them that regarding the scandals like Enron "we really had not seen anything yet". We had literally not seen anything as many of the files for Securities and Exchange Commission (SEC) open cases were destroyed in the mysterious implosion of Building 7, of the World Trade Center on 9/11. I naively professed to those well paid corporate lawyers something that they certainly already knew; "that in light of all the lying, leveraging, fraud, and the diversion of white collar crime enforcement to Home Land Security, what was really needed was BOX (SOXs for bankers)". I then proceeded to further bore them with a mini course in how zombie theories and tools (e.g., the Gaussian Copula) were eating most the brains on Wall Street.

BLACKHEARTS, BLACK-SHOLES, BUT FEW BLACK SWANS

Finance had once been all about building prosperous firms and nations, but within this mission the alchemy of money from nothing became more compelling. With the new millennium the darker dimensions of financialization were put on steroids. In particular, arcane mathematical tools and rapidly expanding computational power were combined and used for massively perverse purposes. Kids trained in physics, math, and computer science (called "quants") were suddenly in very high demand on Wall Street (see, Patterson, 2010). Declining opportunities elsewhere such as the cancelation of the superconducting supercollider served to significantly increase the supply of eager young people with absolutely no understanding of Money & Banking; all-the-better to fool you with my dear. This quantitative manipulation was "not [necessarily] rocket science", however, some manipulations did steal from Ito Calculus (used for guided missile systems). This sleight of hand relied upon faulty economic assumptions such as "neoclassical financial arbitrage" and "equilibrium theory" as well as Milton Friedman's (1953) notion of the stabilizing function of the "rational speculator". When combined with various blackhearted schemes these theories served to obscure the dangers inherent in increasing exotic derivative products and synthetic financial instruments. Moreover, highly creative simulations could convince credit rating agencies that junk bonds and/or subprime loans could be recombined within investment grade tranches in such a way the entire mess deserved the AAA (highest) rating.

Making speculation seem less speculative has been the Holy Grail of the field of finance since long before it was led astray by economists. This quest can be traced back to the work of a brilliant young French mathematician, Louis Bachelier. A student of Poincare, who developed a proof for what is now called Brownian motion (a simple stochastic process) well before Einstein. Bachelier's (1900/2006) Theory of Speculation is the taproot of much of modern finance theory. Essentially Bachelier had developed a formula for capturing, albeit temporarily, a portion the dynamic equilibrium in stock prices, long before Black-Scholes. Black-Scholes is short hand for the Black-Scholes-Merton Options Pricing Model (note, Black & Scholes, 1973) which was recognized by a fake Nobel Prize in 1997 for the latter two (Black had died). I could not help imaging a treacherous seascape sans a lighthouse, but did not know at the time how prescient that image would be. It is a powerful piece of financial hubris, which is widely applied to price composite investments which include diverse levels of risk (e.g., plain vanilla with dangerous derivatives) that quickly metastasized throughout the global financial system. Essentially Black-Scholes is a greatly simplified characterization of the role of volatility in options and futures trading. It assumes that risk is can be readily spread out, but it merely creates the illusion that risk has been dramatically reduced. It fueled a process known as "dynamic hedging", where one attempts to insure their portfolio against risk by continuously changing opposing positions. Robert Merton and Myron Scholes actually signed on with the famed hedge fund of former of Salomon vice chairman, John Meriwether, called Long Term Capital Management (LTCM). Using his banking connections and the unearned intellectual wealth of his two fake laureates, Meriwether was able to leverage LTCM to into far beyond the point of no return. In another dress rehearsal for the 2008 Crisis, this one hedge fund nearly brought down the entire global financial system. However, the Fed and sixteen banks stepped in with a 3.6 billion dollar bail out in 1998 and the fund shut down the following year. You might think that this experience would curb enthusiasm for quant driven derivatives, but it did NOT.

MORE MURDEROUS MATHS

The ill-conceived idea that risk could be smoothed away with clever mathematics had yet to reach its zenith. A new device, called the GAUSSIAN COPULA (Li, 2000) brought forth a deluge of new and more deadly derivatives. The new king of the quants was a Chinese born mathematician with additional degrees in economics, business, and actuarial science (so he should have known better, and probably did). David X. Li (Li Xianglin) was employed by J. P. Morgan-Chase, where bogus mortgaged backed securities were booming. Gaussian (as in Carl Friedrich Gauss) refers to a normalized distribution (e.g., a bell curve), and copula (from the Latin to link or tie) refers to the dependence between heretofore unrelated variables. Hence a GC is multivariate probability calculation that assumes that the marginal distribution is uniform. Consider the miscalculations involved in mortgage backed securities. The central problem with home loans is that they are repaid at various unknown times (each time a home is resold) or occasionally are not repaid at all. Before GCs, it would take mountains of data on repayments and defaults, to calculate the risk. Like Alexander at the Gordian knot, Li just cut through all the complex reality of market killing fluctuations with a statistical leap of faith. It recklessly assumes that if one can dig up a surrogate for risk that correlates with movements in the average interest paid per different types of loans, then they have captured the risk of whole enchilada. Of course it also assumed that house prices never ever fall. And this is the coup de' grass of the copula. The log of crap is still crap. The collateral in the "collateralized debt obligation" (CDO), does NOT refer to underlying assets securing the instrument, but the correlation score via the copula function. And what you might ask is the other variable matched for this purpose? It is the average level of the infamous "credit default swaps" (CDSs) sold. These fake insurance products, which work like naked shorts (an illegal short sale by someone who doesn't actually own the underlying asset), were assumed to be an adequate indicator of actual risk. Thus, the correlation between two highly unstable markets was sold as solid risk measure. Rating agencies merely needed to see the correlation score to issue an investment grade (minimum risk) endorsement. Bundles of shite were turned into gold, and everybody wanted some. Hot money from across the globe poured in. Sales of CDOs and CDSs fueled each other in their copulating copulas. Quants simply ignored the multicolinearity problem, not to mention that fact that systemic risks are nonlinear. The mega–casino just kept rolling. From 2001 to 2007 the number of swaps outstanding rose from 900 billion to 62 trillion, and the CDO market went from 300 billion to nearly 6 trillion. Wait it gets worse, the CDS was only about 10 years old, and during that matched period home prices had only been going up. Thus, the GS correlations for mortgage backed securities made them appear risk free.

Bankers had to know that a small drop in housing prices anywhere would bring down the entire planet. It is not as if it had not happened before. What are now called subprime loans and other predatory mortgages had ballooned during the "roaring" 1920s.

Home and farm foreclosures exploded during the Great Depression. I contend that the bankers knew exactly what they were doing in the recent housing crash. They cannot hide behind the "Black Swan" (Taleb, 2007) defense that these events are so highly improbable that "no one could know that it could ever happen". They were invoking the notion of having a "Minsky Movement" the day of the crash, yet if they really knew Minsky (1992), then they knew how unstable their house of cards was to begin with. The marching orders for the "liar" and NINJA (no income, no job, and no assets) loans came from on high. Moreover, many of those "shitty" mortgage backed securities were created long before the all-out search began for any would-be home buyer who could fog a mirror. Many of my undergraduates (pimply faced kids who could not find their butts with both hands) had already been loan officers at banks. Armies were sent out to convince everyone, irrespective of their credit worthiness, that their homes could be turned into an ATM. One could easily get a home improvement loan to buy a new truck, as the house looked better with it parked in front. It was a dispossession blitzkrieg.

The dirtier little secret of the housing crisis was the sequence of events that only came to light briefly during the "robo-signing scandal" (when state & local laws governing the transfer of titles, etc. were violated), and wholesale foreclosure fraud was revealed (see, Dayen, 2016). Banks were allowed to go back and backfill the required documents to support the mythology of blame. In essence, the tall tale that it all started with unscrupulous buyers and imprudent owners was a complete fabrication. Often model tranche combinations were merely simulated on a computer, excellent ratings were attached, and empty packages of loans were pre-sold to eager investors. Only then were trucks loads of loans ordered up.

DEATH BY DERIVATIVE

Galactic levels of leveraging and increased use of risk diverting derivatives guarantee mutually assured economic destruction (as Warren Buffet calls it). Derivatives (a contract that derives its value from an underlying asset, commodity, or other contract) have been around since ancient times. Keep in mind a debt is an asset to a bank. In relatively modern times, derivatives started as futures contracts. Farmers were always borrowing against their next crop, and used futures contracts to lock in a certain price per bustle well ahead of harvest. It was this offset of agricultural uncertainty that prompted the establishment of Chicago Board of Trade in 1848, but soon thereafter some derivatives became dangerous and laws were passed prohibiting trading in certain food stuffs. Despite their inherent dangers, trading in futures and options quickly spilled over into broader markets as a hedging tool. By the 1870s, famed financier, Russell Sage, was using put, call, and strike prices in such a way as to create synthetic loans (allowing him to charge interest rates much higher than the usury laws of the time allowed). Following speculative frenzies in futures, trading in various commodities were banned for a time in various countries.

Nicholas Hildyard (2007) contends that the primary purpose of derivatives is "permitting the impermissible". He explains that they disguise risk, evade market rules, and allow for unlimited leveraging without maintaining minimum crash reserves (pp. 26–37). The mother-of-all-derivatives is the Credit Default Swap (CDS). Simply stated a CDS functions as if everyone in your neighborhood could, for a tiny premium payment, own a replacement value fire insurance policy on your house. So your 500,000 dollar home could be worth 500,000,000,000 burned to ground. When Wall Street threw Lehman Brothers under the bus, and the Fed and Treasury chose not to act (collapsing the entire economy), yet the very next day they stepped in to bail out AIG the insurance firm (that issued many of the CDSs) and paid them off 100 cents on the dollar; no haircuts whatsoever. You see some of the big banks had purchased CDSs on Lehman (without having to own a single share). AIG also proceeded to pay historically high dividends (4 and ½ bucks a share) with its new public funds. On the 10th anniversary of the Lehman disaster, our three previous partners in crime (Paulson, Bernanke, and Geithner) called for bigger bail out powers next time, including the wholesale purchase of the ailing stocks (at retail prices) for certain feudal friendly firms; So much for free markets.

Since derivatives are mostly unregulated, we have virtually no idea to whom and how many derivatives are out there, and we are a bit vague as to which piece of real or synthetic collateral they are somehow attached. But it is a pretty good bet that there are a lot more entities other than the big banks that are "too big to fail". Recall how a single hedge fund nearly collapsed the global economy with their super-leveraged bad bets. With derivatives the web of counterparties can be difficult to unravel. The first whiff of trouble can send folks scrambling for as much of the ill-valued collateral they can get their hands on whether or not they are entitled to it or not. With an estimated nominal value somewhere north of 1.5 quadrillion it is easy to see why derivatives are more dangerous than nuclear weapons.

Several months before the demise of LTCM, Brooksley Born, the Head of Commodity Futures Trading Commission, sought to investigate financial derivatives and was told by Summers, Ruben, and Greenspan that if she were to shine any light at all on derivatives she might collapse the entire economy. But just in case this bullying did not continue to work, banking lobbyists got Congress to pass a bill that outlawed the regulation of derivatives altogether, and these sacred cows have been sustained even after they helped put economy on life support in 2008.

The next stage of derivatives blackmail is even more subtle. Since so many derivatives contracts are complete and utter fictions (e.g., where the asset itself is merely index of debts twice removed) then it is only the eagerness of governments to avoid total collapse that gives some of them any residual value at all. If "Mark to Market" accountings rules had NOT been suspended, most of the major banks would be insolvent. At the height of the crisis, the Fed violated Generally Accepted Accounting Practices (GAAP) and Basel II (international banking agreements) and allowed banks to use fictitious MARK TO MODEL (or "Mark to Magic") as opposed using fair market values. Then the Fed provided a huge hidden bailout by paying trillions for these nearly worthless securities ("toxic paper") at their magically inflated values. This toxic waste dump gives reckless speculators much more power in the macroeconomy.

NYU Finance Professor and Editor of the Journal of Derivatives, Stephen Figlewski (see, Sheridan, 2007), contends that we really should NOT worry so much about the nominal value of all those derivatives, because they are really just like "lotto tickets". It is only just prior to the drawing where each ticket is a potential winner that collectively the nominal value is the prize times the number tickets. This is a brilliant analogy, but it has a slight problem. With the lotto, once the drawing is held only a winning ticket gets the prize, and all of us with the wrong numbers chuck our ticket in trash. With derivatives, on the other hand, many of those losers were holding on their tickets for dear life, and if they can threaten a Central Banker into giving them some shiny new treasuries in exchange then they might hand them over. What other game of chance rewards the losers so well? Could you imagine expecting a return of your losses, with interest, before you exit Las Vegas? That exit might not be as pleasant as you might have hoped.

SHADOWY BANKING AND OTHER FISCHY STUFF

The financial shenanigans of the last few decades also fueled the growth a monstrous Shadow Banking industry. Shadow Banking (e.g., hedge funds, private equity funds, mortgage lenders, repurchase (repo) markets, credit insurance firms, pay-day and car title lenders, etc.), are often affiliates of the major banks. Lemma (2015) explains that Shadow banks "perform many of the functions of banks", in a "mostly unregulated" no man's land between banking activities. In short, it is where the serious credit gets created. The shadow system is often the source of virtually unlimited leverage and "off balance sheet" misadventures. With activities valued well into in the tens of trillions of dollars, Shadow Banking dwarfs conventional banking, and overwhelms traditional banking and business practices. Some private equity (PE) funds routinely rely upon the creative accounting of the shadow system to hide their liabilities (or their actual stake in a project) when they are attempting to attract investors to big buyout deals (see, Hooke & Yook, 2017). The Financial Stability Board (2013) identified a number of dodgy issues with Shadow Banking, including the curious practice of "self-securitization" (obtaining major and/or central bank funding for instruments that they never intended to sell). Central banks that generally have regulatory responsibilities (a fox in the chicken coop if there ever was one) mostly turn a blind eye to this "heart of darkness", even when regulated entities are implicated. Central banks even engage in making the shadow system more shadowy. For example, the Federal Reserve stopped reporting M3, the only characterization of the money supply that includes the repo market (overnight lending to work around capital requirements). The repurchase market was one of the first things to freeze up during the last crisis, igniting the run on overvalued collateral (e.g., securitized packages of dodgy home loans in this case). Contrary to the all the condemnations of Shadow Banking by regulators at the Fed, they actually encouraged its development as they already had their hands full controlling liquidity and solvency risks at the regulated banks, especially after the elimination of Glass-Steagall. Essentially Shadow Banking provided a way to get a bunch of the risk off the balance sheets of conventional bankers, further fueling the global Ponzi scheme.

However, the folks most responsible for the emergence of the of Shadow Banking were a handful of finance professors, led by Fischer Black (of Black-Scholes fame) then at the University of Chicago, where he was the darling of the Pelerins in their battles with the few remaining Keynesians. A brilliant mathematician (but crappy economist), Black had been hell-bent on having a major role in an intellectual revolution since his student years at Harvard. During his graduate studies, he was expelled briefly for failing to settle on a dissertation topic. After changing his major from physics to mathematics and mathematics to computer science, he finally completed a Ph.D. while working at the very ground floor of Artificial Intelligence (AI) with the legendary Marvin Minsky at MIT. Having worked summers with the RAND Corporation, he chose a consulting career in information systems. After moving to Arthur D. Little, where he was first exposed to finance, he had finally found an enterprise where his wild ideas could make a real difference, or do the most damage, depending on your perspective. The kooky quickly became canon, and Black was credited with completely revolutionizing finance (see, Mehrling 2011). While he did not live long enough to get his fake Nobel, he received numerous accolades (e.g., "Financial Engineer of the Year") as well as having the most prestigious prize in quantitative finance named after him. The gist of Black's ideas can be found in a tiny snippet from one of his short papers (1970):

> *Thus a long-term corporate bond could actually be sold to three separate persons. One would supply the money for the bond; one would bear the interest rate risk, and one would bear the risk of default. The last two would not have to put up any capital for the bond, though they might have to post some sort of collateral (p. 5).*

Bond traders loved the idea that they could remove the risk by spreading it out, and Black's theories caught on like a house-a-fire. The quick conversion of arcane theory to practice was also sped-up by Black moving to Wall Street (with Goldman Sachs, eventually becoming a partner) following another academic excursion to Sloan/MIT, not to mention the overnight success of Black-Scholes in options and futures markets. In the process, Shadow Banking grew by leaps and bounds. Who needed the liquidity backstop of the Central Banks, when idiots like AIG could be coaxed into issuing exceedingly cheap insurance policies, by way of the mathematical illusion that systemic risks were insignificant? Real insurance of course is much more closely regulated. The rapid proliferation of various interest and credit swaps were NO danger if clever formulas could readily convert long-term collateral (i.e., 30-year mortgages) to cover short-term (e.g., 90 day or even overnight) paper. Of course one also has to assume that the underlying loans were sound and that the insurer would also be able to pay, despite having charged gravely insufficient premiums.

I wonder if somebody had an algorithm that translated, in effect, "when the shit hits the fan, then the future Secretary of the US Treasury hands over taxpayers' money to cover fake insurance". Perhaps not, but the models did assume that everyone, including big banks, could act like the dynamically hedged hedge funds and could always be able to get "the greater fool" (e.g., the government) to buy their positions, and find someone to loan them some collateral at a reasonable rate, as values fell. That's right if you know the right shadow banker, then you can simply rent collateral. It is as if you could get a mortgage by pledging the Airbnb you are staying in at the time.

Even before the new finance theories fed the growing chaos in financial markets, the new super-charged financialization was fundamentally altering the nature of business management. In short, financialization moved management responsibilities from production to "rent-seeking." Initially, it helped codify the malicious notion of "shareholder primacy" and by implication diminished other "stakeholders" such as customers, employees, and even vendors (see, Freeman, 1991). Plus, it greatly extended the practice of making heretofore profitable firms mere targets for the corporate raiders. Essentially, shareholder primacy made financial engineering the focal point of corporate management (see, Daneke & Sager, 2015; Foroohar, 2016; and especially note, Lazonick, 2018). Top managers became only tangentially interested in building better products or production at all. During a recent period, 92% of corporate profits went to buying back their own stock shares (once regulated as illegal market manipulations). Still other firms were loaded down with humongous debts to finance stock buybacks, executive bonuses, and hyper-leveraged mergers & acquisitions. In a number of cases corporate executives were NEVER really working for their own general shareholders; rather they served the hit and run speculators, hedge funds, private equity firms, and other Wall Street vultures. Even smart guys like Mitt Romney mistook these economy wrecking crews for good businessmen.

Like oil in an engine, finance is obviously needed to lubricate a smoothly functioning economy, but it is not the engine and as presently constituted it is more sand than oil. Joseph Schumpeter (famed for describing the centrality of disruptive innovation) pinpointed the tendency of credit to shift from productive to unproductive growth in the course of economic development (see, Schumpeter, 1934; also note, Daneke, 1998a). Specifically he described how a first wave of credit expansion is followed a second wave which goes primarily to inflating existing assets and places a drag on innovation and economic growth. All growth in finance is currently viewed as contributing to GDP; however, if we deducted all of the unproductive credit growth and other forms of phantom wealth creation, we would see that little real GDP growth remains. Financialization, by moving heaven and earth to keep the great debt machine alive, can make a mild downturn into a depression.

Our decrepit recovery was not a recovery at all. The real economy remains moribund for the vast majority of Americans, and only the earls of the ersatz economy are profiting. The labor force participation rate (a better measure of unemployment) remains exceedingly low. It now stands at about 70%, and is alarming low for prime aged male (25 to 54 years of age). Another rarely mentioned statistic is labor's share of growth in the Gross Domestic Product (GDP). That number is not just low it is essentially zero, nada, nothing for roughly 95% of the working population. During the prior period from say from the end of the Great Depression through the 1970s, labor's share of prosperity had been nearly 70%. Yet gains in the last few decades have all gone almost solely to the top 5%, and in the last decade (or the era of the Great Recession) the audacious oligarchs (top 1%) have taken virtually all gains. By 2030 this small segment of the world' population will own over 2/3rds of its wealth. This is NOT merely a matter of technology, globalization, or the mythical "secular stagnation". This insidious upward redistribution is the result myriad (yet coordinated) policy choices. To add insult to injury, their ideologically based prescriptions, such as of austerity, further retard growth in what remains of the real economy. In the meantime, a political economy that only seems to work for mostly the top 1% is fertile ground for fascist demagogues.

MERCHANTS OF MAYHEM AND MILITARISM

The most well-worn distraction in times of large scale economic stagnation is a good old fashioned war (see, Veblen 1917; Horner & Martinez, 1997; also note, Plotkin, 2010). Unfortunately, old fashioned wars no longer exist, and weapons of mass extinction have made global conflict problematic to the ultimate extreme. Economies embroiled in the maintenance of empire, however, are hopelessly addicted to militarism. The new millennium began with the Orwellian wet dream of an endless "war on terror", costing 300 million dollars a day for nearly 20 years, with literally NO end in sight. Worse than its material costs are its irreparable social costs. With its suspension of habeas corpus, support for extrajudicial detention, torture, and assassination, our own government has become as terrifying than any terrorist group. Meanwhile despite our all-volunteer forces, militarization seeps into all aspects of society. Pentagon civilian adviser, Rosa Brooks, describes this phenomenon in her brilliant book, How Everything Became War and the Military Became Everything (2016).

Many banks see warfare as a key investment strategy. In the movie The International (2009), vaguely based upon the shadowy, CIA connected, BCCI (Bank of Credit and Commerce International), a bank insider explains this emphasis as follows:

> ...this is not about making profit from weapon sales. It's about control. The IBBC is a bank. Their objective isn't to control the conflict; it's to control the debt that the conflict produces. You see, the real value of a conflict - the true value - is in the debt that it creates. You control the debt, you control everything. You find this upsetting, yes? But this is the very essence of the banking industry, to make us all, whether we be nations or individuals, slaves to debt.

Beyond the maintenance of debt and war profiteering, military action is often undertaken when more immediate corporate and banking interests are at stake. Invasions of numerous developing nations (including China) took place on behalf of specific corporations and banks (see, Butler, 1935). In his famed, War is a Racket speech General Butler confesses that for over three decades,

> ...I spent most of my time being a high class muscleman for Big Business, for Wall Street and for the Bankers. In short, I was a racketeer, a gangster for capitalism.... I helped in the raping of half a dozen Central American republics for the benefits of Wall Street (see, Butler, 1933).

More recent events in the Middle East seem to revolve around threats to the global banking and monetary system. The swift establishment of a congruent central bank by a ragtag group of rebels in Libya is especially suspicious. Apparently Gadhafi should have been more circumspect regarding his plan for a new Pan-African currency pegged to his gold-backed dinar.

Nothing makes people more collectively stupid than the call to arms. Merely tell them that we need to go off to this or that foreign land to "protect our freedom" and they will line up at the recruiter's office. Militarism (both at home & abroad) is the lynch pin of crony capitalism. Warfare is such a vital element of financial planning that major banks have a huge revolving door to the Pentagon, and a weapons trading desk. The astronomical levels of war profiteering has become a way of life for much of what remains of US industry. In President Eisenhower's final warning about "unwarranted political influence", he coined the phrase "military industrial complex". We, of course, ignored him and now the traditional military and defense contractors are accompanied by immense intelligence and surveillance industries as well as private mercenaries and militarized police. In addition to providing a playground for finance, militarism is obviously an extremely powerful device of authoritarian manipulation and widespread social control (see, Veblen, 1917). As Sam Johnson maintained, "patriotism is the last refuge of scoundrels".

THE TWILIGHT OF EMPIRE

Americans generally believe they are the good guys. To sustain this myth we have secret budgets, secret wars, secret surveillance, and secret prisons (mostly in violation of US and international law). The average American does not even believe that the US is an empire, despite spending more on its military than most of rest of world combined, not to mention maintaining nearly a 1000 foreign bases in a 130 countries. Defense is the single largest item in the federal discretionary budget (nearly a trillion annually). Plus, scholars at Michigan State University (Skidmore & Henion, 2017) discovered another Trillion in unauthorized spending (mostly on defense) was made between 1998 and 2015. The DOD inspector general recently observed that 3 billion just went missing in Afghanistan alone, our longest war. It is creepily poetic perhaps that the Hindu Kush has long been the "Graveyard of Empires".

Americans prefer to think of themselves as the greatest world power, rather than an empire. They associate empire with large scale colonization of other peoples, as in the Roman or the British Empire, and forget their treatment of the indigenous people of the Americas, as well as several other developing nations (see, Kinzer, 2017). Moreover the US has completely colonized the planet with its currency (one currency to rule them all). In essence, banks virtually everywhere hold their fractional reserve in US dollars. Paul Krugman commenting on the fragility US Reserve Currency Status (with a few nations preferring a new basket of currencies called "Special Drawing Rights" SDRs) said that our "full faith and credit is backed by men with guns". More pivotal yet, was the "Petro Dollar". By way of secret agreements and military intimidations, the US asserted that only dollars be accepted in exchange for oil, and that producers' revenues should be recycled into US treasury bonds and other investments in the US economy (see, Clark, 2005). This "privileged status" for the US dollar is now unraveling as China, Russia, Iran, and soon other nations may seek to trade in other currencies (particularly the Petro-Yuan).

To understand how empire and finance have coevolved requires a broadening of our perspective, globally as well as historically. Giovanni Arrighi in his vast, yet meticulous, charting of the evolution of leading economic and military powers (hegemons) since the beginning of capitalism highlights recurring (but not completely replicating) patterns or macro-cycles, which he labels "long centuries"(1994). As he explains these cycles have special relevance for the US Empire. Each "systemic cycle of capital accumulation" begins with competition in manufacturing and trade, but when profits decline accumulation shifts to financialization. When financialization fails and/or empire unravels, capital simply moves on to a new hegemon (Genoese-Iberian to Dutch, Dutch to English, English to US). He is especially interested in the financial and political machinations that accompany these protracted transitions (Arrighi and Silver, 1999). It is very interesting to note how rewarding residual financial center status could be to particular banking cartels. Certain Dutch were happy to give up hegemony to become bankers to the world. Ditto for Britain and their City of London, which allowed them to punch well beyond their weight long after the sun set on the British Empire (see, Quigley, 1966; Fichtner, 2016). The on-going transition to Chinese hegemony will not be nearly as seamless as in the past. Nor is it likely to be as benign as Arrighi presupposes (Arrighi, 2009). Americans will hardly "go quietly into that good night". Plus Chinese government is not completely welcoming to the incursions of global finance, and despite ancient glories they're not fully prepared pick up the gantlet of global leadership just yet. Moreover, the resources required for a burgeoning new hegemon are rapidly becoming exhausted. Imagine how upset Chinese imperialists might be when they fully appreciate that cupboard is bare, and that much of global economic growth has been a Ponzi scheme.

CHAPTER 6: THE CLOWNS OF ENERGY COLLAPSE

What they've been saying all these years is true, now there is no more, no more morning dew. _____ **Bonnie Dobson**

Anyone who believes that exponential growth can go on forever in a finite world is either a madman or an economist. _____ **Kenneth Boulding**

A great civilization is not conquered from without until it has destroyed itself from within. _____ **Ariel Durant**

Everyone knows the Iraq War is largely about oil. _____ **Alan Greenspan**

We are the first generation to be able to end poverty, and the last generation to take steps to avoid the worse impacts of Climate Change. _____ **Ban Ki-Moon**

Energy policy (or the lack thereof) is by far the most total insanity that humans mind has ever devised. If anyone still needs a paradigm case of our misplaced trust in cartels, energy takes the cake. Profligate energy usage is so built into our very being that that we literally cannot imagine life without it. Our homes, with their average square meter of holes (so that we are heating and cooling the entire neighborhood) an average of 20 miles from where we work were not built with energy in mind. Our massive sprawling suburban communities (devoid of adequate public transportation) were designed around maximum personal automobile usage. In classic monopoly move, auto manufacturers were allowed to buy up lively trolley or street car systems in places like Los Angeles and junk them. Markets don't work without alternatives. Our primary choice of car (the SUV) is actually a truck and might better be labeled the suburban assault vehicle. We have been manipulated by marketing to believe they provide greater safety (when in fact they do NOT). Soccer moms/dads believe their improved visibility makes them safer, but their high center of gravity (and fragile car tires) also makes them more prone to rollovers and their weight will crush the roof. I recall sitting in on the first hearings for the "corporate average fuel economy (CAFE) standards" when the manufactures succeeded in exempting light trucks from fleet averages by arguing that "the tradesmen need their trucks". Little did we know that the average American would own one (van or SUV)? Our archaic technology, the internal combustion engine, in the typical SUV adds 1 ton of greenhouse gases to the atmosphere annually. Yes, that is 2000 pounds from a single vehicle. The average sedan is about half that number, but manufacturers (e.g. Ford) and police departments are abandoning the sedan. When we burn a gallon of gasoline we attach two oxygen atoms to each atom of carbon (so 7 pounds of gas can produce over 25 pounds of CO_2). We now have viable electric vehicles, but still have negligible market penetration. Plus, given the decline of nuclear power, electrical generation is not without greenhouses gases of its own, especially with coal fired plants (Trump's favorite). US cities, especially in the south and the west are a bloody hot mess (more suburbs in search of a city). They are such "brittle systems" (in "resiliency theory" terms, see, Holling, 1973) that the slightest disruption of gasoline would send them into chaos. Our vast nation (without any high speed rail) commits us to the interstate highways or the least efficient and most polluting form of travel (jet planes) to travel between cities. At current usage, a couple of average American 3rd grade class rooms (50 kids), will consume a supertanker full (2 million barrels), with each barrel on average containing 20 gallons of gasoline, 12 gallons of diesel, and 2 gallons of jet fuel, in their lifetimes. Our addiction to oil remains quite acute. So with less than 4% of the world's population, we still consume nearly 20% of the world's oil. What is wrong with this picture? By way of an interesting aside, we also incarcerate 25% of the world prisoners, and have the highest infant mortality rate of all the Organization of Economic Cooperation and Development (OECD) countries. U S A, U S A!

IT'S THE ENERGY STUPID

Given the inherent turbulence of modern capitalism, political campaigns increasingly adopt the slogan "It's the economy stupid", referring to the lack of robust macroeconomic policies on the part of one's opponent. However, the lack of viable energy policies is at the heart of most of our economic difficulties, so it might be more accurate to substitute energy for economy from time to time. Energy (the ability replace basic human labor) is the metabolism of civilization. In fact we define the level of a civilization by the amount and types of energy it uses (or abuses in our case). Distinguished anthropologist, Leslie White (1943) was the one of the first to identify this crucial role of energy in the de/evolution of civilization. He observed that,

> *If we can continue to harness as much energy per capita, per year in the future as we are doing now there is little doubt but that our old social system will give way to a new one, a new era of civilization. Should, however, the amount energy we are able to harness diminish materially, our culture will cease to advance and even recede (p. 350).*

Unfortunately, the ability to marshal abundant sources of extremely cheap energy has caused civilization to expand its complexity far beyond the point of sustainability, and now we seem willing to cannibalize other sectors (e.g., manufacturing, food production, etc.) in order to maintain the illusion of energy stability. Consider hydraulic fracturing (or fracking); we must be out of our fracking minds to poison thousands of acres of irrigable farm land and precious ground water for the sake of a bit of natural gas or shale oil (not to mention impacting earthquakes). When in 2001, VP Dick Cheney met behind closed doors with his oil executive buddies to fashion a secret energy strategy, their only public statement was that "the American way of life is not negotiable". What this really meant however, is that they were willing to bomb countries into the Stone Age to sustain their profits. What Cheney forgot to tell us is that the American way of life was already over.

The crux of energy (and civilization for that matter) is pretty straight forward. It all boils down to energy return on investment (EROI). At the peak of US domestic production it was about 30/1. The much ballyhooed Bakken (North Dakota) and Ford-Eagle (Texas) fields were never more than 5/1, and both are now in experiencing dramatic declines in production. The stripped mined (or surface) Canadian tar sands are about 4/1 and the in-situ (below ground deposits, demanding stream injections) are less than 2/1. Cheney's "American Way of Life", requires at least 12/1, or as much as 20/1 if you include basic health, education, and so on. Plus, it requires geopolitically reliable oil suppliers, who will continue to accept US IOUs (in the form of paper money or low yield treasuries) rather than demand hard currencies and/or precious metals.

Future generations will look back and think "how could you bastards have been so cavalier with the fate of civilization", and so deceitful regarding the centrality of energy. Prolonged warfare over oil rich regions, with the blowback turning into perpetual jihad and/or the new Crusades is merely one symptom of the problem. Incontrovertible evidence of the overwhelming contribution of carbon-based fuels to CLIMATE CHANGE has existed since the 1970s (see, Daneke & Lawrence, 1982), yet the topic remains a source of a carefully cultivated (oil firms spent tens of millions on deniers) cultural civil war in the US. We have already seen sea level rise and the increasing intensity of storms, but they will get a great deal worse. Many of the world's major cities will eventually be underwater (physically as well as financially). Furthermore, as the frozen regions continue to warm, potable water will become much more valuable than oil, and the huge expanses of permafrost and tundra will release their own massive contributions to greenhouse gases.

Heightened militarization is another direct impact of banking and energy strategies. Energy, empire, and a militarized society go hand in hand. Our merry-go-round of energy resource cartelization and associated militarization explains much of our parasitic financial labyrinth. Having their hands on the levers of empire was the ultimate in banker ecstasy, and energy was the ultimate lever. Manipulations could accelerate warfare and debts. Plus, energy is the penultimate source of economic growth, and perpetual growth, in the face of clear limits, is vital to the functioning of our Ponzi economy. Without growth, interest on debt could not be paid, and without interest, banking, as we know it, would swiftly grind to a halt. Much of the bubble blowing in existing assets stems from the recognition that the energy equation for growth no longer adds up. ESSO's slogan from the 1950s "the more energy you use the better you live" is a now a bitter joke. Both the quantity and quality of energy resources are in precipitous decline and substitutions do not occur as automatically as the economic models suggest. Economic feedback loops amplify small snags wherever and whenever they occur in the vast and extremely fragile global energy networks.

THE GREAT OILY EPOCH

In our epoch, energy means oil. Oil is the magical juice that made us the richest civilization in history. It was easy to extract, cheap to process, and completely portable. If our machines were max efficient, a single barrel of oil could yield as much energy as a single human's muscles could render in a dozen years, employed 40 hours a week. Oil allowed our vast consumer economy to flourish, but it also allowed our fundamentally flawed financial systems to mutate into a murderous monstrosity. Cheap oil facilitated immense automotive, real estate, and infrastructure industries. It also fueled transportation for a global market place (via container ships and air cargo), as well as generating sprawling suburbs that could be rendered uninhabitable by even minor disruptions to any of their fragile and far-reaching supply chains. When one adds regional conflicts and global climate change, oil was the most Faustian of bargains. The last time there was this much carbon dioxide in the atmosphere there were palm trees growing in Alaska. Carbon dioxide build-up, resulting from widespread volcanic activity and the ignition of deep coal deposits along with associated acid rain produced the earth's largest mass extinction event some 250 million years ago. It is a bit ironic that the Permian also signifies one of the last oil regions in the lower 48 to be fully exploited (fracked).

The unholy alliance of oil and finance is the deus ex machina of the modern era and the source of many grotesque machinations. They are manifold, and not merely limited the typical price fixing, rent seeking and political corruption. Oil took the inherent macro-cycles of speculation, financialization, globalization and militarization to new extremes. Oil became underlying rationale for the American Empire. If oil were merely tulip bulbs, railroads, steel, or even the entire FIRE industry, then its disruptive patterns might have been containable. Oil is so vital to our civilization that even a minor flux would be analogous to water in the human body, where a loss of only 10% can literally kill you. The "Iranian shortfall" (following the overthrow of the Shaw) was little more than 5% (barely more than noise in the global oil networks), and yet it contributed to a second major oil shock and left drivers sitting in long gas lines in the summer of 1979.

Despite its astronomical profitability, oil remains the most heavily subsidized industry of all time, and that does not include the bearing of externalities (e.g., pollution, military misadventures, etc.). Can you imagine if the price of a gallon of gas included the costs of maintaining two carriers groups in the Persian Gulf (not to mention the trillions spent on various oil wars). By the time muckraker Minerva (Ida) Tarbell's epic history of Standard Oil (1904) was being serialized in the pages of McClure's Magazine (and depicted as a huge octopus), Rockefeller's vast financial empire was literally rewriting the rules on integrated monopolies or "trusts" (including links to European Banking dynasties).

Petroleum (meaning rock oil) that just seeped out of the ground was used by the Native Americans for centuries, primarily for medicinal purposes (but its status as a laxative might be apocryphal) as well as patching canoes. Initially it was this latter use that attracted early investors in Pennsylvania in the 1850s. A Yale chemistry professor was commissioned to study it as a potential replacement for dwindling whale oil supplies. His studies of this alternative lamp fuel proved promising, yet he never received his payment (presaging industry ethics). As another aside, when whales were being hunted to extinction the decline in productivity was blamed on the laziness and low character of the whalers and the increasing shyness of the beasts. Irrespective of the excuses this time (terrorist tree hungers most likely), we really are well past the peak of the cheap oil age.

PEAK OIL AND THE RETARDED TRANSITION

The truth of the matter is that we have been starring at the oil peak in the rear view mirror for a number of years. Keep in mind that peak does not mean the end point, only half way to the end point. In 1956, Dr. M. King Hubbard, chief geologist at Schell (who had discovered rock plasticity in the earth's crust), predicted that US oil production would peak around 1970, and world production around 2005. While much debated, I would contend that he was pretty much spot on (note, Deffeyes, 2005). I was privy to discussions of oil executives in Calgary in the mid-2000s and several expressed concerns that the globe had just passed its peak. The mere fact that we are now turning all kinds of crap into oil suggests that the version that once nearly exploded out of the ground is on the downward slope. If markets actually worked that last few barrels of oil would soon end up in museums and people would have to pay just to see them. And, the guide would ask, "Can you believe that the fate civilizations once depended on this black goo"? Ultimately, oil is much more valuable as a petrochemical feedstock (plastics, fertilizers, insecticides, etc.). This fact should've priced it out of our automobiles (except as lubricant). But oil has never been governed by real market forces. I am reminded of how upset some oil company economists would get each time they contemplated that the cartelized production limits and fixed prices might not hold.

Even excluding the considerable environmental costs (as we normally do) the various new oil supplies (tar sands, oil shale, arctic, biomass, etc.) are much more problematic. A team leader at the General Accounting Office or GAO (now renamed the "Accountability" Office) once related his mission to Parachute Creek, Colorado to check out Exxon's kerogen mining and retorting project. He asked when they might achieve production, and was told "oh we are just here to sell the licensing process".

Many of the so-called "alt-oil" processes are thermodynamically challenged, requiring almost as much energy to extract than they will ever yield. Once the surface Canadian tar sands are stripped mined away, astronomical amounts of boiling water (from yet to be constructed nuclear plants) will be needed to retrieve bulk of the supply buried deep below. Beyond being a nearly net energy wash and a huge greenhouse gas producer (twice that of normal oil production), the vast Canadian Tar Sands, have another dirty little secret. Being mostly carbon they have to add large amounts of hydrogen to make it a suitable hydrocarbon (in route to becoming oil). And, where do they get all the hydrogen you might ask? They extract it from natural gas, a perfectly good (and cleaner burning) oil substitute in the first place. One Canadian journalist referred to the process as "turning gold into shit". It is noteworthy that hydrogen that can be generated by other processes (e.g., electrolysis) and be used to store wind and solar energy would be a great (and cleaner yet) fuel source by itself. But obviously the oil wankers don't want us to have it. Nevertheless, the sheer fact that they seem willing to go to all this trouble and expense suggests that: 1) the cheap oil really has peaked; and 2) that they willing and able to cannibalize the rest of our economy and wreck our environment to get at something that even looks like it might be oil. Meanwhile we the oil addicted are like decrepit alcoholics during prohibition being reduced to drinking poisonous wood methanol.

Past energy transitions (from wood to coal and from coal to oil) were easy, yet still took approximately 50+ years, even when driven by lower costs and increased energy yield as well as vastly enhanced portability. We are already nearly 50 years behind on a transition that we tried to get started in earnest in the 1970s, and still have several decades to go to make a dent in our oil dependency. Given price and yield headwinds, our current transition will require huge amounts of capital investment in alternative technologies at the very time that it is being diverted into re-inflating existing assets and monetizing the monstrous debt overhang. Wall Street is too busy making data manipulation the next big asset class and squeezing every last dime out of oil indebtedness to worry much about an energy transition.

When I worked with the GAO, reviewing national energy planning (mostly the lack there of, see, Daneke, 1981; 1982) we kept arguing that planning should be designed to lengthen the "shadow of the future". Moreover, we maintained that policy should augment markets by gradually blending in the "replacement cost of oil". We concluded that 100 dollars per barrel was probably a good starting point, and that "wellhead tax" could both spur alternatives, and pay for vital R&D in new technologies. Obviously none of this ever got off the ground, and only Osama Ben Laden used that exact number (coincidently), when arguing how the "Great Satan" had been stealing their oil. In the beginning and for several years the US had paid the Saudis a whopping 25 cents a barrel. Even as prices began to rise the OPEC Cartel was mostly able to keep them below the threshold point for alternatives to enter the market in any serious way. British Petroleum (BP) once began an ad campaign touting their investments in alternative energy and saying that BP now stood for "beyond petroleum". One of their executives, however, explained to Prince Bandar that the campaign was mostly cosmetic and they were really only spending 1 tenth of 1% on alternatives; to which Bandar responded: "that is 1 tenth of 1% too much".

Unfortunately for Americans, our Department of Energy (DOE), is an agglomeration of misbegotten pieces from 11 other agencies and is horribly ill-equipped to do anything about energy policy. The lion's share of its budget is in weapons systems. Its efforts at strategic energy planning, of any kind, are tied up with ill-purposed and antiquated forecasting models and other "dogs that won't hunt". When I arrived in DC in mid 1970s, they were still using revamped version of PIES (the "Project Independence" Evaluation System) a simple optimization program from the Nixon and Ford years, yet even after refurbishing it could not really aid planning. Nonetheless, they had renamed it the MEFS (The Midrange Energy Forecasting System). We preferred to call it the "muffs", as in mistakes. To their credit, DOE leaders did hire a student of Jay Forrester and Dennis Meadows (of Limits to Growth fame), Roger Naill to run his huge (1500+ structural equations) systems dynamics model, called Fossil-II, yet I believe this was mostly to co-opt broader concerns. Naill's model could have explored a number of contingencies or "what if" issues, but was mostly only brought out to provide backfill for policy choices already determined without the aid of analysis (other than the profit concerns of bankers and oil companies). Dennis once confided to me that he was upset that more of his students he sent to Washington did not get fired. Meanwhile, most of the standard models used by DOE were completely addled by faulty embedded assumptions (e.g., competitive markets, fungible substitutions, lack of environment concerns, and so on). For example, MEFS had a built in bias for nuclear power, and projected an America in which cheap (if one excludes externalities) electricity from hundreds of new nukes would displace huge amounts of foreign oil. Nukes were already heavily subsidized (see, Daneke, 1978a), but following the near disaster at Three Mile Island, it was more difficult to justify more out pouring of the public largesse. We used to joke that MEFS projections would have jets flying with exceedingly long extension cords.

Near as I can tell, President Carter was the first and only national leader (aside from Al Gore) who attempted to address the problem of societal energy transformation, and was viciously ridiculed for his efforts. Recall that Jimmy called for "the moral equivalent of war" (on energy), and when I relate my experience as an energy policy analyst in DC, I refer to it as "my moral equivalent of war stories". President Carter obviously forgot that William James' lament was that there really is no such thing. While "energy independence" was a perennial political ploy, Jimmy was actually onto something; we indeed needed a Manhattan or an Apollo Project in energy (and still do). The bankers, oil executives, generals, and mainstream economists, however, had another agenda. When one realizes that the lack of any energy transition was an embedded financial gambit, it should be no surprise that most national leaders have more or less conspired to obfuscate the problem since the 1970s. Hence, most Americans are totally clueless that the lack of a viable transition strategy is already a crisis, which is unfolding at this very moment. Hence, they have no idea how their daily lives will be challenged as a result. Like frogs in the pot of water slowly reaching the boiling point, we missed the opportunity to exit.

Worse still, well before resource limits and climate changes boil us, the ubiquitous financial and political machinations used to hide these realities could themselves be the engines of societal collapse. I gave a talk to a group of ecologists at the University of British Columbia in 2006, and told them the good news was that the coming financial collapse might give us few more years to address the problem of climate change. The bad news was that a worldwide depression would delimit options and might produce widespread social unrest as well as the rise of techno-totalitarian regimes. Of course, this deterioration of democratic institutions was yet another ignored slow boiling frog pot.

While Trump is turning up the heat on all us frogs and effectively ignoring the heating up of the planet, he has also made his own personal contribution to our carbon dominated energy policies, by adding coal back into the mix. His policy perspective, which has little rational basis, could be summarized by merely adding "dig baby dig" to Sarah Palin's "drill baby drill". His disdain for the DOE is born of unbelievable ignorance. It is manifested in a number of extremely unqualified appointments, starting with former Texas Governor Rick Perry (who listed but could not recall DOE among the agencies that should be eliminated). A recent article (2017) by Michael Lewis (of Liar's Poker and The Big Short fame) reminds us that the DOE is not just a leaking fountainhead (such as it is) of energy strategy it is also responsible for safe guarding the vast nuclear arsenals as well as overseeing nonproliferation. Lewis contends that Trump's malign neglect of the DOE is tantamount to treason However, his taking a wrecking ball to EPA, OHSA, and SEC, etc. makes this merely par for the course.

ECONOMICS AS THERMODYNAMIC ABSURDITY

Nearly a century ago one remarkable scholar suggested that energy flows should be the focal point of economics, yet in the process he stumbled upon the great horse fly in the economic ointment (i.e., Money & Banking). Frederick Soddy, a chemist by training, was awarded a real Nobel Prize in 1921 for his path breaking work in radioactive isotopes. Having witnessed the weaponization of chemistry in WWI (e.g., mustard gas), it was his terror about the development of radioactive weapons which caused him to take up the study of economics. He recognized that economic conditions as prime source of warfare. Soddy maintained the economy should be viewed as a set of energy relationships, following the basic laws of thermodynamics (e.g., entropy), rather than a monetary system based mostly in myth and mischief. In a series of books (including: 1926; 1934) he challenged the scientific status of economic theories and exposed inherent weaknesses in global financial systems. While labeled an "outrageous crank" in his time, the years since have seen several of his monetary proposals become policy (e.g., floating exchange rates, government stimulus, and the consumer price index). His most pivotal observations regarding debt deflation, endogenous money, and the dangers fractional reserve banking, although correct, are still considered beyond the pale, and he has been relegated to total obscurity. Mainstream economists ferociously maintain the religious dictum "that thou shall never ever mess with the money". All money is generated as debt, and GREAT DEBT MACHINE was built for an era without any energy limitations. Debt at present levels demands explosive future growth, but the entropic decline and associated re-organized complexity make such growth extremely problematic.

An "energetics" approach to economics has been rejuvenated from time to time, particularly during periods of resource crisis (see, Georgescu-Roegen, 1982; Daly, 1996; and note particularly, Hall & Klitgaard, 2011). But few are bold (or energetic) enough to connect the all dots between energy/ecological disasters and mismanagement of Money & Banking (for rare exceptions see, Boyd, 2013: Smith-Nonini, 2016). Roger Boyd is one of the few economists of any stripe who makes direct connection between the mega-mismanagement of macroeconomics and declining fortunes of our energy systems. For him the wholesale printing of money which became the hallmark of Central Bank policy in recent years is a concrete signal that increased energy production in itself can NO longer be relied upon to fuel economic growth. Moreover, he illustrates institutionalized ignorance regarding the real world arrival of inherent "limits to growth". As he (2013) maintains energy limits should fundamentally alter the nature of the financial games we can play. As he explains:

> What all of this means for investors is that, at best, growth may cease at the global level in the relatively near future. Once you accept that growth will cease, all of the current common sense assumptions about investing, such as the assumption of making money from money, cease to be true. Completely different assumptions will be required, including an understanding that the future will be a less wealthy place than the present. This could destabilize and crash the financial system (p. 67).

He proceeds to prescribe that we dramatically reduce our perverse attachment to "fictitious assets" and suggests we prepare for complete financial collapse as much as energy decline.

COLLAPSE AMERICAN STYLE

As mainstream economists encourage us to stand idly by and watch the paint dry on all the warning signs, we are already collapsing. We have been in the midst of collapse for so long that we have barely noticed it. "Rome was not built in a day", and it certainly did not collapse overnight. It is also worth noting that the average Romans (predominantly slaves and peasants) were better off after the Barbarians sacked Rome. Like the Romans, we are fond of our "bread and circuses", and tend to be oblivious to our own decline. If allowed to recognize this "phrase transition", then we might have a chance at a decent society. Collapse is proceeding apace all around us, yet we continue to merely apply pothole repairs to the vast chasms of malinvestment and mounting inequity (as well as iniquity) with our faltering feudalism of fictitious wealth. Given the interdependence and "far from equilibrium dynamics" of global resource systems, not to mention the engineering of cultural and ethnic hostilities amid growing availability of weapons of mass destruction (both real and financial), the potential for much more catastrophic collapse is also ever-present. Director of Havas Media

Lab and columnist for the Harvard Business Review, Umair Haque (2018a) explains "why we're underestimating American collapse". He sees mass shootings (now on nearly a bi-monthly basis), widespread opioid abuse, and the denial of dignity to our elderly, as signs of "the world's first RICH FAILED STATE" (not to mention our crumbling roads, bridges, airports, etc.). Any of these would cause widespread hand wringing and massive policy initiatives among most industrial nations, but we allow them to be exacerbated by government. Haque highlights another core dimension which he refers to as a "disease of the soul" (much as Jimmy did), which when combined with our tacit acceptance of predatory behavior makes us numb to the potential for full scale collapse. In another essay he (Haque, 2018b) explains how our "megatrends of collapse" result from "decades of self-destructive choices", such as:

> ...trickle-down economics, neoliberalism, market fundamentalism, a total lack of investment in people, a culture of cruelty, a modern day caste society, Wal Mart capitalism, all of which added up to Weimar republic style ruin — letting middle classes implode, leaving the poor to die in the streets, because a predatory elite was allowed to capture more than 100% of society's gains, and worse still, Americans were told to believe, by wise men, that all that was noble, righteous, and true: only the strong should survive (p. 3).

The total collapse of the Anglo-American model of civilization is made increasingly likely by the overwhelming inattention to institutional issues. Health, education, and welfare mechanisms are hugely inadequate. And subtle signs of societal malaise abound. For example a recent study (Krueger, 2017) suggests that 20% of the decline in the labor force participation rate by prime age males is attributable to opiate addiction. The mounting societal malaise has already produced grand fissures in the political landscape (e.g., Brexit and Trump) and reactivated various dark forces. Tiny pebble nicks can produce huge cracks on the windshield of society.

A total collapse can be extremely abrupt via the dynamic of "self-organized criticality", where the next grain of sand brings down the pile. Without remedial effort and relatively soon, institutional failures could recombine and spiral out of control literally overnight. Prevailing economic logic compounds human suffering, but what will make life truly "brutish and short" is the shattering of our "brittle" and remote conduits of commerce. With little in the way of local back-up, we could rapidly find ourselves without the basic instrumentalities of life support and experiencing the chaos of crumbling civic order.

Not all collapses are completely fatal, however. Ecologists focus on the "resiliency" conditions which allow socio-ecological systems to "reorganize and recover (see, Abel, et.al. 2006)". From an institutional perspective, one would seek to isolate those arrangements that impede from those that enhance adaptive capacity. Complexity simulations could explore those processes most likely anneal into robust "safe-fail systems", rather than our traditional emphasis on fail-safe devices, because the latter usually fail. As Murphy's 2nd law maintains "it is impossible to build fool proof systems because fools are so ingenious". Despite ample numbers of fools, democratic institutions, with their built-in redundancies and bottom-up processes, can provide a source of resiliency. If informed by complexity economics, participatory channels can more readily reassemble the flotsam & jetsam of unused or pre-adaptations (also called "spandrels" or "exaptations") via civic entrepreneurship. If folks are paying attention, then societal collapses need not be completely catastrophic.

DIAMOND IN THE ROUGH

Most people are only familiar with the concept collapse by way of famed UCLA Geographer, Jared Diamond's (2004) excellent best seller: Collapse: Why Societies Choose to Succeed or Fail. He did a masterful job of highlighting the deadly effects of human hubris. Yet, like his previous Pulitzer Prize winning Guns, Steel, and Germs, it tends to be a tad over-stated. Let's consider the collapse of Easter Island (Rapa Nui) a 63 square mile rock out in the middle of the Pacific Ocean, literally thousands of miles from anywhere. As irony would have it its nearest cousin (over 1000 miles away) was the mis-chartered Pitcairn Island, where the HMS Bounty mutineers hid out. A small group of Polynesians arrived at Rapa Nui around 1200 and developed a primarily agricultural society that thrived sufficiently to support an estimated population maybe

15,000 or 20,000 at its peak. Moreover, its inhabitants possessed sufficient time, manpower, and organization to carve nearly 1000 huge (many over 75 tons) statues (mostly stylized torsos with tall heads) out of stone (petrified volcanic ash) and to install them around the island (as an emblems of status and ancestor worship). Once the island was completely denuded of an estimated 16 million trees, however, life quickly became, nasty, brutish, and short (with famines, wars, and even cannibalism). For Diamond it was a clear case of eco-suicide.

Diamond operates on the theory that the Rapa Nuians slashed and burned the forests for agriculture as well as cut down a majority of the trees in order to roll the huge stone heads to their far flung locations. But a much more plausible theory is provided by two enterprising anthropologists from the University of Hawaii, Terry Hunt and Carl Lipo (2006; 2009). They present wealth of evidence that the decline of population (which was never near the above estimates in the first place) was more genocide, at hands of hands of the Europeans, with their "guns, steel, germs", and sea born rats (who ate the palm roots and seedlings). Furthermore the arrival of slave traders meant that significant number of the more able bodied inhabitants might have left in the hole of ships. More interesting perhaps Hunt and Lipo actually demonstrated how the stone heads were literally rocked and "walked" across the island standing up (requiring a much smaller supply of human laborers) as the island folk lore indicated. Moreover, there is very little archeological evidence of warfare (weapons and fortifications), nor cannibalism. When the going got tough they ate the rats for the protean, and developed swimming contests to regularly rotate their leadership. A Dutch explorer happened upon the island in 1722, reported that they did not appear to be starving and that they "asked for hats instead of food". Hunt and Lipo concluded that given that people of Easter Island were in the wrong place, at the wrong time, for a long time, that it was actually a roaring success.

Diamonds case for self-destruction is perhaps better made with the Norse of Greenland. Their lessons for us stand in starker relief. The famed Viking, Eric the Red (whose son Leif explored America, centuries before Columbus) could easily add land speculation to his long list of crimes. If you have ever flown the northern route to Europe in daylight you noticed that it is Iceland that is green and that Greenland is covered with ice (or was until lately). During his banishment from Iceland for several murders, Eric explored Greenland for three years, and returned with tall tales of a paradise of abundant resources. Hence, the Norse people began settling there around 980, by mostly taking over the abandoned villages of the Dorset (a Paleo-Eskimo people). The Norse colony grew to as many as 5000 at its peak, and was largely a farming and herding (cows, sheep, and goats) economy. As the climate grew colder and growing seasons shorter (especially with the onset of the Little Ice Age around 1300), European style agriculture and animal husbandry became increasing impossible. Trade became more problematic when the ice bergs diverted shipping traffic. Plus, the trade in whale bone and walrus tusks had already fallen off, given the opening up ivory from Africa following the crusades. Rather than abandon their farming practices and/or adapt to the abundant food sources (seals and walrus) of their Inuit neighbors (who thrived, numbering over 50,000 today), the Norse in Greenland simply dwindled, died off, and completely disappeared by 1435. This appears to be a paradigm case of Diamond's cultural suicide, and mirrors our own toxic attachment to elite fatalism and the failure to address climate change. We, however, have more and better choices. We just need get busy experimenting with alternatives.

EMBRACING COLLAPSE

Americans have been in protracted collapse for some time, but our leaders have chosen an admixture of denial, division, and scapegoating. Not only are we needlessly delaying simple adaptations, we are entrusting our choices to an increasing repressive regimes of corrupt oligarchs, their self-serving financial institutions, and their military clients. On this score a much more compelling comparative analysis of collapse is provided by Russian immigrant, Dmitry Orlov (2006), who experienced firsthand the collapse of the former Soviet Union. Unlike our other cases above, the collapse of the Soviet Empire is much more instructive because it mostly about Money & Banking and the rise of hugely corrupt oligarchs. Of course, it is also a harrowing tale of the peoples of Eastern Europe bravely escaping grip of totalitarian states, but perhaps only temporarily (as some are now substituting fascism for communism). Orlov has a more urgent tale to convey, and he does it in an extremely entertaining fashion via his notion of the "The Collapse Gap". Recall Ronald Reagan's famed "Missile Gap", where he got American's worked up for another suicidal arms race, by claiming a widening gap between our total vis-à-vis the Soviet Union. This ploy failed to mention the fact that most of our more than ample supply of missiles had multiple, independently guided, warheads (MIR) or that a single Ohio class, missile submarine, or "Boomer Boat", could destroy most of the Soviet Union. Orlov says a more troubling gap exists between the Soviet preparedness for collapse and our own. In Russia after the collapse, people still had their government provided apartments, public transport, and healthcare. People still went to work and did their jobs (even if wages were sporadic). By contrast, many items of our everyday life would simply stop functioning following a similar financial crisis in the US. Moreover, marshal law would prevail and probably remain in perpetuity in one form or another. Like the Soviet experience, privatization of the commons, amid screaming inequity, would enable and further enrich a small handful of elites. Our collapse gap means that chaos would prevail for an extended period, at which point things would stabilize via serious constraints on basic civil liberties through the extension of the surveillance and social control tools of the ultra-totalitarian state.

Pandering to predators, in the name of economic growth, only exacerbates collapse. Mathematician and public policy scholar, Safa Motesharrei (2014) and his august colleagues (Jorges Rivas and Eugenia Kalnay) modeled modern societal collapse, they conclude that,

> Given economic stratification, collapse is very difficult to avoid and requires major policy changes, including major reductions in inequality and population growth rates. Even in the absence of economic stratification, collapse can still occur if depletion per capita is too high   (p. 101).

Whether or not per capita consumption is too high, was addressed by a legendary set scholars (Arrow, et. al., 2004), and they concluded that most economic studies exhibit insufficient concern for increasing population and decreasing technology.

Meanwhile, concern for resource collapse has been co-opted by pursuit of mythical SUSTAINABLE DEVELOPMENT (SD). Originally coined as a process for adjusting north-south inequities (via tech transfers), by the UN back in the 1970s, it led to a prestigious commission headed by Norwegian, female PM, Gro

Bundtland in the 1980s, and culminating in the famed report, Our Common Future (WCED, 1987, also note, UN, 1992). It started out as more than a bit oxymoronic, as it implied we could have our cake and eat it too, which of course we cannot. It became the battle cry of many a well-meaning group, but was also leap upon by globalization and neoliberal (feudal) forces. As famed journalist, Jeremy Seabrook (2002) summarizes:

> Like all the brave concepts offered up by environmentalists, sustainable development was doomed to go the way of the rest of the treacherous lexicon of developmentalism... Sustainable now means what the market, not the earth, can bear... Sustainable is what the rich and powerful can get away with (p. 2).

Richard Smith (2016) contends that SD as well as much of Green Capitalism is "the god that failed". We will need to be a lot leaner and a little less mean before we can worship at that altar again. If we don't have the cheap energy (or the atmosphere) to sustain our ludicrously complex societies, we need to embrace simpler ones, and in process we might be able jettison some of the jesters of unlimited growth from amidst our more earnest green emissaries.

Unfortunately, limits are rarely politically popular, and in our particular epoch we have a number of fledging fascists telling us we needn't bother. They have the secret sauce of unlimited prosperity we just need to accept unlimited inequality along with their monarchical edicts. They "alone" know the formula for growth without grief. Besides if we just get rid of certain scapegoats (which includes environmentalists), and obliterate resource rich jihadists, we'll be home free. It is very tempting to follow a demagogue down the "making American great again" rabbit-hole. But trust me there are far worse things than graduated collapse.

CHAPTER 7: QUICK, BURN THIS BOOK

Only the mob and the elite can be attracted by the momentum of totalitarianism itself. The masses have to be won by propaganda. _____ **Hannah Arendt**

Those who can make you believe absurdities can make you commit atrocities. _____ **Voltaire**

A fascist is one whose lust for money or power is combined with such an intensity of intolerance toward those of other races, parties, classes, religions, cultures, regions or nations as to make him ruthless in his use of deceit or violence to attain his ends. _____ **Henry A. Wallace**

The great strength of the totalitarian state is that it forces those who fear it to imitate it. _____ **Adolf Hitler**

Looting the future, through currency debauchment, debt accumulation, growth destruction, and techno-industrial retardation is especially easy to conceal, and thus reliably popular. Democracy is essentially tragic because it provides the populace with a weapon to destroy itself, one that is always eagerly seized, and used. _____ **Nick Land**

Since I have struggled to write this book for over a decade, most of the time I was half-joking when I told friends and colleagues that "I hope I get it finished in time for the Nazis to throw it on the pyre". Recently, I've come to question my sardonic sense of humor. With the election of Donald Trump, with all his great potential for becoming the personification of a comic book Nazi, my joking is no longer funny. Despite having warned of the possibility of a much more virulent form of fascism coming to fruition for the last 20 years, I was still stunned when it actually arrived. The experience reminds me of one of those amazing New Yorker cartoons with a bearded figure with the sign stating that "The End is Near", and a passing couple, with the caption that reads, "Oh dear is that Paul Krugman". It is nice to have friends and colleagues who worried about me now see me as less of a nut case, but my feelings are more of fear than of vindication. Frankly, it is quite disconcerting to hear previously unemotional friends exclaim "Oh my god, it is really happening". They ask me about jobs in Canada. They now want me to precisely predict "when can we expect the jack boots kicking down our doors"? I joke "what is this 'we' and 'our' kemo-sabi"? All kidding aside (well mostly), you probably have time to finish this book, and maybe even lend it out a couple of times before you have to burn it. But having said this, I actually believe that free discourse of ideas could soon become dramatically curtailed far beyond "political correctness". However, it will probably take the form massive digital misinformation and propaganda campaigns against much better know and exceedingly more influential scholars and public intellectuals than myself. As for the burning of books and other much more ugly events, it is difficult to say. But the frog water is nearly at the boiling point. Another terrorist attack (real or "false flag"), a financial downturn, or any number of issues could send us over the edge. I fear that a Trump impeachment, even if the evidence of "high crimes" is conclusive, would trigger widespread social unrest and a fascist backlash. Once violence occurs, all bets are off. Perhaps we are nowhere near the point where people will just disappear, except of course those deemed to be members of a terrorist groups (such as the Sierra Club or the Democratic Party, just kidding I hope). But then our definitions of such groups and rules of evidence are changing in our post-habeas-corpus America. While our TVs don't necessarily watch us, they certainly know what we have been watching. Plus, smart appliances and service devices are constantly collecting data that will be used to place you in algorithmically generated behavioral cohort whether you belong there or not. Facebook and Google already have AI systems that they believe capture exactly what people like you are thinking. So who knows when BIG DATA will become BIG BROTHER, and already existing massive surveillance systems will be used to terrorize and intimidate us? All I know is that it could all happen in the blink of an eye. As the guys from Monty Python comically suggested "no one expects the Spanish Inquisition", yet in our neofeudal world we really should.

FASCISM AS AMERICAN AS APPLE PIE

Fascism, like feudalism, has always been latent in the American landscape. In fact, a fully functioning corporatist version has actually been manifest, although subdued, since the beginning of the modern era. Veblen (1899) observed that our fragile civilization vacillates on a continuum of "barbarism". It is always fully able to fall back into more oppressive status. Moreover, he maintained that embedded within our institutions there is a certain "conservation of archaic traits". From this perspective, the fascism of the 1930s was not nearly as aberrant as we might like to believe. The potentiality of full blown fascism remains dormant just below the thin veneer of democracy. Generally speaking it is diffused and contained in less fearsome, yet powerful, subliminal mechanism of social control (e.g., Madison Ave, etc.) and the new surveillance state. With the re-emergence of feudalism, fascism also gathers itself for a brutal reappearance. As Hannah Arendt (1951) observed European totalitarian impulses took root amid the pursuit of empire, and eventually its more virulent tools and concepts, perfected in the oppression of other peoples, came home and attached themselves to existing social undercurrents. Well before Arendt conducted her exhaustive historical analysis, a young Columbia University scholar, Carmen Haider (1934), traveled to Mussolini's Italy and drew parallels to the American-style corporatist fascism arising in opposition to FDR. She was less concerned with whackos like Father Charles Coughlin or the burgeoning KKK and more interested in the bankers and industrialists who sought to undermine his New Deal policies, especially the National Recovery Act. She also highlights how corporate based fascists developed a long range and rather low key strategy of resistance by capturing key legislative seats (in both parties), as well as launching court challenges. She explains:

> Congress could be captured from within, since a powerful fascist movement caught in Republican Party channels would send its own representatives to Congress.... Moreover, a national economic council might be established and the Fascist group, in endorsing economic planning, would probably also approve of occupational representation. Determination of the economic aspects of national life might be turned over to this council as was done in Italy, whereby the power of Congress would be substantially reduced (p. 247).

She also maintained that most of what American fascists sought could be accomplished without a bombastic leader (e.g., Huey Long) or separate party. The more totalitarianism versions of fascism only become necessary if they misplace their grip on the working class, lose their patience, or an interloper steps in and steals their thunder; or all the above.

Another extremely insightful appraisal of American fascism was commissioned by the New York Times Magazine, and written by Vice President Henry A. Wallace in 1944. His grandson wrote a recent op-ed (Wallace, 2017) illustrating it's more prescient elements, in light of the Trump phenomena. Like Haider, the elder Wallace focused on the corporatist and clandestine nature of American fascists and how they would use the democracy against itself. "They demand free enterprise, but are spokesmen for monopoly and vested interests". "They use isolationism as a slogan to conceal their own selfish imperialism". As a further matter, they "poison the channels of public information". By way of "deliberate perversion of truth and fact", they use "their newspapers and propaganda to carefully cultivate every fissure of disunity". Does any of this sound familiar?

In fairness, it is still possible that Trump is merely an wannabe or junior league fascist (more douche bag than Il Duce'); nonetheless, he has somehow gotten his grubby little hands on the authentic authoritarian playbook and is following it chapter and verse. But, he did NOT write it. Unfortunately, if this is a usurpation of the sorcerer's wand, then it only makes our hapless apprentice even more dangerous (i.e., Haider's all-the-above scenario). Regardless, the days of warm and fuzzy fascism may be numbered.

THE RISK OF FRISKIER FASCISM

In case you have not been paying attention, it is high time to wake-up and smell the NEW WORLD ODOR. American is not alone in being over ripe for full-fledged fascism, but it certainly smells like democracy is rotting on the vines. Fascism is always waiting in the wings, and over the years we have diverted so much power to our chief executive that we are increasingly vulnerable to its grip. If our leaders have only a casual commitment to the rule of law, and/or are more than a tad oligarchic, then fascism readily moves out of the shadows. Circumstances also play a major role, especially economic conditions and the level of mass alienation. Like its old buddy feudalism, its latent tendencies await the confluence of forces and personalities we now have in abundance.

Among other things fascism is a system of government marked by ultra-nationalism, ethnocentrism, corporatism, and militarism as well as the generation of extreme anti-intellectualism (even mysticism). Mussolini himself said that "Fascism should more appropriately be called Corporatism because it is a merger of state and corporate power". Italian historian, Gaetano Salvemini (1936), elaborates in his Under the Axe of Fascism as follows "the state pays for the blunders of private enterprise...Profit is private and individual. Loss is public and social (p.416)". Are you feeling the déjà vu yet?

Fascism has deep and diverse philosophical roots in the romantic, anti-enlightenment, and utopian philosophers, as well as occultists, monarchists, and religious fundamentalists. Of late some of the more toxic elements from these bygone philosophies (racism, sexism, and anti-democratic reactionism), have been re-blended with technological determinism in what is appropriately being called the "Dark Enlightenment" (see, Land, 2012). In general, fascism calls for the restoration of a largely imaginary golden age. It corresponds with populist rage and coalesces with widespread social inequities. Thus we should expect to see more virulent and violent forms gaining momentum. Numerous distinguished scholars have been sounding the alarm for some time now. In the process of synthesizing these observations, two UCSB Sociologists (Robinson & Barrera, 2012) produced a seminal contribution of their own in an article entitled, Global Capitalism and Twenty-first Century Fascism: A Case Study. They describe the new fascism as a direct result of the crises brought on by "neoliberal over accumulation" and "dispossession". In particular they highlight "militarized accumulation", defined as: "making wars and interventions that unleash cycles of destruction and reconstruction and generate enormous profits for an ever-expanding military-prison-industrial-security-financial complex... (p. 6)". They also conclude that the new improved fascism, American style, will draw extensively on our racism, misogyny, religious zealotry, and national exceptualism.

What is especially devastating is that women (more than half the population) who were just beginning to emerge from their long standing second class status, are now just another scapegoat for rising feudalism and fascism. A recent report from the Anti-defamation League (ADL, 2018) When Woman are the Enemy: The Intersection of Misogyny and White Supremacy, describes how anti-reproductive rights activists, angry and violent involuntary celibates ("Incels"), and various white male victimhood movements, have coalesced under Trumps manifest misogyny to place women in the crosshairs. A George Mason University (a new bastion of neofeudalism) economist, Robin Hanson (see, Douthat, 2018), has entertained the notion of the REDISTRIBUTION OF SEX, for all those horny under-achievers. A TV adaption of Margaret Atwood's (1985) dystopian novel, The Handmaid's Tale, has taken on greater currency, and is less unimaginable in light of recent revelations, especially the secret SS breeding program, called Lebensborn (font of life) during WWII. The burgeoning #MeToo (anti-sexual harassment and assault movement) has had the unintended consequence of fueling greater fear and hate, among mediocre white males, as well as entitled executives. Perhaps our new feudal lords will reintroduce jus primae noctis (right of the first night).

IS TRUMP A REAL NAZI OF DOES HE JUST PLAY ONE ON TV?

Ever since his election a somewhat trivial (academic style) debate has raged over exactly whether and what kind of fascist Trump might be; place your bets. His obvious pandering to various neo-Nazis and white nationalists notwithstanding, some contend that it still remains to be seen whether or not he is the real deal, and/or how much we can contain him. Overly meticulous historians and political pundits apply some seriousness, but also a bunch of nitpicking silliness. The debate sounds much like he can't be a Hitler because he does not have a tiny mustache. Similarly, he can't become a Mussolini because his "Benito score" is only about half of the possible total (McNeil, 2016). Much of the debate seems to turn on misconceptions of what fascism was or is, for example its lack of a "coherent governing philosophy" (see, Kagan, 2016). Yale historian of tyranny, Timothy Synder (via various news interviews) suggests that we be vigorously vigilant regarding Trump's staging of a "Reichstag Fire" (i.e., a "false flag" attack). My own appraisal of King Donald is that he would score well north of 80 (the pathological point) on Adorno's famed F (for Fascist) scale, which melds anti-intellectual and, anti-democratic tendencies with various other personality traits (see, Adorno, et.al. 1950). However, it is all speculation since getting him to take a test is about as likely as him releasing his tax returns. It is noteworthy, however, that back in 1989 Trump spent 85,000 dollars on a full page ads in four premier newspapers, including the New York Times, to call for frontier justice for the "Central Park Five" (black youths who were eventually completely exonerated of the brutal rape of a jogger). He wrote in all caps "civil liberties end when attacks on our safety begin"; so maybe we "don't need no stinking" test after all. I believe he will be every bit a real fascist dictator if we allow it.

Bonafide conservative Republican (W speech writer), David Frum's book (2018), Trumptocracy: The Corruption of the American Republic, really does say it all. Frum believes Trump is seriously dangerous for democracy. Plus, he makes the unusual observation that in his inordinate lassitude that leads him to seek more than shady short-cuts in business and government, as well as knowing so very little about the latter. This suggests that he does not have the energy or the attention span to be a serious dictator. I am not so sure, myself, yet it does explain his preternatural propensity for lying, beyond the basic need to deceive and to protect his fragile ego. He might just be too lazy to learn the truth. When caught out, he simply doubles-down with more focused lying. He seems to believe that has mastered the Jedi mind trick (and so far he has): "these are not the droids we're looking for, move along", and "even if they were colluding with droids is not a crime". He constantly harangues how every fact he does not like (or understand) is "fake news" (by a vast Democratic conspiracy) as well as attempting to erase many well established scientific or historical facts (e.g., Climate Change). Thus far his serial unfamiliarity with reality only appears to work on his ardent supporters and cowering Republicans; however, his constant assault on anyone trying to question his fantasies, especially the legitimate news media, is a huge step in a very dangerous direction. When combined with his apparent lack of respect for the rule of law, it places the open society in extreme jeopardy, giving the phrase "trumped-up charges" an ironic twist. If we continue to accept this behavior as the new normal, then fully fledged fascism will not be far off. Many would-be fascists believe that the tedious pretense of civility and the tepid pursuit of the public interest should be set aside completely. While we still can, we need to have a much more urgent public discussion of how our deeply damaged democracy can be repaired and then quickly move on to economic redesign. But the first item on our agenda should be how we can survive such a clearly illiberal (in both the classic and modern sense), ill-prepared and irreparably damaged individual in a position of virtually unlimited power, irrespective of idiosyncratic scoring and/or arm chair psychoanalysis. No matter who holds the office our checks and balances are in dire need of repair and rebalancing. If any good comes from Trump, it is that he is a huge orange CHECK ENGINE light that can no longer be ignored.

LET'S NOT PUT THE TOTAL BACK INTO TOTALITARIANISM

If our president is going to retain all his/her imperial powers, then we better pray that a cool headed and judicious statesperson is at the wheel when the energy/financial excrement finally "hit the fan". As a general rule I subscribe to "Godwin's Law", which roughly maintains that the first person to mention Hitler forfeits the argument. If I had a nickel for every time I hear the word Nazi these days, I could join the elite. However, if everyone is a Nazi, then Hannah Arendt was correct about the "banality of evil". But if you have a president who seems willing to condemn as "enemies of the state" people who merely questions his erratic behavior and panoply of lies then "Houston we have a problem". Are we really willing to accept that a lack of enthusiasm for our feckless fuehrer is "treason" (even as a joke), or that anti-fascist demonstrators are equivalent to the KKK? Will we allow our neighbors or our athletes who march or take a knee to assert that "black lives matter" to be labeled traitors and terrorists? If you are ambivalent on any of these items, then we might already be well down the path to totalitarianism. With budding brown shirts (now in polo shirts) using fear and nativism to provide increasing cover for corporatism and militarism, where do we go from here?

Are we just one more major terrorist attack away from a total police state? We have already given the surveillance state all the toys and most of the permissions it needs. Trump may not be Hitler, but just being himself is already bad enough; and, "we ain't seen nothing yet". Okay, I violated Godwin's Law and I will have to take my chances on the outcome of the on-going debates. Yet, I belabor all these red flags (or hopefully red herrings) to make a slightly different point. If the mere election of one individual can raise the specter of brutal totalitarianism, then our democratic republic is far too fragile.

Severe forms of fascism are like some viruses that cannot be completely cured. It merely becomes semi-dormant in the body politic. In our case, totalitarianism has been ever present and yet deeply submerged and modified within our system of corporatized or "Managed Democracy" as legendary political theorist, Sheldon Wolin (2007) called it. He suggests this submersion has created an "inverted totalitarianism". As he explains:

> ...while exploiting the authority and resources of the state, it [inverted totalitarianism] gains its' dynamic by combining with other forms of power, such as evangelical religions, and most notably by encouraging a symbiotic relationship between traditional government and the system of "private" governance represented by the modern business corporation. The result is not a system of codetermination by equal partners who retain their distinctive identities but rather a system that represents the political coming-of-age of corporate power (p. xiii).

Beyond battling our corporate overlords, our pressing need at present is to prevent total totalitarianism from reasserting itself within are increasing authoritarian world (with its manufactured as well as real crises and enemies). The global bankers and industrialists along with German generals thought they could contain their little Austrian corporal, but once tolerated the trajectory feeds on itself and becomes nearly inexorable. Famed philosopher, Hannah Arendt, who narrowly escaped the Holocaust, provides an assiduous study of The Origins of Totalitarianism (1951) and it is back on the best seller lists along with Orwell's dystopian novel Nine-teen Eighty-Four (1949). In it she describes how it all begins with a subtle, yet vast, popular atomization, alienation, and division within the public sphere. All existing parties, leaders and policies are widely ridiculed. And, members of the free press are vilified. The masses that have never had much involvement with politics become agitated and mobilized. Ancient ethnic or cultural differences are amplified and scapegoats identified. These processes produce a dramatically diminished dedication to discussion and deliberation. Moreover, they cripple collaborative power sharing which is the raison d'état of democratic republics. But for Arendt really distinguishes totalitarian fascism from merely the run of mill fascism is the "systematic use of terror" as the primary instrument of social control.

Terror comes as much from the state itself as from any actual insurgencies. Agent provocateurs infiltrate and discredit legitimate opposition. Consider how off duty policemen disguised as

Antifa were the most unruly element by far at the G-20 in Toronto. Furthermore, False flag attacks ("Remember the Maine", Gulf of Tonkin, etc.) and make-believe threats (e.g., W's WMDs) are especially useful in manufacturing militarism and fueling further fear and violence. Ultimately the overwhelming fear that totalitarian fascists create literally turns neighbors, friends, and family members against one another. Orwell's Winston has his "do it to Julia" (his insufficiently secret love) moment, when faced with his greatest fear (rats). Where are the Rapa Nuians when you need em? Mark Zuckerberg, the NSA, or both probably already maintain lists of our personal terrors.

Long before the internet and social networks, Herbert Marcuse (1964) warned of how the subliminal control mechanism of the mass media could turn democracy in on itself, and yet most citizens would remain unaware of this "warm unfreedom". When I heard him lecture I thought, if this is true, then is it not more humane? And, I am still a tiny bit bivalent today. I doubt, however, if we will have the comforting subterfuge of our "Brave New World" much longer. More axiomatic versions of feudalism and fascism are chomping at the bit. Continuing failures to maintain the illusion of fairness will fuel unrest, and in turn, hasten calls for taking off the gloves and ushering in an era of much more brutal repression. The line between concerned citizen and "insurrectionist" as well as many other "alternative facts" will become distorted, to say the very least. Since 9/11 the state has acquired monstrous surveillance capabilities, and burgeoning AI and deep learning devices can reprocess BIG DATA any way you like. The million square foot NSA Data Center in Utah is merely a small example. Surveillance, of course, has been complimented with massive domestic control capabilities (including fully militarized police forces and the anti-social media). Now all these new totalitarian toys are in the hands of a madman and his merry band of crooked businessmen and messianic misanthropes. Irrespective of how long or short their tenure turns out to be, they may have already poisoned our political discourse for generations to come. The search for antidotes needs to begin in earnest.

This is where a little bit of institutional ecology can go a long way. For example, Erich Kaufmann (2017) of the University of London made use of an Economics and Social Research Council grant to explore how complexity theory explains much of the "horizontal", "peer to peer" and "network effects" in the "inverted" (bottom–up) spread of nationalism and tribalism we have experienced of late. He applies the concepts of emergence, feedback, tipping points, and distributed information to explain how small identity issues can explode into ethnic and regional conflicts. We might extrapolate from this to type of research to delve into how fascism can grow with or without a top down tyrant. If Haider, Wallace, and Wolin were telling us we don't need a Trump to bring the fascists out of the woodwork, then we need the epistemological equivalent of the termite inspector. We have known for a while now that "social capital" can become anti–social, but we remain a bit vague about at what point "bowling alone" (see, Putnam, 1995; also note Adler & Kwon, 2002) becomes bombing alone (or with other atomized individuals). Mainstream economists, of course, have never had much use for the concept, either way. But software designers with absolutely zero understanding of these social systems are already developing predicative algorithms and hoping to cash in on the culling of society.

REBALANCING WORLDVIEWS

While greatly over simplified, the late great Jane Jacobs provides a useful heuristic in her prescient little book, entitled: Systems of Survival: A Dialogue on the Moral Foundations of Commerce and Politics (1992). She uses a Socratic approach to trace the problems of imbalance between two world views, which she calls syndromes. Her "Commercial Syndrome", (see; Figure 1) involves the set of social traits and beliefs which made trade and economic development possible. Meanwhile, her "Guardian Syndrome" (Figure 2) seems better suited to our deep feudal past. Yet, for Jacobs both syndromes are vital to the survival of society at different times and under difference circumstances. In times of war, society wants those guardians "on that wall"; however, most members would probably prefer that they not engineer conflicts to maintain their privileged position in society and/or to create vast wealth for themselves and their industrial colleagues. Plus, society might not want warlords to run the banking system (or the government for that matter). Jacobs contends, however, that the really dangerous folks are the "monstrous hybrids" (who employ their guardian traits in the commercial sphere), such as "the Mafia and drug cartels", as well as monopolies of all sorts. The institutional failures of the last few decades have allowed toxic hybrids to become the crown of creation. A truly rational and decent society would seek to marginalize rather than deify these monsters. Yet it must also recognize societal participation processes that create them. It would also seek to ameliorate the institutional failures that fuel alienation and undermine the distribution of power and influence. In our ancient tribal past, anyone who exhibited and overabundance of self-interest was simple exiled. I am not suggesting that we lock-up all these folks; however, I doubt if they would extend the same courtesy to us. We merely need to dramatically curb their most destructive impulses, and reinstate our various the institutional safeguards (e.g., antifraud & antitrust laws, progressive taxation, charter revocation, etc.) as well as enforce the basic obligations once spelled out in articles of incorporation (note: Bakan, 2004).

Figure 1: Commercial Syndrome

- *Be collaborative*
- *Respect strangers*
- *Promote innovation*
- *Honor contracts*
- *Be open and honest*
- *Be thrifty*
- *Be forgiving*
- *Promote optimism*
- *Seek investment*
- *Expect fairness*

Figure 2: Guardian Syndrome

- Be competitive
- Respect only your own tribe
- Honor tradition
- Promote hierarchy
- Be secretive & deceptive
- Be ostentatious
- Be vengeful
- Foster fatalism
- Seek exploitation
- Demand privilege

In Veblen's The Theory of the Leisure Class (1899; also note Plotkin, 2010), the latent barbarism inherent in institutions of Capitalism drives the system toward greater stratification, with the several slots in the higher ranks reserved for the "men-at-arms", dynastic rentiers, the "captains of industry" as well as their counterparts from the criminal world. These groups merge with one another to form a corrupt ruling class. Like the feudal lords of old they expect that they and their descendants will command vast wealth and power. They contend that the basic rules of society to not apply to them.

EXPROPRIATORS VERSUS ENTREPRENEURS

These same self-appointed royals lay claim to most of the surplus of society via unproductive rent-seeking (George, 1879), yet they do not actually value the traits upon which broadly prosperous society built itself. Recall all the British period dramas where tradesman (or anyone with a vocation) are looked down upon. Of course those who toil via their "pride in workmanship" are also brainwashed to value and seek to "emulate the status of their betters" through "conspicuous consumption". Elsewhere Veblen (1904; 1919), much like Jacobs, drew a dramatic distinction between "business" (which was mostly extractive, parasitic and rent-seeking) and "engineering" (which was mostly creative, problem solving, and productive). Veblen viewed his mission as the restoration of classical political economy by adding social psychology and institutional evolution to observations made by the likes of Henry George.

George's great contribution was the discovery that our processes of progress produce crushing poverty. George reconciled his governmental activism and libertarian ideals by invoking the whole of Adam Smith's two part treatise and integrating laissez-faire with anti-monopolist features. Beyond land rents, George was especially concerned about the money monopoly and the rise of "seigniorage rents" following the demise of Lincoln and his Greenbacks.

Another fan of Henry George was the distinguished modern economist, William Baumol (2004). He found in George's attack on the rent-seekers of his day vital clues to our own battles over the expropriation of the commons. For Baumol, it is all about the misrepresentation of ENTREPRENEURSHIP. In one path breaking piece (1996) he explains:

> ...while the total supply of entrepreneurs varies among societies, the productive contribution of the society's entrepreneurial activities varies much more because of their allocation between productive activities such as innovation and largely unproductive activities such as rent seeking or organized crime. This allocation is heavily influenced by the relative payoffs society offers to such activities. This implies that policy can influence the allocation of entrepreneurship more effectively than it can influence its supply (p.3).

In another piece Baumol (2004) directly invokes George and asserts that society would be much better served by discouraging, rather than facilitating the accumulation of "unearned wealth". To this end he might have us extend George's notion of a "land tax" (the only tax without a deadweight loss) to common intellectual property, etc. Since it is the provision of public infrastructure (university research and the internet as well as roads and canals) that initiate the value of various holdings, we should tax those rather than income of the commoners. Baumol points out:

> The Enrons of the economy—along with the proffision of top corporate managers who have been able to provide themselves with obscenely high incomes even though the

performance of their firms had little or nothing to commend them—are today's more obvious counterparts of George's Landholders (p. 9).

Ultimately the old mythology of the heroic entrepreneurship fails to provide as much intellectual cover for this new generation of landed gentry, especially the instant billionaires of Silicon Valley and similar tech centers (Route 128 around Boston, Seattle, etc.) who expropriate so much of the publicly provided military and scientific infrastructure, as well as engage in restraint of trade and monopolistic labor tactics (e.g., wage suppression, non-compete contracts, and use of temps and H1-B visas). These clever nerds and geeks have thus set about fashioning their own apologia which, of course, places them at apex of human evolution as the miscegenation of men (and they are mostly men) and thinking machines. Their mythology is an odd admixture of eugenics and other science fiction (e.g. cyborgs) with Ayn Rand, Nietzsche, and even more toxic fellow travelers (e.g., Julius Evola). It is crucial to note that breakthroughs that allow editing of the human genome (particularly CRISPR CAS9) may serve to rekindle the socially repugnant EUGENICS agenda (for pros as well as cons see, Kozubek, 2016). In addition to the unmitigated racism of the Dark Enlightenment, their political agenda is purely reactionary (i.e., reacting to feminism, multiculturalism, and social justice, and democracy in general), in fact they often call themselves "Neo-reactionary"(or NRx for short). I would have to agree with its many critics that it is mostly "Moldbuggery" from the blog name of its most outspoken spokesperson Dencuis Moldbug (alias: Curtis Yarvin of the Orbit Platform). NRx Program has roots in right-libertarianism and anarcho-capitalism, but is also decidedly authoritarian and monarchist in orientation. Hey, as Emerson said, "consistency is the hobgoblin of little minds", and these guys have big minds and bigger wallets. It is this latter attribute that connects them with old school gentry; however, I suspect that existing elites are pretty upset about having their dirty ideological laundry flying in the breeze. Moreover, neither they nor the new silicon social Darwinists view themselves as remotely akin to their skin-headed and swastika festooned brethren. Yet these street level storm troopers are basking in these racist, sexist, and fascist vindications, as well as feeling they have kindred spirits in the White House.

UN-GILDING THE GOLDEN GOOSE BEFORE THE GOOSE STEPPING BEGINS

Most, but not all, of my Stanford colleagues would be shocked to learn Silicon Valley is now not only the center of the technological universe but also a fountainhead of neo-fascist philosophy in America. Somehow various arcane anti-democratic and even occultist philosophies have a certain appeal among would-be instant billionaires. Obvious they like being told that they are the master race, or Nietzschean ubermenschen. While the tech sector has always enjoyed a high level of public tolerance for their "move fast and break things" modus operandi, we should be less sanguine about their new moving slow and monopolizing everything approach. Much of their new ideological agenda seems to be in anticipation of any coming political back lash, when it is only barely on the distant horizon. It is funny to see the most pandered people on the planet prepping for victimhood. In particular they have already laid elaborate plans to take their ball and go home (e.g., regional secession or merely floating away on their Seasteads) should the rules of the game allowing them to always win become altered in anyway.

It is no accident that our once powerful entrepreneurial engine that spread bay wide, nationally, and internationally from near the campus of Stanford University is now sputtering. It has now become more a conglomerate of huge monopolistic platforms and select unicorns (astronomically overvalued start-ups, stemming from skillful scams and/or speculative frenzy). The dot.com bubble that so dramatically burst in late 1990s has been effectively re-inflated. It is ironic that Silicon Valley and entrepreneurship generally which benefited so substantially from the antitrust crackdown of the New Deal is now controlled by a few of mammoth monopolies. Silicon Valley was also a great experiment in public support for innovation, yet it is now just another playground for crony-capitalists and rentiers. The outpourings of public largesse have been so continuous for so long that they are now widely mistaken for private initiative. Even when I taught there during the free market 1980s, the fake chip wars with Japan were prompting huge public expenditures (e.g., the Strategic Computing Initiative and Sematech).

It is worth pointing out that Stanford has 6 different economics departments (if you include the conservative think tank, the Hoover Institute), and they rarely speak to one another. Across campus in the plain vanilla econ department leading economic historians (e.g., Nate Rosenberg and Paul David) were illuminating the curious dynamics of technological change, but engineering economists rarely ventured over there. Meanwhile back at the Terman Engineering Center, many of our students were already shifting from resource to financial systems. Furthermore, the multiple venture capital firms on nearby Sand Hill Road that employed them were already evolving into "vulture capitalism" and playing "pump and dump" games. After the dot.com debacle and the housing crash these trends intensified and a new version of malicious mythology was rekindled. Essentially the myth, fortified by Wall Street, is that this tiny haven of techno-geeks can somehow replace our rusting and deported industrial base, and it is now back in full to bloom. BIG DATA/AI is now the new asset class.

If you believe that just because the Facebook monopoly paid a billion dollars for Instagram (which had 13 employees) that it is just good for the economy as the bankrupt Kodak (which once employed 140,000), you may already be brainwashed. At its core this well cultivated mythology is that these firms are so vital that they should be allowed to regularly "break all the rules" (e.g., antitrust laws, corporate tax and accounting codes, governance and employment practices). Yet the larger myth is that they are the quintessential entrepreneurs, who took all the risks, so they deserve all the rewards. This, of course, is pure horse pucky. In particular, LSE Professor of the Economics of Innovation, Mariana Mazzucato (2011) contends that much of the risks and rewards belong to the state and its tax-payers.

The actual history of the Silicon Valley substantially confirms this alternative viewpoint. In true medieval motif, this new generation of robber barons has direct links to American's original robber barons. A group of western regals, with vast landholdings, but little experience with building or running a railroad, were tapped to provide their portion of the transcontinental project. As Stanford historian, Richard White (2011), documents, the transcontinental railroad was a new plateau for crony capitalism. It involved huge tax breaks and subsidies, mammoth land grabs, creative topography and book keeping, the torture of migrant labor and indigenous populations, not to mention repeated tax payer bail-outs. Essentially it was a real boondoggle for California Governor, rancher, and raconteur, Leland Stanford, and his buddies (e.g., Mark Hopkins, Charles Hinde, and Collis P. Huntington).

Upon the untimely death of their beloved son, Leland Junior, the Stanfords decided to memorialize him by starting what was originally to be a tiny technical college on one of their race horse farms in the hills at the edge of the Santa Clara Valley, 40 miles south of San Francisco. Following a tour of world's great universities and the death of her husband, Jane Stanford developed a more grandiose plan for what was still to be primarily an engineering school. Only one thing stood in her way, Leland had defaulted on 30 million (a tidy sum at that time) in Government Bonds, and the US Treasury was suing for at least half of it back. Jane took the matter all the way to the Supreme Court, but also secured the intervention of family friends (including President Grover Cleveland) and won her case. This, of course, would not be the last government handout to what would become an integral engine of technological change.

Early on Palo Alto (the small town near the campus) became a hub for developments in electronics. Federal Telegraph (which produced some of the first vacuum tubes) started there in 1909. It initiated a pattern of defectors from local firms and students joining in new ventures. Researchers left Federal Telegraph to establish Magnavox and Litton Industries. Legendary Stanford engineering professor, dean and electronics pioneer, Frederick Terman (who returned to Palo Alto in 1925 from MIT where he worked with NSF founder, Vannevar Bush) encouraged his students (which included Hewlett, Packard, the Varians, and many others) to stay in town and start their own companies if necessary. Yet, it was not until the war years that Silicon Valley began to significantly emerge from sprawling plum orchards.

It was massive military spending, that originally put Silicon Valley on the maps, and this spending has continued (often from "black budgets") over the years, intensifying again during the relatively recent explosion of the surveillance state, following 9/11. During WWII the valley was home to Moffett Naval Air Station, and its gigantic anti-submarine blimp hangars were still gracing the landscape in the 1980s. Much of Moffett would evolve into branch of the Ames Research Lab (of the DOE). It is worth reminding you that most of the Department of Energy's research budget is still in weapons and warfare systems. During WWII, Terman went east to lead research into counter measures to the Germany's superior radar and he brought the best of his team back with him to Stanford afterwards. As attention shifted to the Soviet Union, Palo Alto became the center of secretive electronic warfare and ballistic missile research as well as developing most of the microelectronics for the "space race". Much of the work done in the Applied Electrics and Integrated Systems labs as well as the Stanford Research Institute (SRI) remains classified. I could tell you more about it, but then they would have to kill me (kidding I hope).

Local and federal governments supported one of the first research parks (early 1950s) in Palo Alto, but it was less about entrepreneurship than intrapreneurship, housing skunk works (corporate research shops) from various industrial giants (e.g., GE, Lockheed, and Xerox). It is noteworthy that the term "skunk works" came from the chemical industry, which removed research from their factories and headquarters because they stank to high heaven and also occasionally exploded. Spin-offs into new start-ups, of course, could never be completely contained, in a small region with so much surplus engineering talent. Another war time radar researcher, solid state physicist and Nobel laureate, William Shockley, returned to Palo Alto (with his team from the Bell Labs) in 1955 to set up Shockley Semiconductor. Shockley was brilliant scientist, but terrible manager, and his "traitorous eight" (including Julius Blank, Victor Grinich, Jean Hoerni, Eugene Kleiner, Jay Last, Gordon Moore, Sheldon Roberts, and Robert Noyce) left in 1957 to start Fairchild; taking a pile of defense dollars with them. In 1959, Noyce would patent the first integrated circuit (or silicon micro-chip). Demand for more microelectronics literally skyrocketed via DOD/NASA applications. No single company could meet all the demand. By the late 1960s, defectors from Fairchild would join National Semiconductor, start-up Intel and Alemco (now Teledyne), as well as become venture capitalists in their own right (most notably Kleiner). In 1971, Intel's Ted Hoff, invented the first microprocessor (computer on a chip), and a journalist coined the phrase "Silicon Valley".

It could have just as easily been dubbed "surveillance valley", as national security research was expanded into all the dark nooks and grannies of the information age. Specific agencies were developed to channel mountains of government funding into a variety of projects. ARPA became DARPA (the defense advanced research projects agency) and funded everything from the internet and high definition signaling to satellite servicing robots and remote controlled insects. The CIA developed their own version of DARPA called Peleus (now In-Q-Tel), which while based near their Langley HQ, funds a wide array of secret projects in Silicon Valley.

DEATH VALLEY DAYS

As the microelectronics industry shifted from hardware to software, the character of the valley began to change. Bill Gates was so compelled to build his empire on clunky software that he avoided the valley altogether (except when grabbing up others' intellectual property or crushing software competitors). He set up in Seattle where he would not have to compete for coding talent, nor foster many spin-offs. Apple flew the Jolly Roger over its headquarters, but Microsoft was the more consummate buccaneer. From their expropriation of DOS and sand-bagging of IBM's OS2, to their bundling of their browser and alliance with Intel on the "Wintel Platform", Microsoft's apparent role model was the brutal British East India Company (EIC). While not as bloody perhaps as the "Storming of Seringapatam" (that ended Indian resistance in 1799), it was equally as effective. The message went forth "get on the Windows bus or be thrown under it". Microsoft was twice convicted of acting in restraint of trade (violating of antitrust laws), but it was too big to be broken up and only received a minor slap on the wrist. We have no idea what cool, non-crashing, software we could have had if Microsoft had not strangled them in its crib. However in fairness to William Gates Junior, he knew which road to stand in, waiting for the money truck to hit him (twice). While sitting in his dorm room at Harvard, with a copy of January 1975 issue Popular Electronics (the one with the Altair personal computer on the cover) in his hand, he and his buddy Paul Allen had their flash of inordinate awareness. Thinking that they might already be late, they dropped out of school, moved to Albuquerque (across from the plant that built the Altair) and started writing code (BASIC) for the hobby kit toy. It is noteworthy, that Altair's founder eventually returned to dentistry, while Bill Gates went on to become the richest man on the planet.

Now it is this global monopoly or bust model which prevails in Silicon Valley. The likes of Facebook (which started on stolen ideas and hacked private files, and now buys up most potential rivals with impunity) and Google (which started with DARPA funds, in a quonset hut behind the Terman Engineering Center, I could see from my office), have certainly mastered this new monopolistic as well as the militaristic ethos. Google recently received a large contract from DOD's Algorithmic Warfare Division to work on AI system for enhanced drone targeting (which might allow them to pick their own). Back when the defense funded ARPANET was becoming the "world-wide-web" (now just called the Internet) and the vast system of Global Positioning Satellites (GPS) was a still mostly a military toy, the valley was already a circus of ruthless want-to-be billionaires and galloping dot.com lunatics, as well as fledging feudalists. This new generation of Robber Barons is perched atop their vast information castles are mostly extorting tolls from a system of technologies that they did NOT build. US tax payers build the information super highway, but we now allow a small handful of new elites to claim it and rent it back to us. Moreover, their plans for things like autonomous vehicles have already received anticipatory regulatory relief, so we can look forward to the old fashioned highways being rented back to us as well.

If Henry George were here today, he would say that we should "tax the shite out of em". And if they hide their bread in a multinational "sandwich" (tax arbitrage), then we should seriously look into new strategies. Apple (the first trillion dollar firm) used its infamous "double Dutch, and Irish sandwich" to pay no taxes whatsoever on either side of the pond. If firms threaten to leave the US altogether we should counter threaten to levy huge fines and tariffs to access to our markets (as well as freeze their assets until they repay all the public funding they received with interest). Prices to consumers will obviously rise, but this would provide incentives for new domestic entrants and their acquisition could be limited by stricter enforcement of antitrust or competition laws. Meanwhile existing conglomerates should be broken up. It should go without saying that the monopolies and their armies of well paid lobbyists would fight this tooth and claw, but laws governing our great bribery machines can be changed as well. Plus, the same populist pressure that gave us Donald Trump could be rechanneled into purposive policies. It nearly was with Bernie Sanders. Strangely enough, Bernie agrees with Alt-right guru, and former White House senior advisor, Steve Bannon that Google and Facebook should be regulated like public utilities, and I assume by that they mean the way utilities used to be regulated.

I might also be naively assuming that politics can somehow be reset to the level of functioning dysfunctionality it had before Trump ran it completely off the road. Some optimistic folks believe that if we survive Trump, a renaissance of more reasonable regulatory processes will result. I honestly don't know. I think we can clearly see where our corporatized feudalism is taking us. While I generally agree that "more government is rarely the answer to bad government", those who routinely run on libertarian promises are not the least bit timid about spending trillions on the military and their banker friends. The rare exception is radical Texas Representative and Presidential also ran, Dr. Ron (not Rand) Paul (note his various books, including: Swords into Plowshares, 2015, and his continuous calls to "AUDIT DA FED"). He understands that ultimately the more we spend on defense the less secure we become, and they greater the compromise of our liberty. As President Eisenhower (1961) expressed, the "military industrial complex" not only distorts our economy, it undermines our democracy. He explained:

> The total influence—economic, political, even spiritual—is felt in every city, every Statehouse, every office of the Federal government... Our toil, resources, and livelihood are all involved. So is the very structure of our society... The potential for the disastrous rise of misplaced power exists and will persist. We must never let the weight of this combination endanger our liberties or democratic processes.

As we rush headlong toward becoming another "banana republic", the specter of tiny junta equipped with an endless supply of planetary search and destroy technologies is disturbing to say the least. Our over-reliance upon leadership from the ranks of Jacob's guardians has brought with it a flood of monstrous hybrids. They are so emboldened now that they no longer feel obliged to hide their incongruous gangster ethics and antics from their religious partners in crime. It is truly medieval moment when our new unholy alliance of church and state seems willing to fully embrace an amalgam of completely sociopathic generals, bankers, tech moguls, and associated power addicts.

In a recent Atlantic article Jonathan Bachman (2018) claims that Trump Made Socialism Great Again. But on the right they would never admit to their socialism only for the wealthy and on the left, new candidates "feeling the Bern" or the fresh breeze of AOC (Alexandria Ocasio-Cortez) are still a bit premature. The average American has been well programed by Neofeudal propagandists to regard socialism as somewhere between child molestation and premeditated murder. Many of the classical economists and even some modern economists were proud to call themselves socialists, before the Pelerins poisoned the well and fake socialist systems proved to merely be just far less subtle versions of oligarchic corruption. The classical economists held socialism to be the provision of public infrastructure, protection of the commonwealth, and enforcement of a level playing field for private enterprise, as well as the capture of windfall rents. I have often thought modern day socialists will need to choose a different terminology, calling themselves the Stewards of the Commons or some such thing. No, that won't work, COMMONISTS if too close to communists, for the semi-literate masses. We might have to look elsewhere for inspiration. How about some universally beloved fiction?

CHAPTER 8: THE FELLOWHIP OF THE RINGFENSE

I found it is the small everyday deeds of ordinary folk that keep the darkness at bay, small acts of kindness and love.
_____ **Gandolf (J.R.R. Tolkien)**

We'll never be royals. It doesn't run in our blood. That kind of luxe just ain't for us. We crave a different kind of buzz.
_____ **Lorde**

The equal right of all men to the use of land is as clear as their equal right to breathe the air — it is a right proclaimed by the fact of their existence; For we cannot suppose that some men have a right to be in this world, and others no right.
_____ **Henry George**

In times of tragedy, of war, of necessity, people do amazing things. The human capacity for survival and renewal is awesome.
_____ **Isabel Allende**

There are historic situations in which refusal to defend the inheritance of a civilization, however imperfect, against tyranny and aggression may result in consequences even worse than war.
_____ **Reinhold Niebuhr**

In the amazingly life-affirming prison movie, The Shawshank Redemption, the note that Andy leaves for Red under the volcanic rock reads, "if you have come this far, perhaps I can get you to come a little further". If I have at least piqued your curiosity regarding the revival of feudalism (and its first cousin fascism), perhaps I can get you to come bit further and imagine for a moment that our struggles with this Neofeudalism is analogous to the fictional Battle for Middle Earth (with far less head chopping, I sincerely hope); with all apologies to Lord Tolkien. He is best known for the trilogy, The Lord of the Rings (1954/1968). It has captivated generations all over the world. With his inspiration and your indulgence, I will, in this chapter, wax a bit more whimsical, if I may? If you have only seen the truly marvelous movie series of LOTR from Peter Jackson (2001-2003) and not read the book, then you will need to bear with me even more. The episode I most wish to invoke is NOT in the films. Jackson, for apparently dramatic reasons, chose to exclude the important final chapters which involved the "Scouring of the Shire" and the further fate of the Hobbits. It matters, because we are Hobbits and because we matter (in all our various skin tones, ethnic backgrounds, sexual preferences, and religious affiliations). This is not "identity politics" (IDP), it is humanity politics. Besides IDP divides I want to unite. Any political economy that does NOT promote a chance at well-being for all is an affront to the entire enterprise. SERFS UP, is not just a play on terms from the beaches of my youth, it is my take on the human condition, and a worthy battle cry.

HOBBIT LIVES MATTER

Serfs, "debtcroppers", the "precariat", "deplorables", Hobbits, "commoners" or whatever you choose to call us, we are mostly peasants in the new feudal system. Most Americans, even those with meager prospects, would never admit to being serfs, but they are. Duke University, economic psychologist, Dan Ariely (2012), of Predictable Irrationality fame, conducted some amazing surveys (with Michael Norton) comparing actual levels of inequality with what the average person thinks it is, as well as what they think it should be. Jane Q. Citizen has absolutely no idea where they stand and how much of the wealth has been institutionally redirected toward the top. Assuming that top 20% had earned it, most respondents would like to reward them about 30% of the pie, when in fact they take over 90%. Moreover, like my students, most Americans are overly optimistic about probability of upward mobility. Yet, if one is born into the bottom 40%, that is pretty much where they remain, except for those who fall further into the very bottom quintile (no pie for them). Phillip Alston (2017), Special Rapporteur on Extreme Poverty to the UN Commission on Human Rights, visited the United States in the fall of 2017, and concluded that those who fall into that bottom 20% experience the greatest loss of basic human rights of any of the other OECD (Developed Nations). He also observed that the obscene level of inequality in the US is mostly the result of conscious policy choices, rather than individual misfortune. When you add the insult of feudalistic political power to the injury of dispossession, any way you cut it we are the little people.

Hobbits, of course, really were the little people (standing about three foot tall). Half as tall as an average man, so Tolkien also referred to them as "Halflings". However, what they lack in size, they make up for in bravery, compassion, and sense of community.

He introduces us to them, in his earlier book (1937), The Hobbit, the prequel to the LOTR, and the amazing adventures of Bilbo Baggins (Frodo's great uncle). They live in "The Shire" (from the British word for county), the most beautiful little rural valley with their tiny homes built into the terrain. The Hobbits refer to themselves as "Shire Folk", and their simple, peaceful way of life, stands in stark contrast to the turmoil of Middle Earth (the larger region, with its various kingdoms, creatures, and conflicts). Okay that is enough background, so let us jump ahead now to the very end of the LOTR (beyond the great battles over the kingdoms of men).

Upon the return of our tiny Hobbit heroes to their once bucolic Shire they find it transformed into squalid Dickensian nightmare. Sam exclaims, "This is worse than Mordor" (Sauron's volcanous realm). Unlike the film version having helped Frodo destroy the ring of power Sam does NOT immediately live happily ever after with his blushing bar-maiden. The actual Tolkien story goes on for another hundred pages following the defeat of Sauron (of the burning eye). Our fearless four: Frodo Baggins (Frodo), Samwise Gamgee (Sam), Meriadoc Brandybuck (Merry) and Peregrin Took (Pippin) return not to their rural paradise but to a devastated industrial landscape, on the brink of ecological collapse. Worse still, the corrupt officials they confront are controlled from behind the scenes by their old arch nemesis, the evil wizard of Isengard, Saruman, who has reinvented himself as a financier/industrialist of sorts named Sharkey. Sharkey's hired thugs are captained by another familiar villain, Grima Wormtongue (one time evil advisor to King Théoden of Rohan), He appeals to the greed of some of the Hobbits and terrorizes the rest. Our small band of small folk must battle these powerful predators without the aid of their extended Ring cohort (i.e., no Wizards, Elves, Dwarfs, nor Giant Eagles (if I recall correctly), and very little magic.

In this final segment of his epic saga, Tolkien wants to remove any doubts as to who are the real heroes of the Lord of Rings. Aragorn the Ranger turned King of Gondor, Gandolf the Grey turned white wizard, Gimli the ax wielding Dwarf warrior, and Legolas the agile Elf archer are all certainly stout of heart and very handy in scrape. Yet, it is unskilled and unschooled Halflings who carry the day. Recall it is the meekest Hobbit, Frodo, who is the only one pure enough of heart to carry the ring without being corrupted by its power. Even the good wizard Gandolf could not take it.

Without Frodo's compassion for the treacherous Gollum and Sam's unflagging loyalty, they may never have made it to Mordor. Meanwhile, Merry and Pippin were gaining military and organizational experience as well as growing in confidence and stature (apparently Treebeard's ale promotes physical growth). It is noteworthy that Merry and Pippin are not the dim witted, bumbling buffoons as Jackson portrayed to provide his movies a bit of comic relief. In fact, Merry is a gifted strategic planner and Pippin a skilled community organizer. Starkey has atomized the villagers into fearful acceptance of fascism, but our four returning Hobbits are able to re-weld them into a cooperative resistance. Eventually together the citizens of the shire complete its re-capture and begin restoring its civic and natural environment. In others words, our tiny troop of Hobbits did not need kings and wizards to decisively win the battle for their own self-directed way of life, and neither do we.

DUDE, WHERE'S MY COMMONS?

The Shire was not necessarily an equalitarian paradise. Lest we forget, Sam was Frodo's servant (gardener), despite his voluntary valor. Moreover, it was partially the avarice and greed of the Sackville-Baggins that led the shire into fascism. Nevertheless, the communal life of the shire provides a set of signals for present day society. Noble Smith (2013) finds in the shire a "guide to a long and happy life". The shire is somewhat emblematic of the commons (a region that is self-managed for the collective benefit of the peasant community). As we begin to accept our status as serfs, a key question should be, "where are our commons"? During the middle-ages, commons were quite common. The name "commoner" was given to anyone lacking a title of nobility. Lands and titles, of course, were originally acquired by force of arms and/or through service to the sovereign. Yet amid these titled holdings there still existed certain common areas which peasants were allowed to share. Arable farming and herding was organized as a cooperative, and peasant village co-opts were empowered to manage the affairs of commons. Over-grazing was prevented by community consent and policing called "stinting" (limiting the size of herds). The "reeve", an official elected by the peasants, supervised the commons and conducted relations with the titled landlord. This system worked amicably for centuries. However, when profligate kings (such as Henry VIII) needed increased taxes to pay for their wasteful wars, landlords were forced into greater levels of production agriculture. The requirement of more peasant labor for these enterprises, prompted the passage of laws for the elimination (or "enclosure") of the commons. George Orwell of 1984 fame (1944) summed-up this process nicely in his Tribune (London) column as follows:

> Stop to consider how the so-called owners of the land got hold of it. They simply seized it by force, afterwards hiring lawyers to provide them with title-deeds. In the case of the enclosure of the common lands, which was going on from about 1600 to 1850, the land-grabbers did not even have the excuse of being foreign conquerors; they were quite frankly taking the heritage of their own countrymen, upon no sort of pretext except that they had the power....

Various local rebellions accompanied these enclosures, but generally were swiftly and brutality put down. Eventually few commons remained across Europe, outside of a handful of Alpine meadows. Nevertheless, the inspirational aspects of the commons have been sustained. David Bollier and Silke Helfrich (2012) gathered together some 73 essays aimed at reviewing the history and rekindling the concept, which they characterize as a prosperous "world beyond market and state".

The concept of the commons or "common pool resources" has played a particularly potent role in environmental or resource economics over the years, and that research has been extended to clarify a number of broader issues of public policy. One of my professors, the biologist, Garret Hardin (1968) initiated one of the contemporary conceptual uses of the commons in his classic essay, "The Tragedy of the Commons", that kindled an intellectual controversy as well as launching a sub-branch of resource economics. Using it as a metaphor for how individual exploitation can push a common pool resource toward exhaustion (rational individual decisions cause collective harm); he turned the actual commons on its head. One political scientist, Lin Ostrom (1990), set out to prove that Hardin's commons was not only historically inaccurate, but unhelpful as a policy perspective. She and her students from Indiana and Arizona State Universities spent their careers discovering various contemporary (mostly third world) examples of where voluntary associations of individuals cooperated to manage a particular resource (such as a fishery) in a more or less sustainable fashion. Interestingly enough, her findings were often perverted to support privatization just as Hardin had been distorted to defend large scale government intervention (see, Gardiner, 2001). Her relatively successful (some eventually failed) examples require an extensive list of what economist call "priors" (preconditions). Among others, Ostrom requires the following:

1. *Accurate information about the structure and flow characteristics of the resource;*
2. *Absence of extreme conflicts of interests among appropriators;*
3. *Ability of appropriators to communicate with one another and establish trust and shared norms;*
4. *Low transaction costs as compared to potential benefits;*
5. *Knowledge of the effects of diverse rules on behavior and outcomes; and,*
6. *Availability of social entrepreneurship either within the set of appropriators or in the surrounding governance structures. (pp. 205–211).*

Obviously, these preconditions are rare and difficult to maintain. Nevertheless, Ostrom's concrete examples of community-based resource management rekindled interest in the commons as alternative form of governance.

I have to admit to a change of heart regarding Lin's work. I now regard her as one of the most accomplished scholars of her generation. Early on I was more than a bit put off by her assertions, in keeping with the Public Choice ideology, that government interventions were always and everywhere bad. Despite her apprehensions about government in general, she seemed to be enthusiastic regarding certain elite institutions. Her dissertation at UCLA appeared to extol the virtues of particular secret governments (e.g., special water districts in Southern California), despite the failure to cope with sea water and gas intrusion and the types of shenanigans portrayed in the film China Town. I also felt she was a bit abusive of her students in that she required them to live in exotic locations and conduct elaborate ethnographic studies. More than one contracted some awful tropical disease. However, their contributions speak for themselves (even without her fake Nobel Prize), and her lessons regarding the evolution of shared communities are of inestimable value. Her "eight principles for the design of the commons", have become canonical. She (1990) lists them as follows:

1. Clearly defined (clear definition of the contents of the common pool resource and effective exclusion of external un-entitled parties);
2. The appropriation and provision of common resources that are adapted to local conditions;
3. Collective-choice arrangements that allow most resource appropriators to participate in the decision-making process;
4. Effective monitoring by monitors who are part of or accountable to the appropriators;
5. A scale of graduated sanctions for resource appropriators who violate community rules;
6. Mechanisms of conflict resolution that are cheap and of easy access;
7. Self-determination of the community recognized by higher-level authorities; and.
8. In the case of larger common-pool resources [CPRs], organization in the form of multiple layers of nested enterprises, with small local CPRs at the base level.

Current advocates (e.g., onthecommons.org) of the commons use it as a rallying point for a variety of broader public policy issues, from the patenting of genes and net neutrality to public spaces and collective creativity. They have invented policy initiatives such as the "Sky Trust" (Barnes, 2003) and "Copyleft" (general public licensing, for open source software and other collaborative work). They also speak of the "tragedy of the anti-commons" (see, Heller, 2007) in which "too much ownership wrecks markets" and stifles scientific innovation. These reaffirmations of the productivity of shared enterprise directly fly in the face of neofeudal maxims regarding the utility of concentration. Overall these broader conceptualizations of the commonwealth battle mightily on many fronts against the onslaught of dispossession.

As with any instrument of the popular imagination, the commons is in real danger of being hi-jacked by Astroturf (fake grass roots) spreading elites. Consider how expropriators and fascist fueling fanatics have perverted the spirit of the "Sagebrush Rebellion" (Thompson, 2016). Don't let their cowboy hats fool you, these guys serve the wealthy elite. Ammon Bundy who led a group of heavily armed militia in the attack on the Oregon Wildlife Refuge actually owns a large truck fleet maintenance business in Phoenix. He admitted at a press conference that he was NOT just standing up for loggers, small farmers, and ranchers, but also "the auto industry, the health care industry, and financial advisors". Yes, the financial advisors are so damn oppressed. After all they had to pay their lobbyists a bundle to strike down regulations suggesting that they might have some fiduciary responsibilities.

David Bollier (2014) muses that the average American finds it is "easier to envision the end of the world than the end of finance capitalism". Perhaps we'll have both. He notes that the left is completely bereft of ideas as to where we go next, so they should apply "the commons" as a "template of transformation". From an evolutionary perspective it is an "exaptive" (note, Gould & Vrba, 1982) institutional relic, worth recycling. Obviously, not everyone can move to a rural community, however, there is many a shire in the midst of Manhattan (beyond Zuccotti Park). Everyone can seek to reclaim a portion of their patrimony, especially those currently being enclosed by the new technological gentry and other expropriators. Bollier points out that,

> The commons—a paradigm, discourse, ethic, and set of social practices—provides several benefits to those seeking to navigate a Great Transition. It offers a coherent economic and political critique of existing Market/State institutions. Its history includes many venerable legal principles that help us both to imagine new forms of law and to develop proactive political strategies for effecting change. Finally, the commons is supported by an actual transnational movement of commoners who are co-creating innovative provisioning and governance systems that work (P. 1).

RING THOSE RASCALS

Transnational revolt or not, recognizing the rise of the new feudalism suggests the need to renegotiation the SOCIAL CONTRACT or at least the fleshing out of some basic socioeconomic rights. But don't hold your breath on any formal provisions. Yet in the meantime, our own benighted bands of Hobbits and other lowly creatures should erect barriers to further economic damage; ergo our fellowship of the RINGFENCE. In finance, a ringfence is an accounting gimmick, designed to shield assets from creditors, and it is has been proposed by bank reformers in Europe as a device for separating out "retail banking functions", along the lines of a watered down Glass-Steagall. As we might expect bankers are already probing for weaknesses in the fences before they are even erected (e.g., issuing special assurance bonds to select investors). A better example perhaps is the case of Portland General Electric (see, Schwarcz, 2013) where Oregon regulators successfully ringfenced customers from the bankruptcy of Enron (which had acquired a large number of heretofore public utilities). However, until banks are rigorously converted to and regulated as public utilities (as the "mediation theory of money" suggests), we Halflings may have to move our savings to local credit unions and building societies. Some scholars contend that states should have their own banks, like the one in North Dakota which is credited with reducing the severity of recessions there (see, Lemov, 2012). America Samoa finally got approval from the Fed to have a PUBLIC BANK after having been abandoned by full service banking for the better part of a decade. Their experience has inspired explorations by other states and some localities (e.g., LA and SF) especially those whose legalized cannabis industries have been equally void of financial services. Plus, a nationalized version of local banking functions has been proposed for the ailing US Post Offices.

Community based banking is integral yet only a small element of building more resilient regional economies. Diversifying the economic base is essential. The rusting and ruined remains of single industry towns dot the landscape across the United States. Boarded-up industrial spaces can become low cost business incubators. Building viable communities often requires more fellowship than ringfencing. Like the motley mix of beings from the LOTR, those who would seek to have a real economy need to form alliances with many a strange bedfellow (Trump supporters, anarcho-capitalists, and even Dark Enlightenment types). Initially, fellowships might be a bit heavy on libertarian/anarchists, as well as assorted progressives, yet the hard work of actually building socially viable economic institutions will soon sort out the hard core monarchists, monopolists, and other mother-frackers. Ringfencing would be like the camp sites in the Canadian Rockies, where they fence in the tourists at night, rather than attempt to control the mercurial grizzly bears.

Another vital element of fellowship strategy is the provision of alternative currencies, the other side of the coin if you will. In his excellent little review of alternative currencies, Boyd Cohen (2017) blames many of the ills that I have categorized as neofeudal dispossession on the existence of a single fiat currency (Federal Reserve Notes). He contends that alternatives (from Bitcoin to BerkShares) "discourage passive investment" and facilitate the emergence of a "post-capitalist economy". Prior to the Civil War, 1600 corporations and private banks circulated their own notes (theoretically redeemable for gold or silver), and recall that during the war Lincoln issued a series of non-interest bearing currency (greenbacks) to pay the union troops and avoid the usurious interest of the northern bankers. Prior to the greenbacks, the US treasury only issued coins, but following the war they issued Gold and later Silver Certificates, the latter from 1878 up to 1965. Sanctioning of the banking cartel via the Federal Reserve Act in 1913, also brought with it a private monopoly in the production of money, and Richard Nixon removed any remaining pretense to precious metals in 1971. Only the words "In God We Trust" printed on the Federal Reserve's interest bearing notes since 1957 implied that anyone was watching over their actual value (down 97% since 1965). Thus, the primary role of currency as "a store of value" has fallen by the wayside as well. Aside from the so-called crypto currencies, most of the experiments with alternative money address the second major role of a "medium of exchange". Notes such as Berkshares (in the Berkshires region of western New England) have become a viable community solidarity device. Other barter upgrades and/or service exchange systems such as "time banking" are breaking out in localities across the country. Ultimately ringfencing experiments would serve to highlight how a real economy could function on the basis a more ecologically and anthropologically accurate model of society; a FRODONOMICS if you will.

A FUNCTIONAL FRODONOMICS

Frodonomics is quite simple. In the words of E.F, (Fritz) Schumacher's classic, Small is Beautiful (1973), it is "economics as if people mattered". Frodo is not just the main hero of LTOR, he and his Shire represent the basic societal principles of Community, Compassion, and Cooperation. These elements were once present in Classical economics (e.g., Smith, 1759) and have been reconfirmed by various anthropological as well as from complexity economics studies of diverse societies (see, Gintis, et.al., 2005; Henrich, et. al., 2005; Bowles & Gintis, 2013; and, Stanish, 2017). Items such as "active altruism" have been vital to human evolution (see, Fehr & Fischbacher, 2003). Viewed from this perspective, mainstream economics is not only anti-historical but also anti-scientific, as they attempt to ideologically override our more natural trajectories.

For those who still think that economic theories don't matter, I would direct you to an excellent study by an intrepid troop of sociologists (Bellah et.al. 1985) that follows up on Alexis de Tocqueville's observations about community values in his Democracy in America (1835). Invoking his notion of the "habits of the heart", they document instances in which the extreme atomization extolled by modern economists undermines various vital community functions. However, when left to their own devices, shire-like communities often emerge. They observed that in small town America, it was necessary, but not sufficient that someone runs a scrupulously honest business (e.g., car dealership). To be considered a "community father" (or mother); they needed to take the added step of giving back to the community. Those of wealth would always be a bit suspect until they demonstrated their non-aggrandizing "commitment" to local affairs. Frodonomics would explore how our new feudalism lost this sense of nobles-obliges.

A functional Frodonomics would also seek to understand how communities have actually thrived by extending the greatest level of opportunity "to the least advantaged parties" (see, Rawls, 1971; also note Weithman, 2016). John Rawls (1971) presents us with a simple situation like castaways on deserted island choosing our leader as well as rules for governing. He argues that if we were really rational as the economists contend, then we would accept that we are mostly peasants and seek to constrain our leaders (in case their power goes to head) with rules of "distributive justice". Rawls also invokes his "vail of ignorance" (not knowing our class status) as a tool for generating greater objectivity regarding distribution and mobility rules. Frodonomics would not merely draw upon these thought experiments and formal proofs (see, Alexander, 2000) as mainstream economist often do, but would also draw upon real world studies of industrial and community cooperatives (e.g., Mondragon). Furthermore, it would invoke findings of how the individuals and institutions co-evolve using "reciprocal processes" and cooperation rather than competition (see, Bowles & Gintis, 2013: Henrich, 2006). UCLA Economic Anthropologist, Charles Stanish (2017) discovered a number of co-operative rituals from his studies of "stateless societies" which further undermine homo economicus. If we are to be the commoners among the new royals, this type of research might be useful in the negotiation of rules. Moreover, we might draw upon increasing examples of the active restoration of "the commons" via shared ownership (see, Adams, 2015) strategies. Even the "everybody an entrepreneur" semi-libertarians have a number of useful ideas (see, Posner & Weyl, 2018). In general, we simply do not need to be overwhelmed by erroneous economic ideas and institutions that resurrect barbarism, and ultimately yield debilitating social conflict and collapse. Myriad ideas and examples of community based economic alternatives as well as national reforms are found in the pages of Yes Magazine (co-founded by former Harvard Business School professor, David Korten of When Corporations Rule the World fame, plus several other very stimulating books; e.g., 2009). In a recent essay, Korten (2018) spells out the choices before us. He suggests that,

> Transformation begins with clarity on the nature of the choice and its cultural and institutional implications. Our defining cultural value must become cooperation. And we must transfer power from institutions that reward predatory competition to ones that facilitate and reward cooperation in service to the common good (p.2).

In essence, the scholars of Frodonomics should strive to hold as many big, hairy feet as we can get our hands on to the fire emanating from the actual co-evolution of agents, their ideas, and institutions.

UNCORRUPTING THE ORCS WITHIN

Before we let our hulking golden Goblin King (see the resemblance to the goitered, bug eyed ruler in The Hobbit movie) corrupt us all irreparably, or worse (i.e., rush us down the road to dystopia), perhaps we should strive to divert as much of this acculturated narcissism as we can. Tolkien tells us the Orcs were once Elves that had been tortured and corrupted. Let's face it there is a bit of Orc in us all. Our own "mindless rabble of Orcs" (as Gimli called them) are one of the most dangerous elements we must confront, because once corrupted by populist demagogues they are difficult to retrieve, and they lead many of us to question the viability of democracy itself. Full on sociopaths (the Urak-hai) are pretty much impossible to uncorrupt, but they are a much smaller portion of general population and we might be able isolate and marginalize them. Recall these were the muscle bound warriors that Saruman's minions dug out of the mud, and who wore his white hand face paint. Only in the case of our Urak-hai (e.g. certain hedge fund managers and investment bankers) it is probably cocaine dust. Our financial systems are especially designed to pander to these groups of sociopaths and we need to seriously address these institutional deficiencies.

We also need to focus on our own orcishness, which is also a product of our Culture of Narcissism (Lasch. 1979). This was the title of Rochester Professor, Christopher (Kit) Lasch's classic study. He explained how modern American society came to make certain relatively rare personality disorders pandemic. Jimmy Carter called him to Camp David to help him fashion the speeches that helped, along with Reagan/Bush dirty tricks (e.g., cutting a treasonous hostage deal with Iran), to cost him re-election. We could not handle the truth, then or now. Lasch's amazingly prescient, and posthumously published (1994), The Revolt of the Elites: and the Betrayal of Democracy, never actually received the recognition it deserved. It is curious that at the very time that a few scholars were questioning the cultural psychology of American, the dark wizards of Sauronomics were capturing academia (and policy-making) and closing off any deeper discussion. Nevertheless, at this juncture we need take another stab at altering our cultural imperatives or else prepare to meet its by-products at the barricades.

The psychological disorder of Narcissism is a destructive level of self–absorption and exhibiting a distinct lack of empathy, bordering on sociopathy. It draws upon the Greek myth of Narcissus, a young hunter who devalues those drawn to his physical beauty. A rival, Nemesis, draws him to a pool, where he is so captivated by his own image he cannot leave it and dies. The term is often misunderstood as self-love; rather this pathology stems from a weak self-concept, demanding constant reaffirmation. At the individual level it manifests itself in an inability to form healthy human attachments, well beyond seeing one's fellows as mere instrumentalies. It often involves ego-maniacal grandiosity, and given the underlying fragility even minor criticism is met with rage and aggression. Sound like anyone we know? At the cultural level, natural patterns of group empathy are suppressed by increasing atomization. A bizarre cult of celebrity emerges, where the figures are admired for merely being in the public eye. Unearned status and admiration becomes the norm, and average individuals either expect their own 15 minutes of fame or to experience it vicariously through celebrity worship. Everyone demands recognition of one sort or another, and resentments grow when it is not forthcoming. In the US, cultural narcissism goes hand in hand with our sense of "American exceptualism" (that we are not just unique, but chosen by God to be beacon to all mankind) and pursuit of empire.

Cal State San Diego psychology professor, Jean Twenge, famed for her studies of the Millennials (2006) and the "hyper connected generation" (2017), undertook an overview of research into The Narcissism Epidemic. She and her colleague, W. Keith Campbell (2009) review a diverse range of empirical research, including reporting on 1000s individuals who took the NPI (narcissism personality inventory) or NPD (narcissistic personality disorder) test. They point out that, not only were most of the parental and educational efforts at engendering greater self-esteem (i.e., everybody gets a first place, and so on) a dismal failure, but when combined with personality displacement stemming from the new interconnectivity (e.g., smart phones and social networking, etc.) has spread narcissism like the flu in a preschool. "The T-ball Generation" (baseball with the ball set up on a tee, and where players get as many swings as they need to get a hit) is particularly ill-equipped to secure healthy self-affirming and socially enhancing opportunities.

My own take on the narcissism plague relates to perverse economic ideology and institutions. This poses a bit of a chicken and egg problem, but it seems relatively clear that neofeudalism and narcissism are mutually causal. Consumer driven economic growth demands narcissism and vice versa. Marketing attacks one's self esteem, yet also gives them a way to purchase a projected personality, which our current culture convinces us is just as preferable. This vicious cycle can spin into another triple whammy for the newest generations, who may be mediocre, but feel entitled to riches and fame. They are not equipped to earn it, nor even purchase a fake version of it in the economy of rapidly declining opportunities. They have been robbed of the community based activities which would offer healthier ways to gain a stronger sense of self, and become the Merry or Pippen (or Frodo) they were meant to be. Only in Lake Wobegon can "all the kids be above average".

Neofeudalism also clearly breeds narcissism on a cultural scale and this pathology fuels further feudalism. Professor Lynne Layton (2014) of the Harvard Medical School, points out how narcissism is a "psychic effect of neoliberalism" (i.e., the Pelerin Paradigm). She describes "individual, group, and relational effects of social repudiations of vulnerability and dependency needs" that result from "the widespread disavowal of the interdependence of privileged and marginalized populations". Earl Gammon (2017) Professor of Political Economy at the University of Sussex maintains that "narcissistic rage" is a vital part to understanding "the underpinnings of neoliberal resilience". That is, the combined anger of having suffered personal slights has exploded onto the cultural level. And this vicious cycle has sustained this destructive dogma far past its sell-by-date. Harvard trained psychologist and Emory Business Professor, Emily Bianchi (2014), conducted a large sample empirical study correlating one's coming of age era and their level of narcissism. She hypothesizes that "entering adulthood during a recession tempers latent narcissism". Conversely, entering during "prosperous times" encourages increased narcissism. I suspect that narcissism takes on even more grotesque permutations, amid our hidden and slow simmering depressions marked by Herculean efforts to maintain the illusion of widespread prosperity. Given how tightly interwoven are the isms (feudalism, fascism, and narcissism) it is difficult to address any of them in isolation. Only a new economics (or Frodonomists) could recognize and unwind them, particularly those features that reward predation and impede adaptation.

CHAPTER 9: THE BATTLE FOR MEDIEVAL EARTH

When plunder becomes a way of life for a group of men living together in society, they create for themselves in the course of time a legal system that authorizes it and a moral code that glorifies it. _____ **Frederic Bastiat**

Our passivity has resulted in much more than imperial adventurism and a permanent underclass. A slow-motion coup by a corporate state has cemented into place a neofeudalism in which there are only masters and serfs. _____ **Chris Hedges**

While tech billionaires and sycophantic journalists who report on them laud the hipster friendly 'Sharing Economy', the reality is, this is just a buzzword for a new economy that badly screws the poor. _____ **Robert Reich**

People of privilege will always risk their complete destruction rather than surrender any material part of their advantage.... But the privileged also feel that their privileges, however egregious they may seem to others, are a solemn, basic, God-given right. The sensitivity of the poor to injustice is a trivial thing compared with that of the rich. _____ **John Kenneth Galbraith**

I wish it need not have happened in my time, said Frodo. So do I, said Gandalf, and so do all who live to see such times. But that is not for them to decide. All we have to decide is what to do with the time that is given us. _____ **J.R.R. Tolkien**

My father was part of what is called the "Greatest Generation", because they faced the challenges of a full scale depression and a massive world war (he served as a medic in Patton's 3rd Army). Famed historian, Stephen Ambrose (1997), implies that the US citizen soldier, with their individuality and creativity, actually had an advantage over the better trained, equipped, and disciplined Wehrmacht. Be that as it may, the generation currently coming of age has even more monumental challenges to face (including Nazis). They will obviously spend a good deal of time blaming my generation (the baby boomers) for destroying their birthright, and deservedly so. Given the chance they would probably turn us all into biodiesel. But if they don't put down their smart phones for a second and step up to their challenges then their children (assuming they ever have any) will surely blame them for their duplicity. The first major challenge is to slow the wholesale destruction from within of the institutions they will need to harness and reassert their own basic rights. Next they will need to rediscover their own humanity. The new feudal warlords have been very systematic in dismantling and undermining the very traits and mechanism we will need to contain them, and will pull out all the stops trying to convince them that all government is useless and corrupt (in their hands, it is really is), and that many institutions (such as habeas corpus, freedom of the press, open meetings laws, etc.) are superfluous anyway. When government is so corrupt, both Right and Left Libertarianism have a certain basic appeal. But anti-government rhetoric is more than a little disingenuous when offered up by oligarchs. Some voices bellowing forth from places like Silicon Valley are insisting that we should abandon our pursuit of liberal democracy, such as it is, and embrace a full blown revival of aristocracy (see, Finley 2013). One instant multi-millionaire, Anthony Levandowski, could re-establish the divine right of kings via his church that has AI as its godhead (Brean, 2017). The once lovable nerds have evolved into bankers but without any of their social graces. Okay, a lot of these guys have merely overdosed on medieval themed video games or binge watching all the episodes of the Game of Thrones, but a few of them have the rents and misplaced resources to buy great power and privileges, and they are every bit as aggressive as their Wall Street role models. Their "narcissistic rage" over past slights and their perpetual adolescence (via stunted socialization) create attachments to simplistic and cynical world views (e.g., Ayn Rand) that the rest of us left her behind in our teens. The revenge of the nerds will not be nearly as humorous as the B movies. The younger generation's battle against neo-medievalism might be the greatest test our democratic adventure has ever faced. Underpayment and precarious employment affords little time of resources for organizing, and for many the battle is just to get out of their parents basement. Furthermore, when they do venture forth, they are often misled by simplistic sorcery of the dark wizards.

FROM DARK MONEY TO DARK AGES

If future historians are allowed to write the postmortem of modern democracy the cause of death will be an overdose of DARK MONEY, as much as any "Dark Enlightenment" (note, Land, 2012). They would tell a tale of how the creation and maintenance of fake wealth allowed small cadres of elites to gain immense political power. In other words, in an era where elites could create money out of thin air, they could then spend as much as they needed to acquire ever greater political power. Historians would identify how the institutions which our Founding Fathers designed to provide a brake upon power had themselves become corrupted. They would chronicle how Supreme Court decisions like Citizens United should join Dred Scott and Bush v. Gore as one of the greatest judicial mistakes in American history. They would explain how it defies logic that money could ever be equated with free speech. They would conclude that when money became speech, dispossession became nearly irreversible.

Despite having lived briefly under a very mild form of monarchy (yet Elizabeth II is no mere figurehead) in Britain and Canada, I still do not get our desire for royalty. But then I don't get the Kardashians either; especially since their cardinal claim to fame is their papa removing OJ's gym bag (Louis Vuitton) supposedly full of his bloody clothing and knife. Maybe Balzac is correct, "behind every great fortune [and/or fame] is a great crime". All I can say for sure is that our own "return of the king(s)" will NOT be a cause for celebration. Various uberlords and uberladies and their obsequious sycophants have been returning without much fanfare for decades now. The dark wizards (mega-wankers) and their worm-tongued minions (mainstream economists) have mostly worked behind to scenes to insure the restoration of the feudal order. They have enlisted brigades of politicians and bureaucrats, as well as otherwise ordinary citizens, into the rancorous ranks of incurious Orcs, toxic Trolls, and vainglorious Goblins. When they come fully out of the shadows, how will we respond? While our emerging "Game of Thrones" is missing some elements, we have enough billionaires (and soon some trillionaires) to serve as White Walkers, and able to purchase their own Army of Dead (or Blackwater version 2.0). Many of us will become their zombie bitches if we don't wake up.

Latent feudalism has been an ever present hidden partner of democratic institutions since their beginning. To his vast credit, George Washington refused requests for him to stay on as "king". He then returned to his more lucrative pursuits in land speculation. In essence, he had a third career selling of western lands out from under the tribes that had been promised them "forever" as reward for fighting on behalf of the colonists and the Crown in the French and Indian War. While the titles, pedigrees, and semblance of nobility may be missing in most of our current generation of overloads, the medieval motives remain intact. Hedge funds and private equity firms are the new dukes and earls of dispossession. Consider how PE firms bought up hundreds of thousands of foreclosed homes in the nation's most crushed housing markets and turned them into rentals, then securitized the rental stream, and sold it to eager investors, leveraged to the hilt coming and going. A feudal land grab not seen since the Norman Conquest. Recall that Obama had promised to have the banks set aside a 100 billion to rescue the home owners but only a small fraction of that sum ever reached them. Homes, of course, are now just another global commodity. The phrase "safe as houses" came into popular usage following the rail road collapses in the late 1800s, heralding the return of the ancient source of unproductive wealth creation. Land speculation and manipulation of bubbles remains an essential oligarchic device. The ghost cities in China and large ghost neighborhoods in Vancouver and Toronto are testimonials to the lengths that Central Banks will go to maintain these hugely inflated asset values. Furthermore, the displacement of the middle class from prime housing markets by "absentee landlords" is feudalism revisited (see, Veblen, 1923). But since land (as in land, labor, and capital) was surgically removed from mainstream economic theory (or Sauronomics, if you will) no one is supposed to have noticed (except Gaffney, et. al., 1994). Add to this unreality the fact that luxury and commercial properties became the primary vehicle for laundering the gain from criminal activities and you begin to get the picture. President Trump certainly gets it. Between pandering to mobsters (first Italian and then Russian, see, Unger, 2017), creative tax avoidance, and strategic bankruptcies he is the poster child for the unreal use of real estate. Beyond amply representing the current trends in the evolution of "gangster capitalism", Trump also embodies the authoritarian mind set, and thus portents a return of a Dark Age, of super anti-enlightenment. Just as we are beginning to develop a deeper understanding of our unique social ecology we are confronted by forces that are impervious to scientific observations as well as dismissive of democratic processes.

HONEY, HAVE YOU SEEN MY CHAINMAIL UNDERWEAR?

A few serious scholars have been touting and outing the revival of the pre-democratic/pre-market economy for a while now. Distinguished UCLA professor, Karen Orren, in her classic Belated Feudalism (1992) laid waste to the mythological view that the pristine US shores had never been touched by the filthy fingers of feudalism. She points out that as a creature of British Common Law, with its own history of repressive labor relations (not to mention slavery); America is still a bastion of the "master-servant model". Moreover, she contends that it was organized labor that spawned ingredients we associate with liberalism, rather than the inverse. It is well to note that the modern multinational corporations, including many US based firms, have deep roots in medieval guilds, patents, as well as the organization dynamics of the fiefdom (see, Sicard, 2015).

One of our most venerable founding fathers, John Adams, was so concerned about the persistence of feudalism that he cautioned constant vigilance. In his 1765 work A Dissertation on the Canon and the Feudal Law, he picked apart its ideas and key features, and found them completely antithetical to basic human "rights". He suggested that the colonies should dedicate continuous scholarship to the institutions of liberty to combat the corrupting influence of latent feudalism. He explains:

> Let the public disputations become researches into the grounds and nature and ends of government, and the means of preserving the good and demolishing the evil. Let the dialogues and all the exercises become the instruments of impressing on the tender mind, and of spreading and distributing, far and wide, the ideas of right and the sensations of freedom (vol 6, no 4).

Our new feudal lords see themselves as the only viable alternative to chaos, much of which they carefully create. Recall (back in chapter one) that "creation and manipulation of crises" is a complimentary tool to financialization in the process of dispossession. Like Urak-hai dug out of the bowels of the earth, unscrupulous characters come out of woodwork to thrive and contrive in bubble economies. In essence, fledgling feudal lords (and associated sociopaths) are nurtured in engineered turmoil, such as ours (note, Nace, 2003). Consider how former apparatchik (with copious funding from global bankers) quickly morphed into the oligarchs (and Trump buddies) following the collapse of the Soviet Union. Phillip Mirowski (2013) chronicles how our neoliberal overlords continue to use these financial crises to forward their own ideological agenda.

Wharton Finance Professor, Stephen J. Kobrin (1998) observes that "neo-medievalism" has been accelerated by globalization and the rise of the "digital economy". He contends that under such systems sovereign states become increasing irrelevant to multinational trade cartels. Apparently nation states only exist for purposes of protecting private property, underwriting bail outs, and the providing compliant human cannon fodder for various wars of choice. Kissinger Associates VP, Joshua Cooper Ramo confirms much of this reality of the new globally networked economy. With digital information as its own asset class, computer hackers from the "cult of disruptors" join the Nietzschean pantheon in a "new caste system" in his bestseller, The Seventh Sense (2016). Elites, particularly freshly minted ones, love to hear this type of rubbish, crowning them as the result of some sort of natural processes of evolutionary selection. As suggested above, this revisiting of Social Darwinism from a previous Gilded Age, is now back in vogue in places like in Silicon Valley (see, Pein, 2014). From an institutional ecology perspective it is more like SURIVAL OF THE MISFITTEST.

FROM DOLDRUMS TO DARKNESS

While mostly metaphorical, many commentators have noted that there is a good deal of the "dark ages" in the so-called "sharing" or "gig economy" (note, Slee, 2017) that fully emerged with the onset of the on-going economic doldrums. In fact, they refer to it as "serfdom" (see, Evans, 2013). Even the pro-business consultants at McKinsey Global Institute (see, MGI, 2016) contend that this trend is a throwback to a "pre-industrial economy". Plus, the boys at Brooking (Hathaway & Muro, 2016) report that gig economy is growing faster than anyone imagined, as government employment measures miss much of it. Nearly half American workers could be freelancers in the next decade. The Congressional Research Service (Donovan, et.al. 2017) warns that in the "Gig Economy" worker well-being is highly problematic. They point out that independent contractors are NOT covered by Fair Labors Standards Act or the National Labor Relations Act. They further observe that,

> ...certain other benefits [e.g., paid sick leave, health insurance, retirement benefits] that are often associated with traditional employment relationships may not be available in the same form to workers in the gig economy (p.2).

Mellissa Chadburn (2017) went undercover into what she calls the "Ghost Economy" and noted that among other things that gig workers are often sent out to dangerous work environments with virtually no safety training, and that injuries (and occasionally death) result. She elaborates:

> I get notices on my cell phone to dig a ditch or clean up construction sites or serve cocktails at a corporate party. People live like this for years, responding to a text message every day, holding out for the promise of a permanent position. The city is alive and abuzz with Hail Marys. Hail Mary, give me a job. Hail Mary, may I not get hurt. No health insurance, no unemployment insurance, no workers' comp. There's no maternity leave, no way to plan a life, sign a lease, pay off debt (p 2).

In short, one person's "taskrabbit" is another person's serf. More traditional forms of indenture and even slavery, of course, are also on the rise worldwide. When combined with burgeoning "debt serfdom", accelerating abuse of common resources, and incomprehensible levels of inequality, they paint a pretty feudalistic picture.

Historians who study the original feudal period often question whether our all-purpose caricature of diverse periods ever actually existed (Brown, 1974). Feudalism was never much like a Robin Hood movie (especially the one with Kevin Costner). If you take out the Spanish Inquisition (and other religious persecutions) and certain other aspects of the Dark Ages (which treated science as witchcraft), then in general feudalism was not all that bad, unless the absence of any social mobility is a problem for you. You might be extremely lucky and get the lord to recognize you as his bastard, but that is about it. The original serfs, however, did have more leisure time than the average modern gig worker. Furthermore, brilliant blogger, Ian Welsh (2015), reminds us that modern day serfdom is more accurately "wage and debt slavery", and that the new feudalism might actually be far worse than the ancient version. He explains:

> One of the things that we forget about Feudalism is that serfs had rights: economic rights. They had the right to farm common land, they had the right to take wood from common forests, and they had the right to live where they had lived before... [Today] absent a job, or charity, you will probably wind up dead. If you don't, you will be miserable....Serfdom? You should be so lucky.

Obviously, few who invoke feudalism today are envisioning jousting knights, despite the number of police in their full body armor on our streets. As an aside, I recall that my policeman father was quite upset when required to give up his tan uniforms for black (very dark navy), and not just because of the heat factor in Southern California. He said, "It made them look like the German SS". In a moment of sardonicism, I bought him a death's-head tie tack, but he never wore it. I'm glad he did not live to see much of the far more menacing accoutrements and heavy ordinance. Having grown up around the cops of a very different era, I used to think how it was a good thing that the bad guys did not know what truly gentle souls most of them were. I still recall how unsettling it was when I first traveled to foreign places where cops had machine guns slung across their backs. But I digress. At any rate, all the symbols of medievalism aren't found within the theme restaurants, re-enactments, and Renaissance Fairs. It is very interesting how many "alt" groups from anarchist nerds to neo-Nazis (see, Devega, 2017) and ultra-rentiers to presidential advisors want to be linked to ancient knightly orders. It is noteworthy that raging medievalism is also a primary recruitment tool for radical Islamist groups. Hence, the re-emerging feudalism is much more than the militarization of police forces; it is a thorough-going reversal of modern society back to an era of myth and magic, where the serfdom of the masses is taken for granted.

Who could have imagined when the Berlin Wall came down that ancient religious wars would be rekindled to replace the clash of cartoonish economic ideologies? Or that in an age of science, the finding of the vast majority of distinguished scholars regarding energy and climate change issues would be dismissed for the sake of short-term pecuniary motives or displaced by perverse cultural imperatives? It has been several centuries since human enlightenment and progress have been so hobbled. Greed and pretty political motives are cloaked in a shroud of willful ignorance and superstition. Even the acquisition of raw power demands the conjured legitimacy via occult iconography of fake chivalry. It completely defies any logic with which I am familiar that such battles would need to be re-fought in the so-called modern age. Famed French Anthropologist of Science, Bruno Latour (1993) is probably correct in the title of his classic, We Have Never Been Modern. For him our notion of modernity is based on a set of grave misconceptions about the separation of culture and nature, and what elements are socially constructed versus unconstructed. We are now suffering from deeply deceptive ideological project that sought to make that which is unconstructed appear cultural (e.g., resource limits) and that which is constructed appear natural (e.g., the feudal economic order). If we cannot extricate our natural head from our cultural excretory canal, it really will be an exceedingly dark age indeed.

TASK RABBITS UNITE, YOU CAN ONLY LOSE YOUR TAILS

This new serfdom is diverse, but generally entails an intense level of socio-economic dislocation, personal insecurity and organizational disenfranchisement. Guy Standing (2011, 2014) former Chief Economist for the International Labor Organization, labels the new serfs "the precariat" (as in precariously employed proletariat) with peripatetic employment their lot in life. He calls them a "dangerous class" since they are easily taken in by fascist demagogues. He also uses the medieval term "denizens" (groups with no status and/or only partial rights that existed on the fringes of medieval villages) to refer to the growing number of non-citizens, refugees, and migrants laborers that are exploited to push down wages and working conditions for all. He further invokes the Charter of the Forest of 1217 (which followed the Magna Carta) in his arguments for a "precariat charter" (2014) of basic employment rights (and responsibilities). He develops a unique perspective regarding the future of work and remuneration (e.g., "guaranteed income") that go well beyond traditional labor movements. Cities, across the globe (e.g., Stockton, Glasgow, etc.) are experimenting with these ideas. These experiments are vital given that ruling class has pretty much demolished conventional labor unions. As suggested above the precariat must spend so much of their week in the unpaid search for their next gig, they have little time left for politics or civic engagement of any kind (also note, Shippen, 2014).

The new war upon organized labor and collective bargaining, of course, predates the precarious economy by several decades. Early unionists paid for their rights with their blood over a century ago. The modern anti-union movement began in earnest with Reagan and Thatcher in the late 1970s (along with other Pelerin party-favors), and was followed close behind by full scale outsourcing. It was also augmented by additional policy choices, including down grading the middle class to service jobs and/or simply removing large numbers of working class (to the military, prison, sweat shops, and now to the gig economy). It is ironic to note that Uber, the quaking pillar the new erstwhile "sharing economy" is betting their monstrously overvalued store on self-driving cars to eliminate the bulk of their labor altogether. It reminds me of the old economic conundrum that "a robot can build a car [and now drive car] but a robot will NEVER buy a car".

The wobbling warlords at Uber, like other new rent extracting firms (e.g., Airbnb, etc.), profess anti-establishment motives. Uber says they want to take down the "oligarchy of cab medallions holders", ignoring those individuals who saved for decades and/or borrowed a bundle to buy one. Yet all the while, these types of firms have hitched their star to the emergent ultra-conservative policy pushers (e.g., the Koch Brothers). Their ultimate goal is replacing all sorts of community services with new government sanctioned cartels that employ mostly independent contractors. They recognize the "sharing economy" as another "enclosing of the commons" game. Via "zero-hour contracts", the new serfdom grabs up most of your civic time as well as resources. Already having laid claim to the publicly financed infrastructure of the information superhighway, they have set their sights on actual highways as well. The self-driving car industry has already hinted that they need their own lanes on "freeways" (soon to be toll roads) and that they would appreciate more public funding for the address various tech snags. They also imply that "bothersome bystanders" will have to undergo "behavioral retraining" at public expense (see, Brooks, 2018). When the robotic learning fails, they want us to change. They may even get their new political friends to banish conventional cars to the back roads. Eventually they could outlaw private car ownership altogether, much like the EIC outlawed food crops from poppy fields (source of opium) throughout a starving India. This particular gambit, of course, may not work, but it wouldn't even be imaginable, were it not for the dark wizards and their various minions toiling away in economics departments, think tanks, as well as the Federal Reserve (see, Lepers, 2018) to fashion the new feudal order. They rail against the "Nanny State" and yet aid those who seek their own personalized Leviathan. The heart of their mission is to misrepresent all this expropriation and rent extraction as entrepreneurship. As Aragorn would say, it is an economics "bred for a single purpose, to destroy the world of men". Only the over-men shall thrive.

DESTROYING THE RING OF MISPLACED POWER ONE INSTITUTION AT A TIME

If we cannot figure out how to wrestle away the Ring of Power from our reigning ubermenschen and design institutions which prevent power from being so concentrated even again, then Feudalism will be the least of our worries. Our "imperial president", no matter who he or she turns out to be, is a big problem in an era of burgeoning authoritarianism and perpetual war. If we are not willing to directly curb their power, we should at least seek to rejuvenate checks and balances. Our Founding Fathers hated partisanship and factionalism. Madison maintained that "the public good is disregarded in the conflicts of rival parties". They would certainly soil their breeches if they could see our highly toxic partisanship today.

Campaign finance reform and redistricting laws (anti-gerrymandering) are absolutely critical, but our seriously damaged two party processes with both parties pandering to elites, must be remedied as well. It is important to point out that our winner-takes-all elections are designed to only support two parties. By contrast the many parliamentary democracies allow multiple parties proportional representation and coalitions have to form across party lines in order to run things. The Prime Minister is merely the leader of the majority party (or the party with the most votes in a minority coalition), and they can be removed with a legislative vote of "no confidence". I doubt that the US will have anything like a parliamentary system any time soon, but we should at least begin to reform our divided and dysfunctional system by facilitating greater proportional representation. We can do very little about the fact that the Dakotas (pop: 1.6 million) has 4 senators and California (pop: 40 million) only has 2, but some measures could easily be implemented at the state and congressional district level. The presence of even minutely viable third parties might create greater policy discussion and reduce reliance on simple demonizing the party in power. Additional small adjustments, such as proportional distribution of Electoral College votes (which a few states already have), and rule changes from the Commission on Presidential Debates, might even allow a third party to get national traction. Legendary Harvard Business professor and record breaking consultant, Michael Porter (of the 5 Forces fame or infamy) recently joined with Katherine Gehl, former corporate mogul, public servant, and prime mover in the Centrist Project to apply "competitive strategy" to the "political industrial complex". Viewing the political parties as an impenetrable and completely self-serving duopoly (e.g., Pepsi vs. Coke) they have come up with a number of excellent practical changes for candidate selection and electoral processes (Gehl & Porter, 2017). For example, they recommend nonpartisan top four primaries, rank-choice voting with automatic run-offs, and nonpartisan redistricting, and new debate access rules, as well as public campaign funding

The spillover of bitter partisanship and ideological litmus tests for judges have greatly degraded the safeguards once provided the court system. This has become particularly problematic with the appointment of judges who exhibit an inordinate attachment to the new feudal order. Now we have pure ideologues or complete ciphers, and the Supreme Court has become such a partisan battle ground that otherwise well-meaning voters were willing to hold their noises and vote for Trump on the mere promise that he would appoint pro-business and anti-abortion judges. I am not sure how we can restore neutral competence and independence to these life time appointments, but we should think carefully about it.

Our Money & Banking systems are larcenous and must be brought to serve their original mandates. A Glass-Steagall style firewall must be reinstated immediately. If bankers want to gamble, they do it with their own funds. Next we should explore the re-introduction of competing currencies, including an interest free treasury issue. Clearly the systemically vital banks are far too powerful. If they are indeed too big to fail, they are too big to exist in their present form. Mark to marker accounting rules must be reintroduced, and zombie banks must be nationalized until they can be re-privatized. Shadow Banking should be brought out of the shadows. Systemic risk in capital markets must be addressed with anti-contagion firewalls as well as other new international measures aimed at over-leveraging (e.g., larger reserves requirements and rehypothecation limitations). Moreover, financial insurance instruments (e.g., interest and credit default swaps) should be regulated like any other insurance product. Finally, the rating agencies should be made authentically independent and completely transparent (as well as responsible for willful mistakes).

We already have a number of hard won antitrust laws (e.g., the Sherman Act of 1890 and the Clayton Act of 1914), but they need to be updated for the tech/information monopolies. It is noteworthy that the rest of the world calls them "competition laws", making them positive rather than negative. We need re-enforcement when it comes to enforcement. In recent decades, antitrust enforcement has been overwhelmed by minions from "Law and Economics Movement" (including joint degree programs), pushed by the Pelerins and the infamous "Powell Memo" (1971), the Mein Kampf for corporate America. It is noteworthy that Lewis Powell was rewarded for articulation of corporate victimhood with a Supreme Court appointment. Many lawyers and judges now toe the line that antitrust has been rendered pointless by continuous technological progress. Except that evidence suggests the exact opposite (see, Stiglitz, 2017). Moreover, original antitrust systems recognized that concentration of wealth meant concentration of political power and not merely higher consumer prizes. All forms of monopoly (especially our new tech darlings) should be broken-up and/or converted into public utilities. Since all mergers must be reviewed we could at least stop most of them from going forward. New laws and regulations which reflect the political as well as economic power of the new data-driven firms need to be written and implemented vigorously. With specific reference to the new tech monopolies, former Senior Congressional Advisor, Matt Stoller (2017), told an audience at the Harvard Law School that "the platforms" represent a new era of "lawlessness". Oxford Professor of Competition Law, Ariel Ezrachi and his colleague Maurice Stucke

(2016) contend that "algorithmic driven economy" with its "super platforms" pose entirely new threats of "collusion", and "dominate data-opolies".

Civilian control of the military as well as military influence of the government should be ameliorated immediately (i.e., stop granting overrides for generals to prematurely serve in government). Moreover, universal service should be restored (even in times of peace, with very few deferments). Young people, of course, would have the option of the Peace Corps (or other such select civic groups). Some might find their inner Frodo in the process. Meanwhile, lobbying should be dramatically curtailed and turnstile between the government and industry (especially defense industries) should be shut down. The permanent war mentality and "Bush Doctrine" (allowing preemptive attacks upon imaginary threats) should be subjected to the War Powers Act of 1973 (requiring Congressional approval for armed conflict) and additional strictures introduced.

Our tax system is ludicrous, and has reached the height of repressive absurdity under Trump. FINANCIAL TRANSACTIONS, corporate, property, inheritance, and particularly "windfall" should all be taxed at much higher rates and combined with value added and luxury taxes in order to eventually do away with the regressive income tax. In the meantime, the CEILING (or cut off) on social security and medical contributions via the Federal Insurance Contributions Act (or FICA Tax) should be raised substantially (if not eliminated altogether). Why should the rich only pay on the first $127 thousand of their income while the rest of us pay on every penny we earn?

Campaign finance restrictions should become draconian. If Citizens United cannot be reversed, real transparency needs to be vigorously enforced. Election seasons should be substantially shortened, as in England, with a small fixed number of TV and social media ads allowed (with all advertisements approved by the candidate). If we adhere to the silly idea that money is speech, who is speaking should be exposed. Moreover, internet fake news and slander blogs should be subject to libel and defamation laws as well as campaign restrictions. Perhaps we need new "truth in advertising" laws applied to candidates as well as well as any group seeking their election.

Education should be recognized as a basic right, and higher education should be made much more accessible. Publicly supported universities in particular, however, have seen their budgets continuously slashed by increasingly hostile state legislators, and have been raising tuitions to cover the shortfall. But this political situation only partially explains why the costs of higher education has gone up over a 1000% since the early 1980s (more even than medical costs). Given the dramatic conversion of the bulk of the teaching to low wage/few benefits/non-tenured graduate students and adjunct instructors, faculty wages do not explain the increase either. Have you ever wondered what university presidents have done with all the money they saved on faculty wages, aside from wildly rewarding their cadre of cronies and coaches? Consider the following example: after another lack luster football season in 2017, Arizona State University fired their head football coach, but he will still be paid 13 million dollars (the full value of 4 years contract) whether or not he lands another job. Costly sports programs are merely the most obvious tip of the iceberg.

A far less obvious, yet more profound, trend is the increasing number of administrators. In the name of running things like a business, they have become as heavily bureaucratized as some of the worse run (and mostly defunct) corporations. Most universities now have many more administrators than faculty, and the costs of this academic overhead has skyrocketed. Private universities have not escaped this pattern either. John Hopkins Professor, Benjamin Ginsberg (2013) documents this pattern in his tome, The Fall of the Faculty: The Rise of the All-Administrative University and why it Matters. He points out that administrators used to be chosen from distinguished faculty, but now we have armies of administrators who have never ran the gauntlet of academic promotion. Many come from and return to their departments with their immaculate promotions, unpublished and unskilled at teaching. So want begins as the blind leading the lame and infirmed, leads to particular departments becoming complete turkey farms. SCHOOLS OF PUBLIC AFFAIRS are prime examples; with faculty slots for life awarded to failed administrators and orphaned politicians.

Only a few academic administrators could make it in real corporate environments. The touted efficiencies of all their bloated bureaucracies is a tragic joke. Ginsberg explains that while student populations rose 56%, in the period from 1975 to 2005, faculty only increased by 51% (with most of those temps and adjuncts). Yet, administrators rose 85%, and their staffs rose 240% during that same period, and the salaries of many (if not most) administrators far exceed those of the faculty.

Higher education needs a complete overhaul. It should probably begin with thorough reassessment of licensing and certification requirements for many fields, especially professional programs. Tuition at public institutions should be dramatically reduced, and for-profit colleges should be carefully policed, especially those with poor graduation rates and unpaid government insured student loans. Clear frauds, like Trump University, should incur extreme punishments (including perhaps prison time). If public support cannot be increased then cost cutting needs to be blended with curriculum redesign, and be redirected to student outcomes.

Instruction could obviously be enhanced (as well as costs cut) via the application of information technologies, on line, peer-to-peer, and other innovative learning modes. However, if university administrators merely use the savings to increase their ranks the cost advantages will be moot. The application of artificial intelligence and machine learning could not only eliminate a substantial amount of the administrative overhead, it could provide a ready-made lab for students to learn about state-of-art applications. All students, irrespective of major, should at least be exposed to objective-oriented computer languages, and simulation tools.

Many in higher education have maintained for some time that the average 18 year old is not ready for college. My universal service idea would not only automatically address the delayed entry that some prescribe; it would also afford a once-in-lifetime experience of wider world for some, as well as just increased maturity for most. Once more serious learners do enter college at 20 or 21, steps should be taken to keep them on-track toward completion within allotted times. No more 6 year plans for 4 year degrees, plus many programs could be reduced to 3 years, or even 2 year + 3 summers.

Aside from these simple educational reforms, very few of the items (especially political reforms) above have much a chance in hell at present. However, once an institutional ecology perspective is taken and reforms tested, with simulations of artificial adaptive agents, new paths of practical reform will emerge and discussions can begin in earnest. However, if conservatives are successful in their plot for a new Constitutional convention, who knows what crazy shite might emerge. Increased taxation may be particularly difficult but the FICA ceiling could be adjusted more rapidly to shore-up social security and tax rates on the top portions of top earner's unearned wealth go up more than a bit, while alternative taxes are tested. Dark Money is particularly difficult, yet a greater level of campaign transparency might have a chance even in lieu of a constitutional amendment. Public (and private who get public funds) universities can be made to identify big donors; especially those that seek to hand pick their own faculty, in violation of contracts and charters. Given their political power, Money & Banking reforms are really a long shot, but if discussions have started before the next crisis, who knows what might happen when the hall of mirrors is exposed again. Glass-Steagall will be on the lips of many in coming campaigns, and we need to actually get them to deliver. While the arm forces probably don't want most our universal service draftees, all the more for the Peace Corps, etc. Our crumbling infrastructure could also benefit from a new Works Progress Administration (WPA) or Civilian Conservation Corp (CCC), as service options. Young people could learn a trade while serving their country, as well as reducing the alienation of military. Military service would still carry GI bill type benefits and premiums to make it the preferred choice of many.

Short of another world war, restoring the blue collar middle class of 1950s is probably an empirical impossibility. Leading business guru, Polanyi friend, and self-proclaimed "social ecologist", Peter Drucker (1994) cogently observed that widespread membership in the American middle class was mostly an aberration to begin with. Even if we could overcome the massive misallocation of financial resources and restore a major portion of our old industrial base, it would mostly employ robots. As the joke goes, the factories of the future will employ one human and a one dog. The human is there to feed the dog and the dog is there to keep the humans away from the machines.

We would be better served to focus our efforts at reducing the growing gap between lords and serfs, as well as making serfdom less onerous by recognizing "basic economic rights"(see, Chapter 11 below). The realization of our mounting Medievalism should spur a larger discussion of what a decent and just society entails. Inquiries into the prerequisites for happier Hobbits might rejuvenate of LIFE QUALITY ACCOUNTING systems (note, Daneke, 1978b; Lasker, 1981; and, Nussbaum & Sen, 1993), as well as other socio-ecological imperatives. In the process we might actually discover that some of the best things in life really are nearly free.

CHAPTER 10: TAMING THE IMPIOUS TECH PRIETSHOOD

They trust me, the dumb fucks. _____ **Mark Zuckerberg**

I fear that our technology will surpass our human interaction. That world will have a generation of idiots. _____ **Albert Einstein**

Anyone who considers arithmetic methods of producing random digits is, of course, in a state of sin. _____ **John Von Neumann**

I'm increasingly inclined to think that there should be some regulatory oversight, maybe at the national and international level, just to make sure that we don't do something very foolish. I mean with artificial intelligence we're really summoning the demon. _____ **Elon Musk**

The Enlightenment started with essentially philosophical insights spread by a new technology. Our period is moving in the opposite direction. It has generated a potentially dominating technology in search of a guiding philosophy.... This should be given a high national priority, above all, from the point of view of relating AI to humanistic traditions. _____ **Henry Kissinger**

The average American is very suspicious of science (especially when it implies limits) and yet exhibits a strange level of faith in technology. I was once completely flummoxed to find this disconnect among some scientists as well. Long ago I organized a session for the AAAS (American Association for the Advancement of Science) on Energy and the Environment, and one of my speakers was biologist, Barry Commoner of The closing Circle (a bestselling call for ecologically informed policies) fame and US presidential candidate of the Citizen's Party. Another was legendary physicist Edward Teller, father of the Hydrogen Bomb and the inspiration for Dr. Strange Love. The large ballroom was packed and the vast majority of the attendees were there to support Teller and lambast Commoner. When I informally polled some of the audience afterwards, the universal response was that "at least Teller had made something." A few added that Commoner had "given up science for politics".

A more curious element, perhaps, of our technological religiosity might be called the SALVATION EXPECTATION. Even when a given technology produces widespread harm, we assume that some new invention will miraculously come around to correct the situation. I recall talking with a public official who admitted that he firmly believed that climate change was a hoax, and besides he said "guys are working on some sort of chemical spray that acts like a worldwide sunscreen". I told him that it was called "geo-engineering" and that it was very unproven and potentially dangerous technology. Also, I explained that it would do nothing about the carbon's companion crisis of ocean acidification. His reply, "oh those guys will come up with something." At that moment, I did not have the energy to point out his array of contradictions. Rachel Carson (1962) in her classic book on the environmental crisis, Silent Spring speaks about unintended consequences as "elixirs of death" (i.e., where DDT killed the birds and the bees as well as crop destroying bugs). Recall that heroin was created as a cure for legions of morphine addicts that came out of the world wars. Bayer even once marketed heroin as a children's cough syrup as well as a remedy for unruliness. As our visiting anarchist physicist, Shevek, from *The Dispossessed*, came to understand, some breakthroughs should be left less than fully realized. For example, we discovered that the advanced supersonic transport (AST or just SST) was not worth the bother. Of course, ecological as well as economic warnings about the SST (see, OTA, 1980) were ignored until after it proved a financial disaster. When Congress decided to dispense with its Office of Technology Assessment (OTA) in 1995, it decided to purposely fly blindly into the future. But Trump's "magical mystery tour" is a whole new level of enforced ignorance. So we are already faced with medieval level of technological unawareness. Despite our new voodoo technology assessment regime, we still harbor an undying faith in its salvation. We merely trust certain technology industries will provide the type of economic future we desire, with little discussion. Those expecting the second coming of information technology to save our ailing economy really do practice a more ancient form religious observance. Nevertheless, the "market pull" models of mainstream economics merely assume that when a particular resource becomes depleted, an undeveloped technological substitute will just be plucked out of the ether, and brought up to scale without the economy skipping a beat. It is like the joke about a scientist, an engineer, and an economist stranded on a desert island, trying to open a can of beans. The economist says "we can just assume we have an opener". One tiny set back anywhere in our vast webs of commerce with "just in time" supply chains could throw entire civilizations into a cocked hat (see, Korowicz, 2012). A "butterfly effect" could turn into Mothra (Nemesis of Godzilla). That is, interconnected nonlinear systems can easily magnify minor disruptions in such a way to completely shut-down vital elements in our overly brittle and hopelessly complex economies, triggering social unrest and further systemic collapse.

BIG PROBLEMS, BIG DATA, AND BIG BROTHER

We are headed into a "perfect storm" of resource and technological transformations nearly naked, unprepared, ill-informed, with our darker impulses inflamed by ruthless politicians and fake Facebook friends. We face civilization destroying energy and environmental crises, at the very time that we are in the midst of a monumental tech transformation resulting from the linking of learning machines and a global catches of really huge and extensively manipulated data stores, to say nothing of constant digital surveillance. The second stage of the on-going information revolution "the automacene" (where humans are increasingly replaced by machines that think for themselves) is the ultimate dispossession by accumulation. BIG DATA and AI literally converts our very essence and experiences into a digital soup from which it recreates its own reassembled reality and forces us to conform. As machines become more autonomous, humans become less so.

We already have a variety of wildly divisive and anti-democratic forces ready to exploit these mounting piles of overvalued digital assets for more perverse purposes. Meanwhile from within the heart information industry we have voices demanding that we move much faster into an uncertain future, "damn the torpedos" and all that. Furthermore from those same ranks we have a few self-anointed ubermench suggesting that the brave new world of networked everything, as well as a cornucopia of new tech gadgets, is in severe jeopardy unless we forego our democratic institutions altogether and formalize their feudalistic ambitions. After all we are not really using them anyway. Moreover they invoke old style tech gap arguments, only now to compete they contend we must also adopt their authoritarian practices of our global adversaries.

Thus far these NEARLY NAZI NERDS are little more than a blip, but in these chaotic times, fueled by internet frenzies, who knows what the following might become. First they will have to get the existing aristocracy, and the old school fascists, as well as associated skin heads, to move over to make room for them. Oh wait, we have one more monkey wrench to throw into the mix, ultra-conservatives are marshalling for a new blitzkrieg on the courts and the Constitution. While the crises are real, especially climate change, we could be panicked into throwing out our birth rights with the bath water. With some seriously nasty pieces of work waiting in the wings, we need more deliberation, not less, and more safeguards against insanity, not fewer.

Even if we didn't have a bunch of fledgling fascists scurrying around, the information transition poses existential dangers of its own. In an excellent piece for the prestigious publication, Scientific American, Dirk Helbing (Helbing, et.al. 2017) and his colleagues (including the legendary Bruno Frey) review a number threats to our personal liberties and democratic institutions posed by AI and Big Data. For example, algorithmic profiling and dramatically enhanced surveillance is already being experimented with in places like China to give everyone a "Citizen Score". That score then dictates one's future prospects (from education and employment to credit and foreign travel permits). One can easily imagine a dystopia where your score might even produce anticipatory "re-education" and/or imprisonment. Helbing & colleagues describe how individualized targeting not only tells us what to buy, but who to vote for by identifying our bottoms and pushing them continuously using troll bots. They contend that "the trend goes from programming computers to programming people" on a massive scale. Heinrich Himmler would have loved to get his hands on such tools. And, Joseph Goebbels would be ecstatic to have the power to divide, dissembled, and discipline that we cavalierly entrust to our technological overlords.

The raw economic power and impact of our BIG DATA DADDIES poses even more immediate problems. Their networked learning and expert systems will make a huge swath of existing white collar jobs redundant (even as the robots displace the blue collars) and their monopoly power is likely to forestall further innovation and further slow real economic growth, thus curtailing opportunities for displaced workers. The influential members of the Chicago branch of the Mont Pelerins have maintained for decades how monopoly was NOT a problem, since technological innovations would make most monopolies only temporary. Actual economic evidence suggests they were completely wrong. The new platform monopolies are a "huge" problem in this regard (see, Stiglitz, 2017).

The salvation expectation remains the all-purpose solution to, as well as excuse for, declining growth and dismissed as merely temporary secular stagnation. The epic status of technology fuels further institutional fakery from defense boondoggles and failing unicorn farms to the monopoly safe zones. Whenever the plight of American's middle class is raised, it is quickly undermined as mere growing pains in the next technological transition that will subside once one acquires the needed skill set. Sure a robot will take your job, but if given specialized retraining you will find a new one in robot repair. AI and robotics may make your expertise superfluous, yet it also will free you up to pursue a more meaningful and creative work. Smell like bullshit? That's because it is. The threats to future employment from networked algorithms (algos for short) and learning machines is merely a portion of the problem. Information technology (IT) has always been a bit of a mixed blessing, and the new era of data mining greatly accelerates the overhead and diverts the resources of society. The misleading edge of the US economy includes the spoiled offspring of its IT revolution, and they are just getting started. They are known as the FAANG (Facebook, Amazon, Apple, Netflix, and Google), with a market capitalization of over 4 trillion dollars (accounting for 35% of the NASDAQ). Entrepreneur and NYU-Stern Professor of Digital Marketing, Scott Galloway (2017), calls them The Four (minus Netflix), and describes how they have created enormous wealth by pandering to our basic instincts for "God, love, sex, and consumption". Yet he also reminds us that they build "high walls and deep moats" to competition, avoid paying taxes, and "destroy jobs". The "titans" of the 20th Century, such as GM and GE, generated between 100,000 to 250,000 dollars per employee in shareholder value, and employed millions of people at middle class wages and benefits, back in their hay day. GM is now living on bail outs and GE was recently dropped from the Dow. By contrast, Facebook employs relatively few people, but generates shareholder value at a rate of 23 million per employee. What is wrong with this picture?

The spectacle of cities fighting tooth and claw to be the location of a second Amazon headquarters speaks volumes about our technological fantasies. Amazon, of course, is a mammoth on line discount/retail distributor, but less obvious is its huge CLOUD SERVICES branch (which includes extremely lucrative defense contracts). Hence, municipal governments were willing to give away the store, literally, to host its auxiliary headquarters. Fresno promised to allow Amazon to completely replace their local government, and several others would allow it write its own ordinances. Most offer huge tax breaks, free utilities, and services, as well as building all the required structures (including state-of-the-art athletic facilities for Amazon employees). Chicago offered to reimburse income taxes to Amazon employees, and Boston offered to provide a cadre of permanent public employees to an Amazon taskforce and cater to their every future whim. These ill-conceived battles to be the next Silicon whatever (Beach, Mountain, Pasture, Etc.) have been around since the beginning of the IT era (see, Daneke, 1989b), and have only intensified since the crash of 2008.

Distinguished Stanford statistician, Mordecai Kurz (2017) explains how IT not only improved productivity it also gravely distorted the processes of wealth creation. As an industry, IT-based firms fueled monopolies and facilitated what he calls "surplus wealth". In short, IT "is the cause of rising income and wealth inequality since the 1970s and contributed to slow growth of wages and decline in the natural rate" (p.1). According to Kurz, the digital giants with their network effects and acquisitions restrict competition. He adds that they "are also the cause of social losses and a level rising inequality that threaten the foundations of our democratic society" (p. 43). Hence in many ways they are a major contributor to economic doldrums as well as political difficulties. While we are already wedded to the IT/AI transition, it might be time to review and redraft our prenuptial agreements.

DANCING WITH OUR DIGITAL DEMONS

On the 500th anniversary of Martin Luther's 95 Theses challenging corruption in the Catholic Church (e.g., indulgences among other things), Cambridge University Fellow, John Naughton (2017), reported that our digital economy desperately needs our own Luthers. Economic historians (Cantoni, et. al., 2017) remind us

Luther and the Reformation brought "an immediate and large secularization of Europe's political economy". By shifting resources away from the Vatican it also prompted an economic revitalization. Our current church, is the "Temple of Digital Technology", and it is equally if not more corrupt. Naughton elaborates:

> *Most of us are so happy in our obeisance to the new power that we spend an average50 minutes on our daily devotion to Facebook alone without a flicker of concern....that what you once thought of as liberating might actually be malign and dangerous (p. 1).*

If you have ever suspected that Google "protests too much" with their motto to "Do No Evil", then you might be correct. Naughton, who describes himself as a "recovering utopian", points out that contrary to their claims of being above the political fray, internet firms are clearly immersed in political processes and perversions. Furthermore, he maintains that "Facebook is many things, but a community it ain't". This healthy skepticism about Facebook's modus operandi predates the exposure of the Cambridge Analytica scandal. The Director of MIT's Center for Civic Media, Ethan Zuckerman (note his series of articles in The Atlantic), greatly fortifies this critical view and even calls for a "tax payer supported" (yet independent) alternative to our current social networks (see, Metz, 2018). Facebook's former executive, Sean Parker (of Napster fame), even admitted that it set out to "addict its followers" (many of whom check it 150 times a day), and he apologized for the "harm it has inflicted on children" (not to mention adults). Another former Facebook executive, Chamath Palihapitiya (Vincent, 2017) told Stanford Business School students that social media has

> *...created tools that are ripping apart the social fabric....In the short-term, dopamine-driven feedback loops we've created are destroying how society works....No civil discourse, no cooperation, misinformation, mistrust (p 2).*

In a nation that seeks to protect freedom of speech, the misuse of social media introduces serious new difficulties (for an excellent review and research agenda into the "dark side" see, Baccarella, et. al., 2018). If we over react to current trends and require Google, Facebook, YouTube, Twitter, etc. to police their content more carefully, then it could have a chilling effect on legitimate oppositional discourse. But the ill use of vast information stores for political profiling and repression should be less ambiguous. The tendencies of platform monopolies to allow the weaponization of our digital relationships into more potent instruments of social differentiation, commoditization, and CONTROL should concern us all.

THE DISTRIBUTION DILEMMA

Meanwhile back to the future, IT/AI could become an even bigger elixir of bad socio-economic juju, as BIG DATA becomes as asset class in and of itself. Once again we look to the prophetic complexity economist, Brian Arthur (2017), for guidance into the wayward wizardry of this technology. In a piece undertaken for the folks at McKinsey Consulting he asks "where is technology taking the economy"? He points out that IT/AI are now "external to humans" and housed in the "virtual economy's algorithms and machines". This "third morphing", as he calls it, is one of "associative machine learning and dynamic action" without humans involved. Plus, as a good complexity theorist, he points out:

> There doesn't need to be a controller at the center of such intelligence; appropriate action can emerge as a property of the whole system...This sort of intelligence is self-organizing, conversational [between algorithms, not humans], ever-adjusting and dynamic. The virtual economy is not just an Internet of Things; it is a source of intelligent action---intelligence external to human workers (p. 6).

The new AI built upon what is now being called "deep learning" or DL for short (experiential in addition to purely algorithmic, see Goodfellow, et. al., 2016) and inferential leaps of faith displace loads of labor. For example, Stanford AI researcher, Timnit Gebru & her colleagues (2017) demonstrate how DL programs using Google Street View (counting cars and trucks) yield demographic estimates on par with the labor intensive (door-to-door) and expensive (250 million per annum) American Community Survey.

Arthur suggests that machine learning will necessitate a "new economy of distribution", forgetting, perhaps, that our economy and the majority of our economists only know how to redistribute upward (from the masses to the 1%). He contends that "free-market philosophy will be more difficult to support". He also implies that downward redistribution might be more political than economic, per se', but he believes it will be forthcoming. On what planet, you might ask? In fairness, his political examples include those that brought us the present populist demagoguery, yet he hopes these trends are temporary and that "Scandinavian" style ("government-guided by attention to whom gets what") will prevail. I used to chide my Public Choice colleagues for giving up perfectly good political science to become mediocre economists. Brian may have achieved the reverse. His optimism seems to ignore the fact that so much of our economy is tightly controlled by the rentiers who can bend populism to buttress their dominion. Perhaps I am being a bit too harsh as I completely concur that the current generation of IT/IA will greatly intensify distributional problems, and that an even a minutely functioning economy will need to redress them. But what if it doesn't? Why would the more sociopathic elites even bother? A more probable scenario might be like that terrible sci-fi movie with Jodie Foster and Matt Damon, Elysium (2013), where elites withdraw to their orbiting kingdom in the clouds (or private compounds in New Zealand) as well as on "the cloud" (where they have exclusive access to unlimited technological advances). Meanwhile, we peasants must remain in our antiquated police state ghetto below. However, we once knew how to do downward redistribution for a few decades following the WWII, and we could learn to do it again (see; Rawls, 1971; Zajac, 1995: and, Chetty, et. al., 2017). Moreover, if as Arthur implies further advances in Big Data, Computer Vision, and Artificial Intelligence generally hasten the demise of our current version of criminalized capitalism via labor market and consumer debt implosion, then they might be worth the potential widespread disruption.

More importantly, if these new associative intelligence tools can be turned inward to devise adaptive initiatives and institutions, then their wizardry might really be revealed instead of reviled. Spanish scientists (Lopez-Iturriaga & Sanz. 2017) have already applied neural nets and self-organizing maps (SOMs) to allow machines to teach themselves how to predict "public corruption".

In the meantime, we will have to amuse ourselves with imagining what someone like Trump would say if we told them that our expert systems and DL machines analyzed all the data (and discussed it among themselves) so he should act as follows on climate change, or what have you. Trump would rant and rave for days on Twitter about how he is smarter than any computer, despite not knowing what an algorithm is, and telling us to go f--k ourselves!

ALGORITHM AND BLUES

By the way (as you probably know) an algorithm (from the Greek for number) is merely a set of computational steps or activities required to solve a problem, perform a task, or represent a relationship. Expert systems, on the other hand, take the combined "rules of thumb" condensed from the wisdom of thousands of the best practitioners in a given field and convert them into algorithmic expression and/or the use DL (via a neural net algorithm) to create learning machines (e.g. Watson, Deep Mind, self-driving cars, etc.). Moreover, complexity (or "genetic") algos can take matters bit further by representing evolutionary systems that learn, adapt, and are capable of "perpetual novelty" as my late Michigan colleague, the brilliant polymath, John Holland, demonstrated (see, Forrest & Mitchell, 2016). Complexity algos could enhance adaptive pathways built upon entirely unique reservoirs of "transformative information". Or they could just further ENSLAVE us.

Can we really trust our fate to a small and poorly socialized priesthood of math and computer nerds and their sociopathic corporate overlords? The use of algos is already ubiquitous and will be so mega-pervasive in the next few years that they will control our lives in ways we can barely imagine at present (see the excellent Pew study, Rainie & Anderson, 2017). We can only speculate about the jobs that will be replaced by a few lines of code, but the number could be massive. Even if they don't take your particular job, machine learning parameters they will dictate the way your job is done. Computers, however, are far from omnipotent. Plus, an algorithm, even if discovered by machines, is NOT a magic bullet for relieving human fallibility, or a replacement for human creativity. Machine learning is has already been applied to myriad realms with little or no attention to paid to unintended consequences. Judith Donath of Harvard's Beckman Center expresses this concern as follows: "Data can be incomplete, or wrong, and algorithms can embed false assumptions...the decision-making process becomes oracular, opaque yet unarguable (Rainie & Anderson, 2017, p. 22)". University of Maryland Law Professor, Frank Pasquale (2016) reminds us that algorithms place a number of impenetrable "blacks boxes" into the pathways of our lives, and we must merely trust these formal abstractions fit the increasingly messy realities we face. Aside from the mystery of the math, most specific algos are the proprietary creations of private firms; hence the types of data and rules applied are tightly held trade secrets. PREDICTIVE ALGORITHMS are already routinely used to decide who gets into a particular college, or access to a government program, a job, a loan (and at what interest rate) as well as who goes to prison and when they get out. Dartmouth students compared the recidivism predictions of the widely used COMPAS (Correctional Offender Management Profiling for Alternative Sanctions) algorithm and found it was no better than a simple on line survey of non-experts (see, Dressel and Farid, 2018). In Turkey a single error in a one line of code led to 30,000 innocent citizens being briefly imprisoned in a crackdown on a banned phone app. Meanwhile back in the good old USA, Virginia Eubanks (2017) in her excellent book, Automating Inequality, documents how invisible algos are used to further torment the poor, by amplifying cultural biases and creating a "digital poorhouse". Moreover, she suggests that all this monitoring, computing, and sanctioning is much more costly than programs aimed at improving the lives of the unfortunate.

Meanwhile the more fortunate now have an entirely new digital universe to manipulate, mutilate, and metastasize into the real economy. Over half of the hedge funds already rely heavily upon AI. Algorithmic devices in the FIRE industries could prove even more cataclysmic next time around. Jon Danielsson (2017), Director of the Centre for Systemic Risk at the London School of Economics, observes that AI, especially for micro-prudential supervision and/or regulatory compliance, might increase spasmodic instability in financial markets and accelerate the potential for the cascading collapse across far-flung counterparty networks. He explains:

> *A hostile agent can learn how the AI engine operates, take risk where it is not looking, game the algorithms and*

hence undermine the machine by behaving in a way that avoids triggering its alarms...Meanwhile, the very formality and efficiency of the risk management/supervisory machine also increases homogeneity in belief and response, further amplifying pro-cyclicality and systemic risk (p. 4).

MIT Professors Andrew Kirilenko and Andrew Lo (2013) in their cleverly titled article on algorithmic trading, Moore's Law versus Murphy's Law, illustrate the distortion of critical market segments. Moore's law recall involved the period doubling of information contained on a single silicon chip, and they use it as an analog for role of technology in the doubling of the stock market average, recognizing that Murphy's Law of unintended consequences also applies. We have already seen the dangers of algorithmically driven "High Frequency Trading" triggering "flash crashes". Moreover, they can completely overwhelm the regulatory apparatus from the pre-digital era (i.e., the Security and Exchange Act of 1934). As Kirilenko & Low elaborate:

Although legislation has been amended on many occasions to reflect new financial technologies and institutions it has become an increasingly cumbersome patchwork quilt of old and new rules based on increasingly outdated principles, instead of an integrated set of modern regulations designed to maintain financial stability, facilitate capital formation, and protect the interests of investors (p. 52).

Director of ASU's Center for Science and Imagination, Ed Finn (2017), takes a much more optimistic view of algo-omnipresence, yet he also illustrates how they can amplify "magical thinking". Consider the convergence of magical thinking, mathematical legerdemain, financial mistrust, "right-wing extremism" (Golumbia, 2016), and speculative frenzy in the form of BITCOIN. Blockchain may be a brilliant tool, but remains hard pressed to engender a secure store of value or intermediation. Plus, the amount of electricity employed by avid "miners" creates problems for some utilities. Yet these tiny instrumentalities of misguided imagination are only of tangential concern unless we are preparing to unravel the mystical labyrinth of our entire Money and Banking system (with careful attention to cascading nonlinearities). Of greater immediate concern is all the BLACK MAGICAL THINKING influencing our political systems. Historically speaking magical thinking was a primary source of social control, and it serves a similar role in the hands of modern day fascists. Beyond bestowing unbridled power to the fearless leader, it energizes perverse notions of nationalistic and ethnic destiny. But why should we begrudge a bit of more magical thinking, since we are now led by its self-appointed master. To paraphrase the Superman TV show of my youth, Trump is "more powerful than a speeding" super computer, able to construct tail buildings with a single bound (and multiple money launderers), and "leads the never-ending battle for truth" (of the alternative variety) "justice (frontier style) and the America way" (according to Cheney). So what could go wrong?

CHAPTER 11: FROM HOBBES TO HOBBITS

On questions of power, then, let no more be heard of confidence in man, but bind him down from mischief by the chains of the Constitution. _____ **Thomas Jefferson**

Grant me thirty years of equal division of inheritances and a free press, and I will provide you with a republic. _____ **Alexis de Tocqueville**

In the real world, as lived and experienced by real people, the demand for human rights and dignity, the longing for liberty and justice and opportunity, the hatred of oppression and corruption and cruelty is reality. _____ **John McCain**

Human rights are not only violated by terrorism, repression or assassination, but also by unfair economic structures that creates huge inequalities. _____ **Pope Francis**

And the little screaming fact that sounds through all history: repression works only strengthen and knit the repressed. _____ **John Steinbeck**

  If you are less than inspired by presidential super powers, fear not, we have a kryptonite constitution that can contain his/her misadventures. We also have a number of clearly defined constitutional rights that our rulers cannot easily abrogate. Moreover, we also have underlying philosophy of universal rights and a broader notion of the "social contract", which is more John Locke than Thomas Hobbes. Essentially they can be viewed as representing the different sides in the English Civil War (between populists and monarchists, 1641-1652). In his famed Two Treatises of Government (published anonymously in 1689) Locke rejected his earlier pro-royalist writings and took on a decidedly humanistic and democratic tone, while he was in exile in Holland. His ideas add to the bulwark of our democratic traditions. Locke was also very far ahead of his time in his economic writings, which suggested limits upon accumulation and the use of land, a crude labor theory of value, and recognition of the integral role of money (see, Henry, 1999: Vaughn, 2012). Unfortunately as suggested above mainstream economists, and particularly the Pelerins, took a Hobbesian turn, and ended up maintaining a number of contradictory notions, including: the inviolate sovereignty of the state as well as the market, an exceedingly low opinion of human nature, and the primacy of order over liberty (note, Taylor, 2010). Lucky for us, on balance, our founding fathers leaned a bit more toward Locke. However, each generation must restore and rejuvenate Locke's vision of basic of human and economic rights. This requires of course that we press our legislatures and the courts to step up and defend our stake in the system. Moreover, it also demands that we resist attempts to alter the U. S. Constitution by our neofeudal overlords. While our founding fathers were NOT saints nor otherwise superhuman, they were absolutely white-hot brilliant when it came to fashioning a constitution for quelling combative interests. It is noteworthy, however, that the most incandescent portion (the Bill of Rights, or first 10 amendments) was actually an afterthought, added to placate the Anti-federalists. It is important to note that out of the 56 founding fathers of the constitution only 6 were also the firebrands who also signed the Declaration of Independence. Like Tevye in the Fiddler on the Roof misquoting of the Old Testament, our modern leaders often confuse (on purpose) the texts as well as the authors. Neofeudal forces and their confused followers have been working for some time to have a NEW CONSTITUTIONAL CONVENTION. They could completely wreck the safeguards installed some 230 years ago, and shift more power to oligarchs via further counterfeit populism (see, Wines, 2016). Yes, the safeguards have taken a beating the last few years, but they should be repaired not replaced.

From 1776 to 1787 the disunited states operated (badly) as a loose knit confederation. The last straw for the Articles of Confederation came by way of an insufficiently armed insurrection where you might expect it (in Massachusetts) in 1786. U-Mass historian, Leonard Richards (2003) refers to Shay's Rebellion as "the American Revolution's final battle". When word of the uprising reached Jefferson (then an ambassador in Paris) he wrote (to James Madison) that a bit of rebellion was not necessarily a bad thing, including his famed assertion that "the tree of liberty must be refreshed from time to time with the blood of patriots and tyrants. It is its natural manure". The burgeoning merchant class then running Massachusetts was not nearly so blasé. While they could not find the funds to pay the ex-soldiers, like Daniel Shay, their promised war wages, they financed a mercenary army to put down his rebellion (as the national government was too weak to intervene). They believed that since they were forced to use a hard currency to pay their suppliers, they expected the poor (barely subsistence) farmers of the western hills to do the same. The past Governor John Hancock (remember him) had allowed them to pay with debased paper money and did not press them for back taxes. But, the merchant regime of James Bowdoin raised their taxes and took their lands when they could not pay. The farmers had seen their constant petitions to the state and Confederation ignored, so they organized to stop the land seizures. The ranks of the rebels rose to 4,000, but when their plot to move on the arsenal in Springfield was discovered their rebellion floundered. When the delegates met in Philadelphia to draft a constitution, those in support of the existing Confederation were labeled "Shayites" by the Federalists. Yet, the document they fashioned made space for them. And, we Hobbits need to maintain and expand Shay's legacy.

A BIGGER BILL OF RIGHTS FOR THE LITTLE PEOPLE

In his excellent historical analysis, The Heart of the Constitution: How the Bill of Right Became the Bill of Rights, Indiana Law Professor, Gerald Magliocca (2018) describes the evolution of our concept of constitutional protections. His key revelation is that the framers of the constitution did not refer the first 10 amendments as a "Bill of Rights", that designation did not enter the lexicon until after the Civil War, when those restrictions upon the Congress were extended to the state governments via the 14th Amendment. Even their original author, James Madison, did not think of them as special rights, and wanted to merely blend them into sections with the other restrictions upon government, most notably "habeas corpus". Magliocca suggests that our regard for the salience of "Bill of Rights" has grown with certain political uses of the phrase.

Its modern meaning as the pillar of individual freedom was reiterated when FDR used its 150th birthday celebration to answer his critics (who held that the New Deal was an assault on liberty) as well as defend his declaration of war on Germany as well as Japan. FDR would further invoke the revitalized spirit of the Bill of Rights in his famed State of the Union Address of January 11, 1944. In it Roosevelt (1944) recognizes a "Second Bill of Rights" (of "inalienable economic rights") to "complete the work of the framers". He states that,

We have come to a clear realization of the fact that true individual freedom cannot exist without economic security and independence. Necessitous men are not free men. People who are hungry and out of a job are the stuff of which dictatorships are made. In our day these economic truths have become accepted as self-evident. We have accepted, so to speak, a second Bill of Rights under which a new basis of security and prosperity can be established for all, regardless of station, race, or creed (p.5).

He proceeds to list his extended rights as follows:

- *The right to a useful and remunerative job in the industries or shops or farms or mines of the nation;*
- *The right to earn enough to provide adequate food and clothing and recreation;*
- *The right of every farmer to raise and sell his products at a return which will give him and his family a decent living;*
- *The right of every businessman, large and small, to trade in an atmosphere of freedom from unfair competition and domination by monopolies at home or abroad;*
- *The right of every family to a decent home;*
- *The right to adequate medical care and the opportunity to achieve and enjoy good health;*
- *The right to adequate protection from the economic fears of old age, sickness, accident, and unemployment; and,*
- *The right to a good education (p. 5-6).*

Some minor aspects of this list were touched upon via legislation and/or in court rulings (Labor Relations Acts, Brown v Board of Education, FHA, maybe even Obama Care) over the years. Yet, it is perhaps fair to say that notion of an "Economic Bill of Rights" pretty much died with FDR, aside from those included and ignored in the UN Universal Declaration of Human Rights (in 1948, see, Moyn, 2018). The era of "Red Scare" and the rise of Neofeudal Economics, the war on labor, and the cultivation of corporatist judges have enforced a clandestine PREDATOR'S BILL OF RIGHTS. UCLA law professor, Adam Winkler (2018; also note, Cerri, 2018) in his well-researched and written book, We the Corporations, explains how firms waged an unrelenting (with no small measure of subterfuge) war to win for themselves semi-sovereign power and a number of un-civil rights (including personhood), using avenues originally designed to insure rights for us mere humans. For example the 14th Amendment (granting basic rights to freed slaves) was invoked in 604 corporate rights cases and only 28 cases for the groups it was intended. It is certainly high time we begin reconsidering and revoking some of these predatory privileges. However, I doubt whether those calling for a new Constitution have this goal in mind, despite their rhetorical populism.

While many (myself included) can reasonably question the unwarranted power of the Federal government, few can deny the brilliance of the U. S. Constitution. It is neither perfect, nor should it be regarded as somehow sacred, yet it is a prudential foundation for a great experiment in moderated democracy. And, I would contend that it should NOT be altered willy-nilly. It has a number of flaws, but on balance it is one hellaciously amazing contraption. The heavily funded ultra-right wing forces have been anxious to change it and have focused their patience ground game on one particular clause in Article 5 which allows two third's (34) of state legislatures to bypass the Congress and hold their own Constitutional Convention. Via active gerrymandering right wingers already control 32 of the state legislatures. Such a convention would most likely introduce a number of theocratic and xenophobic changes, as well as destroying remaining ingredients of the welfare state. A "balanced budget amendment" is also a high priority for modern Tea Party types (despite their continued support for budget busting military outlays and tax breaks for the wealthy). Some conservatives contend we should return to the Articles of Confederation, completely crippling the central government. For many of these folks the Civil War never really ended over a century and a half ago. Fortunately, any proposed amendments must still be ratified by three fourths of the states. Our creative contraption might well need a bit of tune up, yet it is well to remember that the first constitutional convention met to merely spruce up the Articles of Confederation and ended up junking them altogether. As Michael Wines (2016) points out "holding an amendment-writing meeting with no historical parallel and no written rules [in our contentious times] could open a Pandora's Box of constitutional mischief". Furthermore, our current crop of leaders is NOT nearly as learned as our Founding Fathers, who knew their Greeks and Romans, and read them in own languages. Their ideas of a constitutional republic were shaped by the likes of Aristotle and Cicero, as opposed to Ayn Rand, Jerry Falwell, and David Duke (or even Daisy Duke). It really would be a tragic farce if the document was altered to permanently enshrine various regressive institutions, especially those that seek to reinforce a radically refurbished feudal system.

WISDOM OF THE ANCIENTS

Aristotle, Plato's best known student, was perhaps the first empirical political scientist (see, Barker, 1962). He actually traveled to the various city states and compared their ruling arrangements. While greatly over-simplified, he observed that the functioning of a political system is as much a matter of the character of the rulers as it is the number of rulers one has. For each of his numeric categories there was a bad and good form. In essence, the rule of one (absolute monarchy) was fairly likely to become tyrannical, and the rule of a few or aristocracy (the form he favored, assuming it might be possible to find a few good men) could become oligarchic. The rule of the many or the populace (the demos) was regarded by Aristotle as particularly prone to anarchy (or mob rule). A mob had forced the suicide Socrates. It is worth noting that the best example of a functioning democracy, Athens, was really fairly Aristocratic, given the high property requirements for citizenship (not to mention the institution of slavery). To their credit, however, the Athenians implemented elaborate rotation of authority mechanisms in an earnest attempt to reign in oligarchic forces.

Roman statesman and practical philosopher, Cicero took Aristotle's framework a step further, contending that the ideal republic must "balance and blend" all three elements in a "mixed constitution" (see, Sabine, 1929). His writing on natural law and natural rights were often cited by our original leaders. For Cicero, "freedom is participation in power", and the good republic involves commoners as well as aristocrats. In fact, he contended that without the simultaneous mixture, each type of power would eventually degrade into the next; kings would become tyrants and be over thrown by aristocrats, they would become corrupt oligarchs and be overthrown by "democracy". Democracy would degrade into "ochlocracy" (mob rule), and rabble would eventually seek to end the anarchy by installing a new monarch, starting the cycle all over again. Sabine (1929) explains how Cicero's mixed system was the only hope to break the cycle. As he elaborates:

The blending of these three different elements checks the natural tendency to decay and change which each of the simple forms is infected. It is only when the leaders of the composite fall into exceptional degradation that its constitution will suffer modification (p. 62).

We are obviously pretty near, if not past, the point of exceptional degradation, but before we rush to dismantle our constitution, we need to understand that government was never intended to be run like a business, a church, or a military campaign. Like all complex adaptive social systems, they were designed to run on individual conflicts and arrive at collective improvements (note, Brush, et. al., 2018). In his award winning classic, Seed Time of the Republic, Clinton Rossiter (1953) maintains that the Founders intended a functioning national government that would NOT impede personal liberty. He asserts that they sought "liberty rather than authority, protection rather than power, delay rather than efficiency" (p. 425).

The US Constitution, fashioned as it was on the insights of the ancients was a composite, with competing loci of power forced to cooperate. The different bodies are structured with "overlapping jurisdictions" to have "ambition counter ambition" at every turn. We ate from Aristotelian smorgasbord as it were. It has the rule of one with significant power residing in the President (chosen by people via the buffer of the Electoral College). Yet it is essentially the rule by the few in the Senate (originally appointed by state legislatures, but now popularly elected in each state) and indirect rule of the common people via the House of Representatives. Interestingly enough, given gerrymandering of house districts and the longer senate terms, it is usually the senate that exhibits greatest concern for the public interest, generally defined. We also have a decidedly aristocratic element in the form an independent judiciary (the Supreme, Federal, and State Court systems); however, its independence has been called into question of late. Other democratic elements of our republic enter periodically through the rules by which the loci are chosen and their staggered levels of tenure. The designation of "checks and balances" serves to moderate the concentration of power. Nevertheless, the actual processes by which our rulers are chosen and their operational character (Aristotle's X factor) facilitates a system that often spills over into oligarchy and tyranny. Distinguished University of

Kentucky historian, Ron Formisano (2017), provides detailed analysis of how highly corrupt and oligarchic our legislative bodies can become. Moreover, our President was originally conceived by our founders as a mere administrator, however, the powers of the one have grown astronomically over the years, and along with the politicization of the courts, have made the character issue as critical as it was for Aristotle over twenty centuries ago. Special interests groups seem willing to ignore tyrannical impulses, in the name of their narrow agenda. Trump is a clear a case in point. Nonetheless, the Founder's ingenious Rube Goldberg machine can still tie-up a tyrant, if the other branches and a free press exercise their braking powers appropriately.

Having extolled some of the virtues of the US Constitution, it is also vital to point out that it was also an economic document, created by a "cohesive elite" that, according to legendary historian, Charles A. Beard (1913), sought to protect their property and federal bonds. Of course, critics of Beard are legion, and upshot of a century of debate is that perhaps by accident the Founders did fashion a government capable of extending liberty and prosperity to the masses (see, Commager, 1959; and Gibson, 2004). It is incumbent upon us to hold the nation to its promises, as well as to reline the brakes upon power. If current oligarchic interests get their grimy hands on the document, they are unlikely to leave us much to work with. The paths ahead are largely unchartered, why would we want to destroy one of the few maps we have.

THE TURNING OF THE TIDE

With the controversial election of our contumelious Goblin King many of us were set on a very "unexpected journey". Even those of us who expected something so untoward, did not believe it would begin so soon. Plus, it will NOT end with Trump's term (or terms) in office. Some members of the "Alt-right" imply that he is merely a stalking horse for the real deal duce' yet to come. Unfortunately it matters little whether he is a symptom or source. He is probably both. Trump is not the root cause of all our many problems, yet he is certainly the poster boy for our corrupt economy. Plus, it is our lack of resolution regarding the rise oligarchic forces that left so many of us completely vulnerable to his fake populist bluster. I suspect Trump has little intention of doing anything to alleviate the anxieties of his supporters and will actually expedite our course toward economic catastrophe. As McMaster's Professor for Scholarship in the Public Interest, Paul Giroux (2017), points out Trump is the pinnacle of the most malignant elements of capitalism. According to Giroux, Trump seeks

> ...to destroy all the public institutions that make democracy possible, and to expand a culture in which self-interest, greed, militarism and repression, to expand the ideology, social relations and practices that breathe life into what might be called gangster capitalism, rather than the less odious notion of a Second Gilded Age (p. 6).

Even if you are reading this as Trump the person is little more than a bitter memory, do not overlook all the institutional damage and continuing societal divisions he represents. Trumpism will remain a huge hole in the heart (and the brain) of America for generations to come.

Trump has for most of his adult life has sought to be a larger than life character, but he was too lazy, crass, and corrupt to fulfill his overwhelming addiction to adulation in socially constructive ways. Unique historical factors have given his insatiable narcissistic rage full rein, and awarded him more power than any one individual should ever have. While he was political plotter for decades, the dark stars aligned for him at a relatively singular moment. He was standing in a dark alley of corrupt business dealings, and the ultimate power truck hit him. Yet, all the power in the universe will not give him the recognition and respect that he craves. Plus, he adds a new and far more brazen level of corruption to our increasingly kleptocratic system of government. In fact, Trump has pushed us toward a KAKISTOCRACY (a government of the least qualified and most unscrupulous). Our failure to confront governmental and corporate corruption and address a number of other pressing socio-economic issues (e.g. the peaks) has literally given highly authoritarian forces the "keys to the kingdom", yet they barely know what to do with them thus far. This particular turn of events may have been as much a surprise for them.

As Gandolf proclaims, "I come to you now at the turning the tide." THIS IS THE MOMENT to stand up or lie down and be trampled (as well as Trumpled). I only hope that the next generate will not have to say: "We might tried had we only known how bad it could get". Everywhere we continue to hear "the President cannot do that", and yet with every new affront to our system of government and basic human dignity, fewer and fewer seem willing to step up and say "enough is enough". Trump is so openly outrageous on a daily basis we have become immune to the onslaught, and we are completely disoriented and befuddled. We keep waiting for reason to be restored, but what we fail to appreciate is that his supporters are not merely a cult following, some are an OCCULT FOLLOWING. These darker forces welcome his random acts of ego and induced chaos as some sort of "magick". While it may be giving Trump too much credit, some of his erratic behavior might be designed to trigger hysterical responses and thus further fortify the conspiracy theories he uses to vilify and isolate his opponents (another ploy from the fascist playbook).

It is crucial to note that we have been on this uncharted detour for several years now; before Trump was a sparkle in Putin's eye. While Trump is the personification of unmitigated disrespect of democratic norms, those norms such as "mutual respect" and "forbearance" have been eroding for decades. This erosion coincides with the rise of neofeudal ideology and is a direct result of the toxic political strategy of weaponizing race, religion, and culture. This vast unraveling is explored by Harvard government professors, Steven Levitsky and Daniel Ziblatt (2018), in their riveting book, How Democracies Die. Just when we need all hands on deck to help weather the mounting economic storms many have already jumped ship, inspired by the academic apologies for elite prejudices and prerogatives. The realms we are so blithely entering now are every bit as perilous as any confronted by Bilbo in The Hobbit. We now have our own "Smaug" (awakened dragon) in the form China to face, and we are confused as to who has the Ring of Power. What is even worse, we have cadres of economists and factions of a compliant media making most of our perils invisible. We are NOT completely unarmed, however. We do have many books like this one that seek to direct us toward the historical and political roots of our economic travails. We also have a relatively free press. Hence like "Sting" (the small elfin sword that glows blue when Orcs are near) they might warn us when we are actually surrounded by sociopaths that seek to profit from more societal disintegration. If I have merely provided such a tiny wanker-warning device, then I have done my job. It is up to you join with your neighbors to demand your rights. Despite having their origins in dark corporate board rooms, it is not too late to return various earnest Astroturf "patriot" groups to the light of Hobbithood. Just as scientists have discovered there is only one race (Sussman, 2014) class warfare should give way to the realization that there is really only one class where basic human rights and responsibilities are concerned, irrespective the presence of handfuls of extremely powerful and parasitic individuals.

If all this strikes you as the ravings of an incurable curmudgeon, please know that I was not always thus. As Napoleon once remarked, "If you want to understand a man, you must understand the world when he was 20". In my defense I would point out that I grew up in nearest thing to a classless society (if one were male and white of course) we have had since we left our ancient hunter-gatherer tribes behind. And, even basic "civil rights" for all were on the upswing. Until we got lost in the war in Vietnam, we also had a "War on Poverty". Yet unlike Trump supporters, I don't believe we can return to this halcyon period, and even if we could, he is NOT going to take us there. But it is still worth pointing out that when I was a child the top tax rate was 91% (and the economy was booming). In my youth, we also had presidents and legislators actively fighting against oligarchic forces. My early optimism regarding economic fairness has obviously taken a beating during my later adulthood. Like Johnson's Great Society was side tracked by ballooning military budgets, Trump's canard of re-making of America will soon succumb to his huge tax cuts for the rich and his wacko trade and foreign policies.

Trumps focus is mostly on the top 1%, with merely an extremely faint mist for the trickling-down to the deteriorating middle class. His only slightly disguised elite agenda is expressly designed to further hobble government (except defense and bank bail outs, of course), and enhance the hue and cry for further reductions in social programs (including dramatic cuts to Social Security and Medicare). For example, huge breaks are given to specific elite groups such as those who own lots of real estate, as well as a continuation of the infamous hedge fund "pass throughs". Even assuming Trump's cuts produce a modicum of growth, they will still add an additional 2 Trillion to the National Debt of nearly 23 trillion (well over a 100% of the GDP).

An especially feudal feature of late is the elimination of the "inheritance tax" as it further enshrines the new aristocracy. It was already adjusted to only apply to those with more than 2 million to pass on to their heirs. William Gates Sr. (Bill of Microsoft's dad) once observed that doing away with the inheritance tax completely was like guaranteeing the grandsons of former Olympians a place on the future team, irrespective of their actual athleticism. Can you imagine Bill's performance in any event you might choose? The myth that accumulated wealth will "trickle down" down to masses, simply does not work in a fake financialized world. It should be noted that the preponderance of empirical evidence maintains that "trickle-down" has almost NEVER worked (see, Tcherneva, 2015), particularly in our epoch where the rising tide only lifts the yachts.

Meanwhile, the flow of upward mobility, the essence of the "American Dream", has slowed to barely a drip (see, Chetty, et. al., 2017) and trickle-up does not work either. As comedian George Carlin suggested, "It is called the American Dream, because you have to be asleep to see it". So wake up! A recent study by the OECD, entitled The Broken Elevator, (OECD, 2018) produced some startling facts. For example, in the UK it could take nearly 5 generations for a poor family to raise itself to the national average annual income (27,000 pounds), in other words, never. These types of studies once carried the Pelerin cool aid of the increased austerity solution to economic distress, but now they are beginning to recognize their error.

Just 4 decades ago, despite being low born and lacking an Ivey League pedigree, I moved rapidly into a career full of amazing opportunities and more than ample remuneration (although less than an auto assembly line worker when I taught at the U of Mich.). I could pretty much go anywhere my acquired skills and hard work would take me. In fact doors were open to me that my own ideological biases and naiveté would not allow me to enter. Now I see barriers going up everywhere, and cliques that had been submerged resurfacing. Moreover, entirely new groups are marking their turf and proclaiming their own privileges. But the greatest pile of indulgences and seats at special tables are reserved for the summit predators, and now unabashedly so.

BRINGING BANKING OUT OF THE DARKNESS

As suggested above, American history is heavily preoccupied with a struggle with Money & Banking for the control of commerce. Much of the journey we've been on as a country began when a small group of radicals, called the Sons of Liberty, tossed a ship load of tea into Boston Harbor in 1773. After years of relative self-government, a period referred to as "salutary neglect" by famed Irish statesman, Edmund Burke (also called "Benign Neglect" in our history texts) all attempts by the Crown and its cronies to reassert its control were seen as oppressive, especially when the power to tax was in the hands of corporate cartels, such as the British East India. However, following the real Tea Party, agents of the crown moved more expeditiously, crippling all commerce and ending local government across Massachusetts via what we call the "Intolerable Acts" in 1774. These punitive measures that amounted to marshal law (including the forced billet of troops, and immunity for brutal administrators) were focused upon Boston. But, since Boston was a hub of commerce, these punishments spilled over into other regions and colonies. They are often cited as the primary source of the American Revolution. However, it was also the earlier attempts to completely control the currency and exchange with acts in 1751, 1764, and 1773 that really necessitated independence. It is also noteworthy that the British bankers quickly re-established most of their grip on financial fate of the former colonies soon after the revolution (and we have a Tony winning Broadway musical to memorialize it). The average American has had a dim (if often dim-witted) view of the banking forces ever since. This deep seeded antagonism is hardly undeserved. Money & Banking has always favored the already rich, and is a highly criminogenic ecosystem. It is now apparent that even when regulated it is often little more than legalized fraud. Furthermore, it is a system which benefits from monumental tax payer backstopping and is incentivized toward massive levels of speculation and reckless risk taking. Coupled with near complete immunity from criminal prosecution for banking executives and you have a pretty toxic industry. Yet more often than not we accept a certain level of lawlessness for sake of gravely overstated notions of mediation, money management, and "market making", when actual processes of authentic price discovery are few and far between.

This elaborate mythology allowed all manner of malfeasance, such as controlling entire industries via trusts, rigging LIBOR (the interbank interest rate), laundering huge sums of money, etc. Yet it also facilitated the construction of a galactic time machine that routinely robs from the future to subsidize asset stripping and rent extraction in the present. It is noteworthy that nearly "zero interest rate policies" (ZIRP) and exceedingly easy credit let zombie firms and dying unicorns crowd the landscape alongside insolvent banks, denying the restorative force of "creative destruction". Instead of pursuing a productive economy, we have eaten our seed corn, and have added our young to the menu. Plus, the more cannibalistic features of banking and finance have been greatly amplified through carefully designed deregulation, which is often mutually causal with stagnation. Deregulation, in particular, is prelude to further induced crises, setting the stage for more rounds of bail outs and "bail ins" (conversion and/or confiscation of deposits as in Cyprus). One sign of the times is the arrival in the US of the largely failed European strategy of allowing banks to sell "CoCos" (contingent convertible bonds) and substitute these instruments in lieu of reserve requirements. Certain institutional investors have gone cuckoo for CoCos, despite very modest yields and weak coupons. They obviously know something we don't. While they were still being debated, an elaborate and critical JFK School working paper (Greene, 2016) defined them as "regulatory capital instruments that, upon certain trigger events, automatically convert to common equity", readymade for write downs if required. They also provide an early warning signal for the big bonds holders to bail.

As suggested above, as long as we still have some semblance of democratic processes, citizens should attempt to wrench away portions of elite power embedded in the systems of finance and banking. Consider the recent example of the Swiss Vollgeld (sovereign money) referendum. The mere fact that the initiative made it to the point of a national vote in center of global banking is compelling. Of course, a central bank blitzkrieg that characterized the new public money system as "worse than Bitcoin", carried the day. One can only hope that the ultimate fate of private viz-a-viz public money creation will come up again and soon.

Another cascade of failing banks is completely predictable in the relatively near future via the "systemic risk" assessments of complexity models (see, Haldane & May, 2010; also note, Sergueiva, 2013). Complexity scientists (Battiston, et. al., 2016) have even made a number of regulatory recommendations, including a "dashboard" of complexity indicators for predicting the unfolding of dangerous nonlinear dynamics; however, they conclude that "these effects are unlikely to be routinely considered anytime soon (p. 818)." Meanwhile, the magic money tree is rotting from the roots, its trunk and branches are full of fraud and it canopy is highly leveraged asset bubbles. We need to be fully prepared with serious reforms on hand before the next crisis hits.

REINING-IN RAUCOUS RENTIERS AND ROVING BANDITS

We need to further retard our slow motion economic train wreck. We can remove a few of the cars carrying highly explosive cargo (like derivatives). When it ultimately derails we can limit the causalities by keeping them far from the town of the real economy. The general depositors and tax payers should never be forced to underwrite the gamblers. Once all the fire walls are resurrected and reinforced, we need to address the many sources of unearned wealth (rents) and tax them, rather than lowly wages. For example, even a modest "financial transaction tax" (see, Wilmott, 2017) would discourage speculators, stabilize markets, as well as raise vital revenues. It would also send a signal that we are no longer going to pander so overwhelmingly to forces of money. Rents were once the prerogative of titled lords, and could be tolerated as long they fulfilled their obligations to their tenants (protecting them from marauders). Now our rulers are the marauders. As Schumpeter (1942) predicted we have been displacing our most productive entrepreneurs with unremorseful rentiers. Even Silicon Valley, once our great engine of innovation, is now a rat's nest of neurotic nerds, hell-bent on militarism, monopoly, and even monarchy.

Obviously corporations provide goods and services, yet they also extract rents and privileges from the public patrimony in the form of the internet and information infrastructure as well as the access to natural resources from public lands and the socialization of negative externalities (e.g., environmental pollution) and financial loses. Moreover, many firms are merely platforms for financial manipulation. The rise of the Pelerin inspired "shareholder primacy" model of business management (see;

Daneke and Sager, 2015), led corporations to cannibalize themselves. Asset stripping and debt loading turn many a distinguished firm into an empty shell. Re-investments in research and development are increasingly rare, at the very time that government research budgets, except for weapons, have dramatically declined. Firms now regularly borrow to pay dividends, as well as buy back their own stock (to pump up the price and create the illusion of performance). Rather than building better products, they purchase politicians who create laws that increase barriers to entry and curtail competition in their industries.

The social impacts of hyper-financialization are manifold and devastating to say the least. Near ZIRP arrangements punish savers (including pensioners). The Fed purchasing tons (nearly 16 trillion dollars) of toxic paper (QE) burdens the future generations with a sea of public debt and dramatically reduced expectations. These devices retard capital reallocation and exacerbate stagnation. Plus, they inflate increasingly fragile bubbles and fuel further massive inequality. Major cross sectional studies in rich nations (such as, Pickett & Wilkinson, 2007) also explore deep psychological consequences. They describe how inequality increases childhood stress and destroys trust in society. In sum, elite financial policy decisions readily translate into further alienation and anomie.

In the final section of his opus, *A General Theory of Employment, Interest and Money* (1936, p. 376), John Maynard Keynes contended that a progressive political economy would gradually "euthanize the rentiers". That is, it would crowd out unproductive wealth creation of the "functionless investor class". Instead, of course, it is they that euthanized the rest of us. Financialization which allows wealth to begat greater wealth, without production, is the ultimate revenge of the rentiers. It is, however, a pyrrhic victory if it destroys the functioning of real economy in process. Famed chronicler of the rent-seeking society Mancur Olson was to some the Thurston Veblen of our time, as they were both products of the prairies, and they were fond of history and anthropology. Plus, they both explained how "vested interests" eat away at the marrow of society. Olson (1982), in his The Rise and Decline of Nations, extends his seminal insights into special interest group dynamics *The Logic of Collective Action* (1965) to explore how they gum up the works of nation states. He suggests how these micro processes breed a displacement and derangement of institutions, and in turn, "decreased growth, fueled stagflation, increased social rigidities", and ultimately produced dramatic decline.

In his final and most prescient book (published posthumously) *Power and Prosperity: Outgrowing Communist and Capitalist Dictatorships* (2000), Olson provides a simple yet powerful explanation of why, aside from natural endowments, certain nations prosper and others do not. Stated simply, nations prosper when their rulers and the ruled have an "encompassing interest" in the long term economic well-being of the system. That interest usually takes the form of enforcing contracts and property rights, yet also punishing violations of exchange rules, as well as periodic enhancements to infrastructure, safe guarding of the commons, and providing compensatory opportunities. These benevolent oligarchs he labels "stationary bandits". Unfortunately, in a globalized economy (with free capital flows), "roving bandits" may have again become the norm. Plus, once a leader senses his tenure might be short, s/he intensifies his/her squirreling away piles of cash from the expropriation of public resources, and becomes a willing partner with neo-colonial pillaging. Congolese semi-stationary bandit, Mobuto Sese Seko, once warned his fellow dictators to NOT build roads, as opposing forces would merely use them for attacks. Our first world bandits are only slightly more subtle, and when things go off the rails they tend to abandon much of their subtlety. When kleptocrats fail to maintain the "mandate of heaven" via fake economic growth, they seek to shore-up their power through a combination of real and imaginary external threats, domestic terror, and/or a cult of personality. Sound like anyone you know? What is so curious about US based global rovers is that while owing little special allegiance to the nation that made them, they still feel entitled to the have the US Military provide the muscle for their international misadventures, and have the US Treasury underwrite their bad judgments. Removing this socialism for rich should concern us much more than joining in on the increasing attacks upon Social Security and Medicare that we Hobbits have paid for and to which we are actually "entitled".

A society run by and for the benefit of the rentiers is a direct throwback to a feudal age. Fortified by mainstream economics and its fellow travelers (Neocons, Randians, Straussians, and Nietzscheans) rent-seekers were allowed to obliterate the reality of dispossession and economic displacement. Elites have used their unparalleled political power to alter institutional safeguards (from progressive taxation and unionization to financial and environmental regulation) and push the planet to the brink of another Dark Age. When confronted on these matters they retrench into further feudalism and fascism contending that the democracy, which they have perverted, no longer works. As climate change and resource wars create a vast diaspora of dispossessed denizens, the feudal few and fearful many will demand more totalitarian systems.

In the meantime, increasing inequality, feeds further financialization, diverting increasing amounts wealth to unproductive rent-seeking. People with money realize they can make more a lot more money with little of the risk of potentially productive investments. This vicious cycle is reinforced by the return of vast inherited fortunes. In our new caste system, meaningful employment for the masses and upward mobility become a distant memory.

As Stanford Classics Professor and Fellow in Human Biology, Walter Scheidel (2017) maintains, inequality of the sort we're currently experiencing nearly always results in "violent revolution". What group of citizens is better armed (half the guns on the planet), geographically resourced, and sufficiently narcissistically enraged to pursue another protracted civil war than Americans? Unless we begin immediately to address the various issues discussed above (from peak carbon to peak debt and peak work to peak democracy) it is hard to imagine how we will avoid a future that makes the French Revolution look like a child's birthday party (with scarier clowns). It is worth noting that relatively few royals lost their heads to the guillotine (it was mostly neighbor turning on neighbor); maybe that is what our mega-rentiers are counting on. After all they can merely float away on their private island estates. Their accelerating kleptocracy might merely be final preparations. From a purely practical as well as moral perspective, however, armed insurrection serves NO one's interest. Once violent rebellion begins it will be difficult to contain, and unintended consequences will explode. Do we really want to replicate Afghanistan in the hills and hollows of America? Even isolated violence would hasten the totality of totalitarianism. None of us, including the ultra-rich, should want any version of this future.

BE THE COUNTERVAILANCE

Much of this impending dystopia stems from the fact that the discipline entrusted to address economic issues is hopelessly riddled with deeply deceptive ideological preoccupations. How does one do productive political economy, when mainstream scholars maintains that is does not exist? By excluding political power from their models, they have merely made it more powerful. But the accumulation of unassailable monopoly power over societal as well as economic processes are so completely incongruous with their public pronouncements that it is difficult to accept it was merely an intellectual accident. While cultural devolution was obviously at work, human volition also played a decisive role, and we need to recognize the inherent results of a long and elaborate ideological project. Despite their decided lack of ecological awareness, economists have convinced most of us that their thoroughly artificial world is some type of inexorable natural phenomena to which we should never tamper. By contrast, Karl Polanyi (1944; also note: Block & Summers, 2014) traces the conjuring and institutional "embedding" of this humanity alienating artifice. Plus, he predicted that the "market society" would eventually yield disruptive outcomes. His famed "double movement" illustrates the inherent conflict between capitalism and democracy. Like all "utopian myths", the market would eventually render dystopian machinations, unless democratic institutions accomplish the "Great Transformation" to a constrained and shared capitalism. For Polanyi the key is the maintenance of diverse and ground-up organizational possibilities (such as unions, guilds, and cooperatives, as well as widespread civic engagement) rather than top-down socialism. Published in the same year, his neglected observations are actually much more relevant than von Hayek's popular, *Road to Serfdom*, especially in light of the rise to power of neofeudalism. Market mechanisms obviously have a major role to play (particularly in enhancing product and process efficiencies), but by exalting them as the "end of history" captured mainstream economics has become little more than a doomsday cult.

To his credit, perhaps, President Trump does not set much stock in the economics profession. He is a paradigm case "a little bit knowledge being a very dangerous thing" and that the small smattering of economics in the typical MBA program is like giving a loaded handgun to a small child. He also presents a clearer and present danger in his attachment to the resource, military and industrial agenda of the bygone era. However, his ardor for thuggish oligarchs and his care and feeding of rentiers more generally may prove his undoing. Trump was never nearly wealthy nor respectable enough to be a full-fledged Masturbator of the Universe, he is merely their semi-compliant lackey. But he is also extremely loose cannon. Who knows how long real elites will tolerate his dangerous buffoonery. He provides an ideal opportunity to rekindle the public discussions of the Imperial Presidency (see, Schlesinger. 1973) that followed Viet Nam and Watergate. Poor Jimmy Carter could barely take a piss without permission. Yet with Reagan as figurehead emperor, the imperium came roaring back. His praetorians completely gutted the notion of "neutral competence" in the permanent government and engaged in his secret wars, "guns for hostages", and the CIA drug trade, etc. But even the "Gipper" had to rely upon subterfuge and the huge supply of charisma. Lacking that charisma, Bush senior had to beg on behalf of the "New World Order", as well as trick Saddam Hussein into invading Kuwait. Clinton was a hot mess, and when not preoccupied with scandal, spent a good deal of time pandering to global banking elites and dismantling the welfare state. Following the coup d'état (with gangs of goons lead by Brett Kavanaugh stopping the recount in Florida) that brought us the clan idiot "W", Dick Cheney (who actually ran things) kept crying about restoring executive power (as if 9/11 was insufficient to do the trick). Obama, like Carter, was never really allowed to be president except when he chose to wax warlike. Plus like Clinton, Obama gave away the store to the banks, as well as taking care of health care cartel. Now that we have another Republican (or he has us) the emperor is back in business, yet the empire is more tattered than his hairdo. Trump is claiming powers that the constitution never imaged, and violating rules (e.g., foreign influence and the emoluments clause, etc.) with impunity. Our service men and women are in harm's way across the planet, yet the last actually officially declared war was WWII. If we don't move forcefully to reassert limits, a constitutional crisis will be the least of our worries. The temptation to "wag the dog" into global conflagration is intense.

The real beauty, if any, of the Trump presidency is that he is so ham handed in his kleptocratic aspirations. Take for example how privatization of the public patrimony is the hallmark of his infrastructure renewal scam. With Trump, at least what you see is literally what you get. A century of hide and seek neofeudal dispossession is pretty much over now. The evil wizards are now out of the bag, so-to-speak. We are far past due in realizing our retrospective Hobbithood. We need to band together and insulate ourselves from their macro machinations as best we can. We must also be persistent, yet peaceful in our resistance to fascism. We must strengthen, not abandon the constitutional tools our Founding Father so prudently provided. The Arab Winter provides a powerful cautionary tale, worth reiterating here. It will NOT do for the US to fall into the third world shuffle of sporadically replacing one set of repressive fanatics with another, or always having a new batch of kleptocrats and kakistocrats waiting for their turn to plunder.

The two towers of advanced barbarism (feudalism and fascism) are ever present now, but we should be able to get them to retreat into the background again, now that they have unmasked themselves. Some of them did us a great service lately by sharing their vicious plans so openly. Others only materialize when they need a bailout. If you made it this far in the book you probably won't even need a glowing sword to know them when you see them on your TV (or cell phone) talking out of both sides of the mouth. Even if our empire is in decline, our great experiment with self-government is not over by a long short. The US political system survived a brutal civil war and has sustained a dynamic economy through many monumental trials. We will NOT restore our entrepreneurially based economy by further empowering oligarchic kleptocrats, however. If we need freer markets, then we should enforce and fortify existing antitrust laws. When someone tells you they need additional money and powers to prevent terrorist attacks ask them what they did with the ½ billion you gave them yesterday (and get a detailed accounting).

Remember FEAR is the greatest tool of the tyrant. Practically speaking you have more to fear from your own government than from most terrorist groups. We need to do the calculations, and figure out how much of our liberty we are willing to sacrifice. Recall Benjamin Franklin is credited with having said that "those who would give up essential liberty to purchase a little temporary safety deserve neither liberty nor safety". In Canada, for example, you are 10 times more likely to be killed by a moose than a terrorist. I would add that if you are killed by a moose that you most likely deserved it, but that is beside the point. I have not noticed the Canadian's rushing off to eradicate these compelling creatures (however insect infestations precipitated by climate change might) or continuously monitoring all of their citizens to ensure against close encounters. Okay, it is a silly example, but you get the point. The maintenance of constant threat has been well cultivated strategy of most kings, priests, and their bankers for centuries and modern day fascists are especially adept. We need to look very carefully at those with clear incentives to manufacture a less peaceful and more fearful world. We also need to recognize by the mere fact that they still need to bamboozle us into a militarized society means that their power, which seems so overwhelming, is actually quite ephemeral.

The last great American political economist, John Kenneth Galbraith (1952), suggested that Capitalism only works its magic when there is "countervailing power" (i.e., a free press, strong labor unions, consumer and environmental protections, civilian checks on the military, respect for the rule of law, as well as a real separation of powers in government). The constitutional theories we inherited from Medieval England embodied this notion of "countervailence" (see, Gordon, 1999). Multiple centers of power go well beyond the twiddle dee/twiddle dum of our two prevailing political parties, and it requires multiple forms of civic engagement. Neofeudal economists have sought to belittle all these forms of social organization with their beggar-thy-neighbor ideology. By pretending to ignore POWER, economists have awarded it in abundance to their friends in high places. As Bertrand Russell (1938) pointed out.

> The actual economic power possessed by an individual or a group depends upon military strength and influence through propaganda quite as much as upon factors usually considered in economics. Economics as a separate science is unrealistic and misleading if taken as a guide in practice. It is one element—a very important element, it is true—in a wider study, the science of power (p.135).

If Capitalism, let alone democracy, is to survive, we must seek to restore some semblance of balance. "We the people" are the greatest countervailing force. Our constitutional republic was specifically designed to limit the power of state as well as corporations, and we need to relearn how to use it again (including the brakes on mob rule). We must curb the power and reduce the rewards to roving bandits (global wankers) and inspire our stationary bandits to make the necessary investments in the health, education, and infrastructure as well as alternative energy regimes. Moreover, we need them to begin to design initiatives that flesh out our "economic bill of rights". Beyond medical care for all, we need to consider a broader range of policies to reduce the mounting stress on our precarious work force, including enhancing our labor relations laws in the wake of our anti-union epoch. If defense spending is still justified as a jobs program, we must consider alternatives where we get more societal "bang for our bucks". Real security depends upon a strong domestic, yet low growth economy. We could send tens of thousands to college as well as provide prenatal care for all low income mothers for less the cost of building and deploying another outdated aircraft carrier group. The Chinese are already deploying hypersonic (mach-10) "carrier killers" to defeat their 3-5 defenses.

UNHOBBLING US HOBBITS

In their mighty tome, *Why Nations Fail*, MIT and Harvard economic development scholars, Daron Acemoglu and James A. Robinson (2012) provide a synoptic historical analysis regarding the importance of institutions over geography and nearly everything else. Moreover, they maintain that prosperity is a matter of an "inclusive" political economy displacing an "extractive" one. When it comes to North America they tell harrowing tales of failed colonies (including cannibalism). Only after the Virginia Company spent 12 years trying to follow the Spanish extractive model with numerous failed attempts at enslaving their own colonists as well as the indigenous inhabitants did they reluctantly initiate, in 1618, a new strategy (called the Headright System). It gave their settlers (including the indentured) a stake in the success of the enterprise. It included their own lands and seats in a general assembly (for virtually all adult males), and the rest is history. But the lesson now appears to have been mostly lost as we rush headlong toward becoming just another repressive banana republic.

What I find disheartening are the many Post Millennials that seem quite reconciled to their new indentured status and suspended adolescence. They may never vote or own a home or buy a new car. They will marry later (if at all) and they are being pre-programmed to willingly wander from one slave market to the next in the new feudal economy. They are not merely the dispossessed; they are completely estranged from life as we know it. 50% of adult males 18 to 35 live with their parents. They are told that they merely have to use the fake freedom of the gig economy (and all their non-existent free time) to start ventures and end up as the next Mark Zuckerberg. God help if they did.

More troubling yet, is that a significant portion of the existing Zuckerbergs are beginning to believe their own propaganda. Those in the "Galt Gulches" believe that they are the victims of some Randian passion play. Hence, many a soulless sociopath has come believe that now, of all times, it is appropriate for them to extend their overwhelming advantage. They believe they can with impunity "grind the faces of the poor". That Lasch (1994) posthumously predicted this "revolt of elites" does not make it any less revolting or the "betrayal of democracy" any less treacherous. His criticism of "social divisions", the degradation of "public discourse" and the self-imposed "estrangement" of elites from the "common life" could have been written last week. It is absolutely astonishing that those who have rigged and ravaged our system for decades are now bugging out on the check, which is only chump change to them. In the overall scheme of things the amount of power and purse they must share is miniscule in comparison to the costs of maintaining their dystopian trajectory. As Douglas Rushkoff (2018) of "Team Human" fame, maintains, a number of elites are throwing in the towel. "For all their wealth and power, they don't believe they can affect the future". Some of the biggest rats have already abandoned the sinking ship, while there is still time to man the pumps. Yes, I agree with Rushkoff that it is not too late "to fix the future" considerably.

We humble, yet healthy self-regarding (as well as other-regarding) Hobbits have nothing in our repertoire of experience that allows us to idly accept the mounting level of economic injustice and political alienation. Behavioral economists are already well aware that a "sense of fairness" is a powerful human trait that allows us to reject perverse economic rationality (see, Kahneman, et. al., 1986). Accepting that we are Hobbits, does not mean we are irrelevant. Like the original indentured settlers of American we need to demand our stake in the system. We must use what is left of our democracy to reconnect the historical fibers of an inclusive economy.

Irrespective of who is running the circus we Hobbits can begin preparing for the end of the current energy epoch. We can demonstrate with our big hairy feet what a smaller carbon footprint looks like. Some excellent studies have applied a complex systems perspective (from diverse disciplines) to energy transitions (e.g., Labanca, 2017), and a few have even raised the issue of institutional ingredients (e.g., Koster, 2013) as well as power and politics (e.g., Moore, 2015). Populist tyrants (with all the magical answers) wedded to a fossil-fueled future need to be peacefully pushed aside. A Frodonomics practitioner would appreciate that the best answers begin at the bottom with diverse individuals and come out in the wash of institutional interactions and improvements. And, a complexity scholar can use computer simulations to experiment with generations of "artificial adaptive agents" and legions institutional options in an afternoon.

During the past few decades, mainstream economists presided over the pissing away one of the most universally prosperous economies "the world as even known" (as Trump would say). They also facilitated the mobilization of latent feudalism at the very time that fiat money and world oil/military machinations were accelerating. They skillfully diverted attention from all the financial skullduggery (and skullbuggery) by filling our heads with free market sugar plum fairies. Their underlying worldview was Hobbes's "war of all against all" (note, Kavka, 1983). By design they sought dissemble and disintegrate. Ultimately, Hobbes (1655) boils down to a Hobson's choice of chaos or leviathan. Our democratic experiment begs to differ, and we Hobbits can prove it. In clear contradistinction, the ultimate message of the LOTR Saga (and real anthological studies) is that only when most creatures reject isolation and atomization and seek to and honor their alliances and common aspirations do they prevail over the forces of societal destruction. You might well object, and contend that economic theory, even when constructive and responsible, cannot matter that much. And you would be mostly correct. However, the power of a small cult bound by a handful of extremely inaccurate and perverse ideas can no longer be ignored. As Lord Keynes reminded us "practical men" and women are usually "the slaves of some defunct economist". Worse yet, "madmen in authority, who hear voices in the air, are distilling their frenzy from some academic scribbler of a few years back".

The ideology of atomization have been allowed to breed an increasingly dysfunctional economy. From 1973 to 2016 US productivity rose nearly 75%, and what was the average working person's share? It was zilch, nada, not a bloody dime. In the same period the bestselling pick-up (the Ford F-150) went from 3,500 to nearly 40,000 dollars for a fully equipped version, and when financed it is much more. Throw in a few title loans and you have the cost of a small house. Of course it would hardly buy a tool shed in several of the nation's more bubblicious housing markets (SF, Seattle, etc.). The debt slavery system is far more subtle and less devastating than the legacy of actual human bondage (the clear exception to the universality of post WWII prosperity), but it is still the one of saddest excuses for constructive economy one could possibly imagine. Furthermore, the fact that the purveyors of Sauronomics expend so much effort to keep us in the dark about the more dysfunctional dimensions of our economic system speaks volumes regarding their intellectual dishonesty.

A Frodonomics that seeks to put society back into economics is not as hopeless as it seems. While it appears at present that only the sociopathic prevail, that is NOT human evolution, it is parasitic annihilation. As Adam Smith recognized, without our sense of compassion, community, and cooperation our economy would barely function. If the "affairs of the household" (laundering clothes as well as money) were limited to radical self-interest and never became interwoven with our sentimentalities and communal aspirations we'd probably have gone extinct long ago. As leading human rights expert and Yale professor of law and history, Samuel Moyn (2018) observes without economic rights, all human rights erode overtime. He contends that widespread economic inequality inevitably fuels further repression.

It is high time to make more explicit that which has been implicit in the notion of the SOCIAL CONTRACT debated in philosophy since the ancients and a pillar of the Enlightenment (see, Barker, 1960). Business ethics professors, a handful of corporate executives, and numerous corporate charters continue to allude to the existence of "corporate social responsibility" (CSR). But most business professionals accept Pelerin precepts on the matter (see, Friedman, 1970); in essence, that the there is no such responsibility. At best investments in CSR are mere PR and window dressing. Even if most corporations accepted a broader "stakeholder's view", we would still be a far cry from the practical provisions envisioned by the likes of FDR and Rawls.

The fact that the CEO is paid 900 times their average Wal-Mart worker is not offset by the fact that their HR department helps their Halflings apply for food stamps (now the SNAP program) and other diminished welfare state supplements. Neither should this vast divide be ignored merely because Wal-Mart is now losing ground to Amazon. Of the 10 richest people in America, 3 are the children of Wal-Mart founder, Sam Walton. Allowed to tack his name up on a Woolworths in a tiny Arkansas town, he developed a business model that helped destroy 1000s of the community-based economies across the US. He also led the charge to offshore US manufacturing via his leverage over suppliers. Meanwhile abandoned Wal-Marts (built and maintained by public funds) across the US are converted into mega churches and detention centers. The millions in art given by the Walton daughter to a museum in Little Rock does remotely equate with these destructive consequences.

Since things like community cohesion have no value in Sauronomics, it is not surprising that we are so easily mistaken for mindless Orcs. Yet we still require more brain-washing to believe that cheap trinkets and fake Facebook friends are all we would ever need. Our Hobbit selves know we will need real friends and real community values if we are to face the mega transitions ahead without giving up the remaining remnants of our self-respect to our feudal lords. It is worth repeating that despite their false bravado most of them are actually quite insecure and they require our constant re-affirmation. We would do well to make them actually earn it.

Teachers once had well earned respect (but were rarely well paid). Now, however, they have been thoroughly besmirched by the ideological mud thrown on all public employees by the weaponized minions of the Pelerins. Yet, some are standing up for the nobility of their Hobbithood against ridiculous budget cuts amid public funding for exclusionary (racist and religious) "voucher programs" and/or "charter schools". Miraculously it seems to be working.

Ultimately we will need to move the discussion well beyond a fragile truce with our "stationary bandits" over the lightly increased share of opportunity to the ponderous pachyderm in room, our PONZI PLATFORM economy. The necessity of perpetual financial growth on a finite planet is our core problem and it is the root of much evil, not to mention medieval. It facilitates the vast fabricated wealth that makes our rentiers increasingly recalcitrant. Insane and wildly manipulated stock valuations notwithstanding, finance has made many firms into reckless bets on an inordinately overabundant future. Less than 5% of the wealth currently claimed by investors is based upon present performance. It depends upon a quadrupling of global output in the next half century. Unfortunately this level of peace and prosperity is highly unlikely given dwindling resources and climate issues as well as the associated mass migrations. It was the imperiling of the energy paradigm that engendered the increased manufacture of fake wealth in the first place.

The great debt pyramid is a self-immolation machine. Debt deflation is met with demands for increased austerity and privatization, and the resulting monopolies over the public patrimony increases inflation in basic services amid wage stagnation and declining consumer protections. STAGFLATION sets in as a permanent feature. When central banking policies can inflate existing assets into the stratosphere, little traditional "earned" wealth opportunities can compete. What was once overhead has become overhang, and now is a drag on the entire system. Debt itself becomes the primary asset class and usurious interest and fees become the new RENT, crowding out most conventionally earned wealth and socially viable production. Breaking this vicious cycle is made much more difficult given the premier political status of the FIRE sector. Our own convoluted monetary system makes the specious species (metallically debased coins) of the declining Roman Empire look like diamonds.

Before our military is called upon to cross the Rubicon, our empire needs be allowed to unwind itself in a much more humble and realistic fashion. This does not mean that we'll never get embroiled in global "police actions", but our partially conscript armies and renewed legislative involvement might make them open to more serious deliberation. Our global leadership will still be needed, but only if we provide a respectable role model, rather than a wounded and rampaging bull or a sanctimonious prig. Self-defeating financialization is symptomatic of our weakening grip on global systems. Continued financialization, feudalism, and fascism, as well as environmental devastation await us either way, but it will be an exceedingly short trip if remain wallowing in past glories.

We desperately need new leadership. Aside from purchasing power of dark money, our methods for choosing our leaders are tragically comical. You do realize there is very little reality in Reality TV, don't you? With nearly everyone having a huge digital footprint, it should be possible to get clever hackers to give us a better glimpse of their character flaws. We should require candidates provide their sociopathy scores, if we can't hack them. After all Wall Street firms already use various standardized tests in reverse to make sure that certain hires have lower empathy (seriously). Most candidates would be at least partial narcissists, but we might be able to filter out a few pure psychopaths from the pool. While perhaps more than a bit pie in the sky, it certainly worth discussing some type countervailence to prevailing spectacle of zealots in tiny states sorting the maniacs for us. However, we will still have to greatly strengthen our constitutional safeguards, in case another Trump or other goblins escape our digital dragnet. Actually even a tiny bit of truth (if truth still matters) regarding his extremely corrupt business practices should have placed into the reject pile well before the primaries, even if he were not deeply connected to various Urak-hai and Dark Wizards (mobsters and foreign oligarchs). As for his extramarital adventures and misogynistic attitudes, I not sure that these do not endear him to his many white male victimhoodnics. At any rate a tad more analysis of candidates couldn't hurt. Moreover, in the process we might come to realize that NO lone human being (even an Aragorn), aided by huge amounts of AI and a cabinet full real Nobel laureates (or Elves) can pilot our imperial barge through the turbulent waters directly ahead. Armies of helpful Hobbits with a clear stake in the system will also be required.

We Halflings need to step up and illustrate that we are not half-hearted. We need to let our primitive "habits of the heart" serve as the tiny *Light of Eärendil* amidst the rapidly encroaching darkness. The positive externalities of functioning communities need to be internalized in policy, as well as markets. Ringfences are merely a stop gap measures, we must move on to rebuild broader institutional safeguards against the acquisition of limitless power for the very few. Obviously this will be no mean feat, but it certainly worth the bother. Besides what better have you to do? Watch where you place your big hairy feet, our fake economy is thick with miasmic marsh lands, and there are roving Nazgûl (dark riders) and even more ghostly and ghastly gestapo are lurking in the shadows. But like Voldemort in the early Harry Porter episodes, they are not yet fully materialized. So let us get at them before they gather much more momentum. No amount of orchestrated insecurity should lead us to sacrifice our civil liberties, nor make us abandon our democracy. All the platitudes on the planet, however, will not remotely prepare us for the perils we'll confront, so it is probably time for me to stop. We are in for a very bumpy ride, so hold on to your little Hobbit haunches (as well as hunches). It will be the greatest of adventures, one to proudly tell your grandchildren about as they deliver you up for processing at the biodiesel plant.

REFERENCES

Abel, N., D. Cummings, and J. Anderies (2006). Collapse and reorganization in socio-ecological systems, Ecology and Society, 11(1): 17.

Acemoglu, D. and J. Robinson (2012). Why Nations Fail: The Origins of Power, Prosperity, and Poverty. New York: Crown.

Adams, J. (1765). A Dissertation on Canon and Feudal Laws. 21 (4). https://founders.archives.gov/documents/Adams/06-01-02-0052-0007

Adams, M. (2015). Land: A New Paradigm for a Thriving World. Berkeley: North Atlantic Books.

ADL. (2018) When Woman are the enemy: The Intersection of Misogyny and white supremacy; New York: The anti-defamation League.

Adler, P. and S. Kwon (2002). Social capital: Prospects for a new concept. Academy of Management, 27 (1): 17-40.

Adorno, T.W., Frenkel-Brunswik, E, Levinson, D. & N. Sandord (1950). The Authoritarian Personality. New York: Harper Brothers.

Akerlof, G. & P. Romer (1993). Looting: The economic underworld of bankruptcy for profit. Brookings Papers on Economic Activity (2):1-73.

Alexander, J.M. (2000). Evolutionary explanations of distributive justice, Philosophy of Science 67(4): 490-516.

Alston, P. (2017) Press Conference Held Dec. 15, 2017. New York: UN Commission of Human Rights.

Alt, J. (2017).Monetary mental illness. New Economics Perspectives. Dec. 3.

Alvesson, M. and H. Willmott (2012) Making Sense of Management: A Critical Introduction, 2nd Edition. London: Sage.

Ambrose, S, (1997). Citizen Soldier: The US Army from the Normandy Beaches to the Bulge. New York: Simon and Schuster.

Andelin, H. (1963). Fascinating Womanhood. Santa Barbara: Pacific Press.

Anderson, P., K. Arrow, and D. Pines Eds. (1988). The Economy as an Evolving Complex System. Denver: the Westview Press.

Arendt, H. (1951). The Origins of Totalitarianism. Cleveland: Meridian.

Arrighi, G. (1994). The Long Twentieth Century: Money, Power, and the Origins of Our Times. London: Verso.

_____ (2009). Adam Smith in Beijing: Lineages of the 21st Century: New York: Verso.

Arrighi, G. and B. Silver. (1999). Chaos and Governance in the Modern World System. Minneapolis: University of Minnesota Press.

Arrow, K., P. Dasgupta, L. Goulder, G. Daily, P. Ehrlich, G. Heal, S. Levin, K. Mäler, S. Schneider, D. Starrett, and B. Walker. (2004). Are we consuming too much? Journal of Economic Perspectives, 18 (3): 147-172.

Arthur, B. (2013). Complexity economics: A Different framework for economic thought, SFI Working Paper 2013-04-012. Santa Fe: Institute for the Study of Complexity.

Arthur B. Ed. (2014). Complexity and the Economy. New York: Oxford University Press.

Arthur, B. (2017). Where technology is taking the economy, Mckinsey Quarterly (Oct.). 1-14.

Atkinson, A, (1983). The Economics of Inequality. Oxford: Oxford University Press.

Atwood, M. (1985). The Handmaids Tale. Toronto: McClelland and Stewart.

Autor, D., D. Dorn and G. Hanson (2013). The China syndrome: Local labor effects of import competition in the United States, American Economics Review, 103(6): 2121-2168.

Baccerella, C., T. Wagner, J. Kiertzmann, and I. McCarthy. (2018). Social media? It's serious! Understanding the dark side of social media, European Management Journal, 36, 431-438

Bachelier, L. (1900/2006) Louis Bachelier's Theory of Speculation: The Origins of Modern Finance, Translation and commentary by M. Davis and A. Etheridge. Princeton: Princeton University Press.

Bachman, J. (2018). Trump made socialism great again, The Atlantic, (August, 8), ttps://www.theatlantic.com/politics/archive/2018/08/567245/.

Bakan, J. (2004). The Corporation. New York: Simon and Schuster.

Barker, E. (1960). Social Contract: Essays by Locke, Hume, and Rousseau. Oxford: Oxford University Press.

Barker, E. (1962). Aristotle the Politics. Oxford: Oxford University Press.

Barnes, P. (2003). Who Owns the Sky? Our Commons Assets and the Future of Capitalism. Washington, DC: Island Press.

Bates-Clark, J. (1908). The Distribution of Wealth: A Theory of Wages, Interest, and Profits. New York: Macmillan.

Battiston, S. D. Farmer, A. Flache, D. Garlaschelli, A. Haldane, H. Heesterbeek, C. Hommes, C. Jaeger, R. May, M. Scheffer. (2016). Complexity theory and financial regulation. Science, 351 (6275): 818-819.

Baumol, W. (1996). Entrepreneurship: Productive, unproductive, and destructive, Journal of Business Venturing 11(1): 3-22.

_____ (2004). On Entrepreneurship, growth and rent seeking: Henry George updated, American Economist 48(1): 9-16.

Beard, C. (1913). An Economic Interpretation of the Constitution of the United States. New York: Routledge.

Beer, F. (2001). Meanings of War and Peace. College Station: Texas A&M University Press 2001.

Beggs, M. (2017). The state as a creature of money, New Political Economy, 22(5): 463-477.

Bertotti, M. and G. Modanese (2016) Mathematical models for describing the effects of different tax evasion behaviors, Journal of Economic Interaction and Coordination. http://doi.org/10.1007/s11403-016-0185-9 13.

Bianchi, E. (2014). Entering adulthood in a recession tempers latent narcissism, Psychological Science (May, 8), Http://journals.sagepub.com/doi/abs/10.1177/0956797614532818

Black, F. (1970). Fundamentals of liquidity, Working Paper, Graduate School of Business, and University of Chicago (June): 1-9.

Black. F. and M. Scholes (1973).The Pricing of options and corporate liabilities, Journal of Political Economy 81 (3): 637-654.

Black, W. (2005). The Best Way to Rob a Bank is to Own One. Austin: University of Texas Press.

Block, F. and M. Somers (2014). The Power of Market Fundamentalism: Karl Polanyi's Critique. Cambridge: Harvard University Press.

Bollier, D. and Helfrich, S. Eds. (2012). The Wealth of the Commons. Boston: The Leveler Press.

Bollier, D. (2014). The commons as template for transformation. The Great Transition Initiative. Boston: TELUS Institute.

Borcherding, T.E., P. Dillon, and T. Willett (1998), Henry George: Precursor to public choice analysis, American Journal of Economics and Sociology 57 (2): 173–182.

Bowles, S. and H. Gintis (2013). A Cooperative Species: Human Reciprocity and its Evolution. Princeton: The University Press.

Boyd, R. (2014). Energy and Financial Analysis. New York: Springer.

Brandeis, L. (1914). Other People's Money and how the Banks Use It. New York: Frederick A. Stokes.

Brean, J. (2017). All hail the Godbot: In Silicon Valley artificial intelligence isn't just king, it's literally a new religion, National Post, Nov. 3.

Brooks, R. (2018). Bothersome bystanders and self-driving cars. Rodney Brooks/Robots, AI and Other stuff, BLOG, July 4th.

Brooks, R. (2016). How Everything Became War and the Military Became Everything. New York: Simon and Schuster.

Brown, E. (1974). The Tyranny of a construct: Feudalism and historians of Medieval Europe. American Historical Review, 79 (4): 1063-1088.

Brush, E., D. Krahauer, and J. Flack (2018). Conflicts of interest improve collective computation of adaptive social structures. Science Advances, 4: e160331, January, 17.

Butler, J. and A. Athanasiou 2013). Dispossession: The Performative in the Political. Cambridge, UK: Polity Press.

Butler, S. (1933). War is a Racket: Speech to the Veterans of Foreign Wars. https://www.youtube.com/watch?v=F3_EXqJ8f-0

Butler, S. (1935). War is a Racket: The Profit Motive behind Warfare. New York: Round Table Press.

Byrne, D. and G. Callaghan (2013). Complexity Theory and the Social Sciences: The State of the Art. London: Routledge, Abingdon.

Campbell, H., A. Eckerd and Y. Kim. (2015). Rethinking Environmental Justice in Sustainable Cities: Insights from Agent-Based Modeling. New York: Routledge.

Cantillon, R. (1755/2010). An Essay on Economic Theory. Auburn: The Mises Institute.

Cantoni, D, J Dittmar, and N Yuchtman (2017). Religious competition and reallocation: The Political economy of secularization in the Protestant Reformation," NBER Working Paper No. 23934.

Carlin, W. and D. Soskice (2015). Macroeconomics: Institutions, Instability, and Financial Systems. Oxford: Oxford University Press.

Carruthers, B. and A. Stinchcombe (1999). The Social structure of liquidity: Flexibility, markets, and states. Theory and Society. 28 (3): 353-382.

Carson, R. (1962). Silent Spring. New York: Houghton Mifflin.

Casti, J. (1994) Complexification: Explaining a Paradoxical World through the Science of Surprise. New York: Harper Collins.

Cerri, L. (2018). Birth of the modern corporation: From servant of the state to semi-sovereign power. American Journal of Economics and Sociology, 77(2): 239-277.

Chadburn, M. (2017). The Human cost of the ghost economy. Longreads (December). https://longreads.com/2017/12/13/

Chetty, R., D. Grusky, M. Heil, N. Hendren, R. Manduca, and J. Narang (2017). The Fading American dream: Trends in absolute income mobility since 1940, Science (346): 398-406.

Chopik, W., E. O'Brien, and S. Konrath (2017). Difference in Empathic concern and perspective taking across 63 countries, Journal of Cross-Cultural Psychology, 48 (1): 23-38.

Churchman, W. (1982). Thoughts and Wisdom. Seaside, CA. Intersystems.

Clark, W. (2005). Petrodollar Warfare: Oil, Iraq, and the Future of the Dollar. Gabriola Island, BC: New Society.

Cohen, B. (2017). The rise of alternative currencies in post-capitalism, Journal of Management Studies, 54 (5): 739-746.

Cole, J. (2018).Top 10 signs the U. S. is the most corrupt nation in the world. Informed Comment, Feb, 22. https://www.juancole.com/2018/02/nation.html.

Commager, H. S. (1958). The Constitution: Was it an economic document? American Heritage, 10(1).

Czech, B. (2009).The neoclassical production function as a relic of anti-George politics: Implications for ecological economics', Ecological Economics, 68: 2193-2197.

Daly, H. (1999). Ecological Economics and the Ecology of Economics: Essays in Criticism. New York: Edward Elgar.

Daneke, G. (1978a). The Political economy of nuclear power, Policy Studies Journal 7 (1): 84-90.

_____ (1978b). Life quality accounting and organizational change, The Bureaucrat, 12 (2): 27-35.

_____ (1981). Forecasting alternative energy futures: The case of solar energy, in Perelman, L. A. Giebelhaus, and M. Yokell Eds. Energy Transitions; Long Term Perspective. Boulder: Westview Press, for AAAS. Pp. 147-162.

_____ (1982). Towards a craft of energy policy: Constraints upon and opportunities for strategic planning in the US Department of Energy, Journal of Public Policy, 2 (3): 217-236

_____ (1984). Why Sam can't plan: Industrial policy and the perils of a non-adaptive society. Business Horizons, 27 (6): 50-56.

_____ (1989a). Beyond Schumpeter: Nonlinear economics and the evolution of the U S. innovation system, Journal of Behavioral and Experimental Economics. 27(1): 97-115.

_____ (1989b). Technological entrepreneurship as a focal point of economic development policy: A Conceptual reassessment, Policy Studies Journal, 17 (3): 643-655.

_____ (1999). Systemic Choices: Nonlinear Dynamics and Practical Management. Ann Arbor: University of Michigan Press.

Daneke, G. and A. Lawrence (1982). Life-quality accounting systems and energy transitions, In G. Daneke Ed, Energy, Economics, and the Environment: Toward a Comprehensive Perspective. Boston: Lexington Books. Pp: 69-88.

Daneke, G. and D. Lemak Eds. (1985). Regulatory Reform Reconsidered. Denver: Westview Press.

Daneke, G. and A. Sager (2015). Ghoshal's ghost: Financialization and the end of management theory, Philosophy of Management. 14(1): 29-45.

Danielsson, J. (2017). Artificial intelligence and the stability of markets, VOX, Centre of Economic Policy Research Portal (Nov. 15).

Davis, M. (1994). Empathy: A Social Psychological Approach. Denver: Westview Press.

Dayen, D. (2016). Chain of Title: How Three Ordinary Americans Uncovered Wall Street's Great Foreclosure Fraud. New York: The New Press.

_____ (2017). Special investigation: How America's biggest bank paid its fine for the 2007 Mortgage Crisis—with phony mortgages! The Nation, Oct 23.

Deffeyes, K. (2005). Beyond Oil: The View from Hubbert's Peak. New York: Hill and Wang.

Denton, S. (2012). The Plots against the President: FDR, A Nation in Crisis, and the Rise the American Right. New York: Bloomsbury.

Devega, C. (2017). Alt-right catches the knight-fever—but medieval scholars strike back. Salon, Nov. 30.

Domhoff, W. (1967). Who Rules America? New York: McGraw-Hill.

Donovan, S., D. Bradley, and J. Shimabukuro (2016). What Does the Gig Economy Mean for Workers? Washington D C.: Congressional Research Service.

Dore, R. (2007). Financialization of the global economy, Industrial and Corporate Change, 17 (6): 1097–1112.

Douthat, R. (2018). The Redistribution of sex. New York Times. (May, 2).

Dosi, G., M. Pereira, A. Roventini, and M. Virgillito (2016). The Effects of labor market reform on upon unemployment and income inequalities: An Agent-based model, Working Paper, 2016-24, Observatoire français des conjonctures économiques.

Dressel, J. and H. Farid (2018). The accuracy, fairness, and limits of predicting recidivisim. Science Advances, 4: eaao5580, January 17.

Drucker, P. (1994). The age of social transformation, Atlantic Monthly, 274(5): 53-80.

Dumas, L. (1986). The Overburdened Economy: Uncovering the Causes of Chronic Unemployment, Inflation and National Decline. Berkeley: University of California Press.

Dutia, S. (2012). Private Equity and Entrepreneurship: An Inequitable Match. Kansas City: Ewing Marion Kaufman Foundation.

Ehrenberg, R. and R Smith (1993/2018). Modern Labor Economics: Theory and Policy, 13th Edition. New York: Taylor and Francis.

Eisenhower, D. (1961). Farewell Speech to the Nation. Washington, DC: Government Printing Office.

Eisinger, J. (2017). The Chickenshit Club: Why the Justice Department Fails to Prosecute Executives. New York: Simon & Schuster.

England, C. (2018). John Dewey and Henry George: The Socialization of land as a prerequisite for a democratic public, American Journal of Economics and Sociology, 77(1): 169-200.

Epstein, G. Ed. (2005). Financialization and the World Economy. Cheltanham, UK: Elgar Press.

Epstein, J.M. and R. Axtell (1996). Growing Artificial Societies: Social Science from the Bottom-up. Cambridge, MA: MIT Press.

Evans, J. (2013). Meet the new serfs, same as the old serfs. Techno Crunch, Oct. 5.

Eubanks, V. (2017). Automating Inequality: How High-Tech Tools Profile, Police, and Punish the Poor. New York: St. Martin's Press.

Ezrachi, A, and M. Stucke (2016). Virtual Competition: The Promise and Perils of an Algorithm-Driven Economy. Cambridge, MA: Harvard University Press.

Fama, E. (1970). Efficient capital markets: A Review of theory and empirical work, Journal of Finance, 25 (3): 383-417.

Farrell, J. (2010). Community Solar Power: Opportunities and Obstacles. Minneapolis: The New Rules Project.

FDR (1944). State of the Union Message to Congress (January 11).

Fichtner, J. (2016). Perpetual decline or persistent dominance: Uncovering Anglo-America's true structural power in global finance. Review of international Studies. 43 (1): 3-28.

Financial Stability Board (2013). Global Shadow Banking Monitoring Report. Basel: FSB, report to G7, Nov. 14.

Finley, M. (1973). The Ancient Economy: Sather Classics Lectures, Vol, 43. Berkeley: The University of California Press.

Finn, E. (2017). What Do Algorithms Want: Imagination in the Age of Computing? Cambridge, Mass: MIT Press.

Fisher, I. (1933). The debt deflation theory of the Great Depression, Econometrics, 1: 337-57.

Formisano, R. (2017). American Oligarchy: The Permanent Political Class. Urbana: University of Illinois Press.

Foroohar, R. (2016). Makers and Takers: The Rise of Finance and the Decline of Business. New York: Crown.

Forrester, J. (1971). Counterintuitive behavior of social systems, Technology Review 73 (3): 52–68

Forrester, S. and M. Mitchell (2016). Adaptive computation: The Multidisciplinary legacy of John H. Holland. Communications of ACM, 59 (8): 58-63.

Freeman, E. (1991). Business Ethics: The State of the Art. Volume 1. London: Oxford University Press.

Friedman, M. (1953). Essays in Positive Economics. Chicago: University of Chicago Press.

_____ (1970). The social responsibility of business is to increase profits, New York Times Magazine (September, 13).

Gaffney, M., F. Harrison, and K. Feder (1994). The Corruption of Economics. London: Shepheard-Walwyn Ltd.

Galbraith, J. K. (1953). American Capitalism: The concept of Countervailing Power. Boston: Houghton Mifflin.

Galloway, S. (2017). The Four: The Hidden DNA of Amazon, Apple, Facebook and Google. New York: Portfolio Press.

Gammon, E. (2017). Narcissistic rage and neoliberal reproduction. Global Society 31(4): 510-550.

Gardiner, S. (2001). The Real tragedy of the commons. Philosophy and Public Affairs 30(4): 387-416.

Gare, A. (2002). Human ecology and public policy: Overcoming the hegemony of economics. Democracy & Nature, 8(1): 131-141.

Gebru, T., J. Krause, Y. Wang, D. Chen, J. Deng, E. Aiden, and U. Fei-Fei (2017). Using deep learning and Google Street View to estimate the demographic make-up of neighborhoods across the United States, PNAS, 114 (50): 1308-13113.

Gehl, K. and M. Porter (2017). Why Competition in the Politics Industry is Failing America: A Strategy for Reinvigorating our Democracy. Boston: Harvard Business School.

George, H. (1879). Progress and Poverty: An Inquiry into the Cause of Industrial Depressions and of Increase of Want with Increase of Wealth. New York: Appleton and Company.

_____ (1897). The New Science of Political Economy. New York: Doubleday and McClure and Company.

Georgescu-Roegen, N. (1982). The Crisis in natural resources: Its Nature and unfolding, In G. Daneke, Energy, Economics, and the Environment: Toward a Comprehensive Perspective. Boston: Lexington Books. Pp. 9-24.

Gibson, A. (2004). Whatever happened to the economic interpretation: Beard's thesis and the legacy of empirical analysis, Working Paper, presented at the Midwest Political Science Association Meeting, Chicago.

Ginsberg, B. (2013). The Fall of the Faculty: The Rise of the All-Administrative University and why it Matters. Oxford: The Oxford University Press.

Gintis, H., S. G. Bowles, S. G., R. Boyd, and E. Fehr, Eds. (2005). Moral Sentiments and Material Interests: The Foundations of Cooperation in Economic Life (Cambridge, MA: MIT Press.

Giroux, P. (2017). Gangster capitalism and nostalgic authoritarianism in Trump's America, Salon (Dec. 3).

Glassman, J. (2006). Primitive accumulation, accumulation by dispossession, accumulation by extra-economic means, Progress in Human Geography, 30(5): 608-625.

Golumbia, D. (2016). The Politics of Bitcoin: Software as Right-wing Extremism. Minneapolis: University of Minnesota Press.

Goodfellow, I. Y, Bengio, and A. Courtville (2016). Deep Learning, Cambridge, MA: MIT Press.

Gordon, S. (1999). The Development of constitutional government and countervailance theory in seventeenth-century England. In: Controlling the State: Consitutionalism from Ancient Athens to Today. Cambridge, MA: Harvard University Press, pp. 223-283.

Gould, S. and E. Vrba (1982). Exaptation: A missing term in the science of form, Paleobiology. 8(1): 4-15.

Graeber, D. (2014). Debt: The First 5000 Years. New York: Melville House.

Greene, R. (2016). Understanding cocos: What operational concerns &global trends mean for U.S. policymakers. Working Paper, Cambridge, MA: Mossavar-Rahmani Center for Business and Government, JFK School.

Haider, C. (1934). Do We Want Fascism? Studies in Fascism, Ideology and Practice. New York: John Day.

Haldane A. and R. May (2010). Systemic risk in the banking ecosystem, Nature, 469 (Jan.): 351-355.

Hall, C. and K. Klitgaard (2011). Energy and the Wealth of Nations: Understanding the Biophysical Economy. Berlin: Springer Science & Media.

Haque, U. (2018a). Why we're underestimating American collapse, Eudaimonia and Company. Jan.25. https://eand.co/

_____ (2018b). Three hard truths about American collapse, Eudaimonia and Company, August 11. https://eand.co/

Hardin, G. (1968). The Tragedy of the commons, Science, 162: 1243-1248.

Hartmann, D., M. Guevara, C. Jara-Figueroa, M. Aristara, and S. Hidalgo. (2017). Linking economic complexity, institutions, and income inequality, World Development, 93: 75-93.

Harvey, D. (2003). The New Imperialism. London: Oxford University Press.

Hathaway, I. and Muro, M. (2016) Tracking the gig economy. Brooking Report. Oct. 13.

Hayek, F. (1944). The Road to Serfdom. Chicago: The University Press.

Heller, M. (2007). The Gridlock Economy. New York: Basic Books.

Henrich, J., R. Boyd, S. Bowles, H. Gintis, E. Fehr, C. Camerer, R. McElreath, M. Gurven, K. Hill, A. Barr, J. Ensminger, D. Tracer, F. Marlow, J. Patton, M. Alvard, F. Gil-White and N. Smith (2005), Economic man in cross-cultural perspective: Behavioral experiments from 15 small-scale societies. Behavioral and Brain Sciences, 28 (4): 795-815.

Henry, J.F. (1990). John Locke, property rights and economic theory, Journal of Economic issues, 33(3): 609-624.

Helbing, D., B. Frey, G. Gigerenzer, E. Hafen, M. Hager, Y. Hofstetter, J. van den Hoven, R. Zicari, A. Zwitter (2017). Will democracy survive big data and artificial intelligence? Scientific American, Feb. 25.

Henrich, J. (2006). The Evolution of cooperative institutions: Tracking the problem of equilibrium selection, Science, 312(1): 60-61.

Hildyard, N. (2007). A Crumbling Wall of Money: Financial Bricolage, Derivatives, and Power. London: The Corner House.

Hobbes, T. (1651). Leviathan or the Matter, Form, and Power of Commonwealth Ecclesiastical and Civil. Oxford: The University Press.

Hodgson, G. (2007). A Revival of Veblenian institutional economics. Journal of Economic Issues. XLI (2): 325-341.

Hodgson, G. (2015). Conceptualizing Capitalism: Institutions, Evolution, and Future. Chicago: University of Chicago Press.

Holling, C.S. (1973). Resilience and stability of ecological systems, Annual Review of Ecology and Systematics. 4: 1-23.

Hooke, J. and K. Yook (2017). The Curious year-to-year performance of buyout fund returns: Another mark-to-market problem. Journal of Private Equity, (Winter): 1-11.

Horner, J. and J. Martinez (1997), Thorstein Veblen and Henry George on war, conflict, and the military: An Institutionalist connection, Journal of Economic Issues 31(2), 633-639.

Hühn, M. and Dierksmeier, C. (2016). Will the real Adam Smith please stand up? Journal of Business Ethics, 136 (1): 119-132.

Hunt, T. and C. Lipo (2006). Late colonization of Easter Island. Science 311(5767): 1603-1606.

_____ (2009). Revisiting Rapa Nui (Easter Island) ecocide. Pacific Science 63: 601-616.

Huxley, A. (1958). Brave New World Revisited. New York: Harper Collins.

Jacobs, J. (1992). Systems of Survival: A Dialogue on the Moral Foundations of Commerce. New York; Random House.

Jantsch, E. (1975). Design for Evolution: Self-organization and Planning. New York: Braziller.

Jantsch, E. (1980). The Self-organizing Universe: The Scientific and Human Implications of the Emerging Paradigm of Evolution. Oxford: Pergamon.

Järvensivu, P., T. Toivanen, T. Vadén, V. Lähde, A. Majava, J. Eronen (2018). Transformation: The Economy, Working Paper. BIOS Research Unit, and University of Helsinki.

Jevons, W. (1862). A General Mathematical Theory of Political Economy. London: Edward Stanford.

Just, D. (2013). An Introduction to Behavioral Economics. New York: Wiley.

Kagan, R. (2016). This is how fascism comes to America. The Washington Post. May 18.

Kahneman, D., J. Knetsch, and R. Thaler (1986). Fairness and the assumptions of economics, Journal of Business, 59(4): S285-S300.Kava, G. (1983). Hobbes's war of all against all, Ethics, 93 (Jan.): 291-310.

Kaufmann, E. (2017). Complexity and nationalism, Nations and Nationalism, 23 (1): 6-27.

Keen, S. (2001). Debunking Economics: The Naked Emperor of the Social Sciences. London: Zed Books.

Kennedy, G. (2005). Adam Smith's Lost Legacy. London: Palgrave Macmillan.

Kelton, S. (2001). The role of the state and the hierarchy of money, Cambridge Journal of Economics, 25 (1): 149-163

Keynes, J. M. (1936).A General Theory of Employment, Interest and Money. London: Palgrave Macmillan.

King, M. (2016). The End of Alchemy: Money, Banking, and the Future of the Global Economy. New York: W.W. Norton.

Kinzer, S. (2017). The True Flag: Theordore Roosevelt, Mark Twain, and the Birth of American Empire. New York: Henry Holt.

Kirilenko, G. and A. Lo (2013). Moore's law versus Murphy's Law: Algorithmic Trading and its discontents. Journal of Economic Perspectives, 27(3): 51-72

Kobrin, S. J. (1998). Back to the future: Neomedivalism and the postmodern global economy. Journal of international Affairs, (Spring): 361-386.

Korowicz, D. (2012). Trade-Off: The Financial Systems Supply Chain-Contagion: A Study in Global Systemic Collapse. Research Report, Metis Risk Consulting. June, 30.

Korten, D. (2009). Agenda for a New Economy: From Phantom Wealth to Real Wealth. San Francisco: Berret-Koehler.

_____ (2018). Three questions to lead us away from self-extinction. Yes (July). https://www.yesmagazine.org/

Kosman, J. (2009). The Buyout of America: How Private Equity is destroying Jobs and Killing the American Economy. New York: Penguin.

Koster, A. (2013). An Institutional Approach to Understanding Energy Transitions. Ph.D. Dissertation, School of Human Evolution and Social Change, Arizona State University.

Kozubek, J. (2016). Modern Prometheus: Editing the Human Genome with Crispr-Cas9. Cambridge: Cambridge University Press.

Krippner, G. (2005). The Financialization of the American economy, Socio-economic Review, 3 (1): 173-208.

Krueger, A. (2017). Where have all the workers gone: An inquiry into the decline of the US labor force participation rate, Working Paper. Princeton University and NBER,

Krugman, P. (2014). We are in a new Gilded Age. New York Times, May 8.

_____ (2018). Good enough for government work? Macroeconomics since the crisis, Oxford Review of Economic Policy, 34 (1-2): 156-168.

Kuhn, T. (1962). On the Structure of Scientific Revolutions. Chicago: University of Chicago Press.

Kurz, M. (2017). On the formation of capital and wealth. Working Paper, Economics Department, Stanford University. 1-48.

Labanca, N. Ed. (2017). Complex Systems and Social Practices in Energy Transitions. New York: Springer.

Land, N. (2012). The Dark Enlightenment, http://www.thedarkenlightenment.com/.

Lasch, C. (1979). The Culture of Narcissism: American Life in an Age of Diminishing Expectations. New York: W.W. Norton.

_____ (1994). The Revolt of the Elites and the Betrayal of Democracy. New York: W.W. Norton.

Lasker, G. Ed (1981). Applied Systems and Cybernetics: Vol. 1 Quality of life: Systems Approaches. New York: Pergamon Press.

Latour, B. (1993). We Have Never Been Modern. Cambridge, MA: Harvard University Press.

Layton, L. (2014). Some psychic effects of neoliberalism: Narcissism, disavowal, perversion. Psychoanalysis, Culture & Society, 19(2): 161-178

Lawson, T. (2003). Reorienting Economics, London: Routledge.

Lazonick, W. (2018). The new normal is "maximizing shareholder value": Predatory value extraction, slowing productivity, and the vanishing American middle class, International Journal of Political Economy, 46 (4): 217-226.

LeGuin, U. (1974). The Dispossessed: An Ambiguous Utopia. Harper & Row.

Lemma, V. (2015). The Shadow Banking System. London: Macmillan.

Lemov, P. (2012). The case for a state owned bank. Governing, (April). 1-3

Lepers, E. (2018). The Neutrality illusion: Biased economics, biased training, and monetary policy, testing the role of ideology on the FOMC voting behavior, New Political Economy, 23(1): 105-127.

Lester, R. and D. Hart (2013). Unlocking Energy Innovation: How America Can Build a Low-cost and Low-carbon System. Cambridge, MA: MIT Press.

Levitsky, S. and D. Ziblatt (2018). How Democracies Die. New York: Crown.

Lewis, M. (2011). The Big Short: Inside the Doomsday Machine. New York: W. W. Norton.

_____ (2017). Why the scariest nuclear threat may be coming from inside the White House, Vanity Fair (July, 26).

Li, D. (2000). On Default correlation: A Copula function approach, Journal of Fixed Income, 9 (4): 43–54.

Lietaer, B. (2013). Lecture on Money at the European Journalist Centre, https://www.youtube.com/watch?time_continue=14&v=amvZShTh pg0

Locke, J. (1689). Two Treatises of Government. London: Awnsham Churchill.

Lopez-Iturriaga, F. and I. Sanz (2017). Predicting public corruption with neural networks: An Analysis of Spanish provinces, Social Indicators Research (November, 22), 1-24.

MacLean, N. (2017). Democracy in Chains: The Deep History of the Radical Right's Stealth Plan for America. New York: Viking.

Madrick, J. (2014). Seven Bad Ideas: How Mainstream Economists Damaged America and the World. New York: Vintage.

Magliocca, G. (2018). The Heart of the Constitution: How the Bill of Rights Became the Bill of Rights. New York: Oxford University Press.

Mallaby, S. (2010). More Money than God: Hedge Funds and the Making of a New Elite. New York: Council on Foreign Relations.

Marcuse, H. (1964). One Dimensional Man: Studies in the Ideology of Advanced Industrial Society. Boston: Beacon Press.

Mauss, M. (1954). The Gift: The Form and Reason of Exchange in Archaic Societies. London: Routledge.

May, R., S. Levin, and G. Sugihara (2007). Complex systems: Ecology for bankers, Nature, 451, 893-5.

Mayer, J. (2016). Dark Money: The Hidden History of the Billionaires behind the Rise of the Radical Right. New York: Doubleday.

Mayhew, A. (2018). An introduction to institutional economics: Tools for understanding evolving economies, The American Economist, 63(1): 3-17

Mazzucato, M. (2011). The Entrepreneurial State. London: Demos.

McCumber, J. (2016). Philosophy Scare: The Politics of Reason in the Early Cold War. Chicago: The University Press.

McLeay, M. Radil, A. and R. Thomas (2014). Money creation and the modern economy. The Bank of England Quarterly Bulletin, Q1: 14-27.

McNeill, John. (2016). How fascist is Donald Trump? There is actually a formula for that. Washington Post. Oct. 21.

Meadows, D., D. Meadows, J. Randers, and W. Behrens. (1972) The Limits to Growth. New York: Universe Books.

Mehrling, P. (2011). Fischer Black and the Revolutionary Idea of Finance. New York: Wiley.

Melman, S. (1988). The Demilitarized Society: Disarmament and Conversion. New York: Harvest House.

Metz, R. (2018). Social networks are broken. This man wants to fix them. Connectivity. (Feb.).

Mihalyi, P. and I. Szelényi (2017). The Role of rents in the transition from socialist redistributive economies to market capitalism. Comparative Sociology.16 (1): 13-38.

Mills, C.W. (1956). The Power Elite. Oxford: The University Press.

Minsky, H. (1987). Can It Happen Again: Essays on Instability and Finance? London: Routledge.

_____ (1992). The Financial instability hypothesis, Working Paper 74, Levy Economics Institute of Bard College, CUNY.

Mirowski, P. (1991). More Heat Than Light: Economics as Social Physics, Physics as Nature's Economics. London: Cambridge University Press.

_____ (2013). Never Let a Serious Crisis Go to Waste: How Neoliberalism Survived the Financial Meltdown. New York: Verso.

Mitchell, B., L. R. Wray, and M. Watts (2016). Modern Monetary Theory and Practice: An Introductory Text. Seattle: CreateSpace, Amazon.

MGI. (2016). Independent Work: Choice, Necessity, and the Gig Economy. San Francisco: McKinsey Global Institute.

Moore, S. (2015). Visions of Sustainable Energy Transformations: Integrating Power and Politics in the Mediterranean Region. Ph.D. Dissertation. School of Human Evolution and Social Change. Arizona State University.

Motesharrei, S., J. Rivas, and E. Kaluay (2014). Human and nature dynamics (HANDY): Modeling inequality and use of resources in the collapse or sustainability of society. Ecological Economics, 101: 90–102.

Moyn, S, (2018). Human Rights in an Unequal World. Cambridge, MA: Harvard University Press.

Nace, T. (2003). Gangs of America: The Rise of Corporate Power and Disabling of Democracy. San Francisco: Berret-Koehler.

Naughton, J. (2017). Why we need a 21st-century Martin Luther to challenge the church of tech. The Guardian, Oct. 29.

Nussbaum, M. and A, Sen Eds (1993). The Quality of Life. New York: Oxford University Press.

OECD (2018). The Broken Elevator? How to Promote Social Mobility. Paris: Organization for Economic Development.

Olson, M. (1965). The Logic Collective Action: Public Good and the Theory of Groups. Cambridge, MA: Harvard University Press.

_____ (1982). The Rise and Decline and Decline of Nations (New Haven: Yale University Press.

_____ (2000). Power and Prosperity: Outgrowing Communist and Capitalist Dictatorships. New York: Basic Books.

Orlov, D. (2006). Closing the collapse Gap: the USSR was better prepared for collapse than the US. Resilience, Dec. 4.

Orren, K. (1991). Belated Feudalism: Labor, the Law, and Liberal Development in the United States. Cambridge: Cambridge University Press.

Orwell, G. (1944). On the origin of property in land. Tribune (August 18).

_____ (1949). Nine-teen Eighty-four. London: Secker & Warburg.

Ostrom, E. (1990). Governing the Commons: The Evolution of Institutions for Collective Action. Cambridge: Cambridge University Press.

OTA (1980). Impact of Advanced Air Transport Technology. Washington

Pasquale, F. (2016). The Black Box Society: The Secret Algorithms that Control Money and information. Cambridge, Mass: Harvard University Press.

Paul, R. (2015). Swords into Plowshares: A Life in Wartime and a Future of Peace and Prosperity. Clute, TX: Ron Paul Institute.

Patterson, S. (2010). Quants: How a New Breed of Math Whizzes Conquered Wall Street and Nearly Destroyed It. New York: Crown Business.

Peet, R, P. Robbins, and M. Watts. Eds (2011). Global Political Ecology. New York: Routledge.

Pein, C. (2014). Mouthbreathing Machiavellis dream of a silicon Reich. The Baffler (May 19) https://thebaffler.com/.

Perkins, J. (2004). Confessions of an Economic Hit Man. San Francisco: Berret-Koehler.

Phalippou, L. (2017). Private Equity Laid Bare. Seattle: Amazon CreateSpace.

Pickett K. and R. Wilkinson (2007). Child wellbeing and income inequality in rich societies: Ecological cross sectional study. Business Medical Journal, 335(7629): 1080-1085

Piketty, T. (2014). Capital the Twenty-First Century. Cambridge, MA: Belknap/Harvard University Press.

_____ (2018). Brahmin left vs. merchant right: Rising inequality & the changing structure of political conflict (evidence from France, Britain and the US 1948-2017). Working Paper Series No 2018/7, World Inequality Lab.

Pimentel, D. (2011). World population, Environment, Development, & Sustainability, December: DOI, 10, 1007/s10668-011-9336-2.

Pizzo, S., M. Fricker, and P. Muolo (1989). Inside Job: The Looting of America's Savings and Loans. New York: McGraw-Hill.

Plotkin, S. (2010). War and economic crisis: What would Veblen say? Society, 47: 240-245.

Polanyi, K. (1944). The Great Transformation: The Political and Economic Origins of Our Time. London: Farrar and Rinehart.

Posner, E. and G. Weyl (2018). Radical Markets: Uprooting Capitalism and Democracy for a Just Society. Princeton: Princeton University Press.

Powell, L. (1971). Attack on the American Free Enterprise System. Richman: Memo sent to US Chamber of Commerce.

Prigogine, I. (1980). From Being To Becoming. San Francisco: W.H. Freeman.

Putnam, R. (1995). Bowling Alone: The Collapse and Revival of American Community. New York: Simon & Schuster.

Quigley, C. (1966). Tragedy and Hope: A History of the World in Our Time. New York: MacMillan.

Rainie, L. and J. Anderson (2017). Code-Dependent: Pros and Cons of the Algorithmic Age. Wash. D.C.: The Pew Research Center.

Ramo, J. C. (2016). The Seventh Sense: Power, Fortune and Survival in the Age of Networks. New York, Little Brown.

Rawls, J. (1971). A Theory of Justice. Cambridge, MA: Harvard University Press.

Read J. (2009). A Genealogy of homo-economicus: Neoliberalism and the production of subjectivity. Foucault Studies 6 (Feb.): 25-36.

Ricardo, D. (1817). The Principles of Political Economy and Taxation. London: John Murray).

Robinson, W. and M. Barrera (2012). Global capitalism and twenty-first century fascism: a US case study. Race & Class, 53 (3): 4-29.

Rodrik, D. (2017). Straight Talk on Trade: Ideas for a Sane Economy. Princeton: University Press.

Rojer, R. (2014). The World according to Modern Monetary Theory, The New Inquiry (April 11).

Roosevelt, F. (1944). State of the Union Address to Congress, January 11.

Rossiter, C. (1953). Seedtime of the Republic: The Origins of the American Tradition of Political Liberty. New York: Harcourt Brace.

Ruhl, J. (2016). Financial complexity: Regulating regulation, Science, 352 (6283): 301.

Rushkoff, D. (2018). Survival of the richest: The wealthy are plotting to leave us. Future Human, via Medium (July, 5): 1-6.Russell, B. (1938) Power: The Role of Man's Will to Power in the World's Economic and Political Affairs. New York; W.W. Norton.

Sabine, G. (1929). Cicero on the Commonwealth. Indianapolis: Dobbs-Merrill.

Salvemini, G. (1936). Under the Axe of Fascism. London: Victor Gollancz. (1936)

Scheidel. W. (2017) The Great Leveler: Violence and the History of Inequality from the Stone Age to the Twenty-first Century. Princeton: The Princeton University Press.

Schlaile, M., M. Mueller, M. Schramm, and A. Pyka (2018) Evolutionary economics, responsible innovation and demand: Making a case for the role of consumers. Philosophy of Management, 17: 7-39.

Schlesinger, A.M. (1973). The Imperial Presidency. New York: Houghton Mifflin.

Schumacher, E. F. (1973). Small is Beautiful: Economics as If People Mattered. London: Harper Collins.

Schumpeter, J. (1934). The Theory of Economic Development. Cambridge: Harvard University Press.

_____ (1942). Capitalism, Socialism, and Democracy. New York: Harper and Brothers.

Schwarcz, S. (2013). Ring-Fencing. Southern California Law Review. 87: 69-109.

Scott, J. (2017). Going Against the Grain: a Deep History of the Earliest States. New haven: Yale University Press.

Seabrook, J. (2002). Sustainable development is a hoax we cannot have it all, The Guardian (August 4). http://www.theguardian.com/environment.

Sergueiva, A. (2013). Systemic risk, modeling, analysis, and monitoring: An Integrated approach. Working Paper, Financial Computing Group, Department of Computer Science, University College London.

Sheridan, B. (2007). The 600 trillion derivatives market. Newsweek World, Oct 17.

Shippen, N. (2014) The Decolonization of Time: Work, Leisure, and Freedom. New York: Palgrave-Macmillan.

Sicard, G. (2015). The Origins of Corporations: The Mills of Toulouse in the Middle-Ages. New Haven: Yale University Press.

Skidmore. M. and A. Henion (2017). Press Release, East Lansing, Michigan State University. Dec. 11.

Slee, T. (2017). What's Yours is Mine: Against the Sharing Economy. New York: OR Books.

Slobodian, Q. (2018). Globalists: The End of Empire and the Birth of Neoliberalism. Cambridge, MA: Harvard University Press.

Smith, A. (1759). The Theory of the Moral Sentiments. Edinburgh: Kincaid and Bell.

_____ (1776). An Inquiry into the Nature and Causes of the Wealth of Nations. London: Strahan and Cadell.

Smith, E. (2010). Econned: How Unenlightened Self Interest Undermined Democracy and Corrupted Capitalism. New York: Palgrave Macmillan.

Smith, R. (2016). Green Capitalism: The God that Failed. Glen Allen, VA. College Publishing.

Smith-Nonini, S. (2016). The Role of corporate oil and energy debt in creating the Neoliberal era, Economic Anthropology. 3(1): 57-67.

Soddy, F. (1925). Wealth, Virtual Wealth, and Debt: The Solution to the Economic Paradox. London: George Routledge and Sons.

_____ (1934). The Role of Money: What it should be in Contrast to what it has become. London: George Allen & Unwin.

Standing. G. (2011). The Precariat: The New Dangerous Class. London Bloomsbury Academic.

_____ (2014). The Precariat Charter: From Denizens to Citizens. London: Bloomsbury Academic.

Standish, C. (2017), the Evolution of Human Co-operation: Ritual and Social Complexity in Stateless Societies. Cambridge: Cambridge University Press).

Stiglitz, J. (2017). America has a monopoly problem---and it's huge. The Nation, Oct. 23.

_____ (2018). Where modern macroeconomics went wrong. Oxford Review of Economic Policy, 34 (1-2): 70-106.

Stoller, M. (2017). Lawyers and monopoly power. Harvard Law Forum. https://www.youtube.com/watch?time_continue=2637&v=xM9GMGDsKUU

Stucke, M. and A. Ezrachi (2017). The rise, fall, rebirth of the US antitrust movement. Harvard Business Review (Dec., 15).

Sussman, R. W. (2014) The Myth of Race: The Troubling Persistence of an Unscientific Idea. Cambridge: Harvard University Press.

Sutton, A. (1976). Wall Street and the Rise of Hitler. New York: GSG.

Taleb, N. (2007). The Black Swan: the Impact of the Highly Improbable. New York: Random House.

Tarbell, I. (1904). The History of the Standard Oil Company. New York: First Rate Publishers.

Taylor, Q. (2010). Thomas Hobbes, political economist: His changing historical fortunes. The Independent Review. 14(3): 415-433.

Tcherneva, P. (2015). When a rising tide sinks most boats: Trends in US income inequality. Policy Note 4, Levy Economics Institute of Band College.

Teachout, Z. (2014). Corruption in American: From Benjamin Franklin's Stuff Box to Citizens United. Cambridge, MA: Harvard University Press.

Thompson, J. (2016). A new more dangerous Sagebrush Rebellion. High Country News. (Feb., 10).

Tolkien, J. R. R. (1937) The Hobbit. London: George Allen and Unwin.

_____ (1954/1968) The Lord of the Rings, Complete Trilogy Volume. London: George Allen and Unwin.

Twenge, J. (2006). Generation Me: Why Today's Young Americans Are More Confident, Assertive, Entitled--and More Miserable Than Ever Before. New York: The Free Press.

Twenge J. and K. Campbell (2009) The Narcissism Epidemic: Living in the Age of Entitlement. New York: The Free Press.

Twenge, J. (2017). IGen: Why Today's Super-Connected Kids Are Growing Up Less Rebellious, More Tolerant, Less Happy--and Completely Unprepared for Adulthood--and What That Means for the Rest of Us. New York: Atria Books.

UN (1992). Agenda 21, United Nations Conference on Development and Environment, Rio de Janerio, June 3-14.

Unger, C. (2017) Trump's Russian laundromat, The New Republic. July 13.

Vaughn, K. (2012) John Locke: Economist and Social Scientist. Chicago: University of Chicago Press.

Veblen, T. (1898). Why economics is not an evolutionary science. Quarterly Journal of Economics. 12(4): 373-397.

_____ (1899). The Theory of the Leisure Class. New York: MacMillan.

_____ (1904). The Theory of Business Enterprise. New York: Charles Scribner's and Sons.

_____ (1917). An Inquiry into the Nature of Peace and the Terms of Its Perpetuation, New York: MacMillan.

_____ (1919). The Vested Interests and the Common Man. New York: B.W. Huebsch.

_____ (1923). Absentee Ownership and Business Enterprise in Recent Times: The Case of America. New York: B.W. Huebsch.

Venugopal, R (2015). Neoliberalism as concept, Economy and Society, 44 (2): 165-187.

Vincent, J. (2017). Former Facebook exec says social media is ripping apart society. The Verge, (Dec. 11).

Wallace, H. (2017). American fascism in 1944 and today. New York Times, (May, 12).

Wallace, R. (2017). The Signature of risk: Agent-based models, Boolean networks and economic vulnerability. Economic Thought, 6(1): 1-15.

Weithman, P. (2016) In Defense of a political liberalism, Philosophy & Public Affairs, 45(4): 397-412.

Welsh, I. (2015). Serfdom is better than what the West is heading for. Ian Welsh Blog. www.ianwelsh. Com. March 20.

White, L. (1943). Energy and the evolution of culture. American Anthropologist, 45 (3): 335-356.

White, R. (2011). Railroaded: The Transcontinentals and the Making of America. New Tork: W. W. Norton.

Williams, E. (2010). In the land of the blind the one-eyed are king: How financial economics contributed to the collapse of 2008-2009. Journal of Post-Keynesian Economics 34 (1): 3-23.

Williamson, O. (1985). The Economic Institutions of Capitalism: Firms, Markets and Relational Contracting. New York: The Free Press.

Wilmott, P. (2017). How a Financial Transaction Tax would benefit us all. Davos: World Economic Forum, https://www.weforum.org/agenda/05/22.

Wine, M. (2016). Inside the conservative push to rewrite the constitution. New York Times (August 22).

Winkler, A. (2018). We the Corporations: How American Business Won Their Civil Rights. New York: W.W. Norton.

Winningham, E. (2018). The bond market doesn't control anything; currency-issuing national government does. MMT and Modern Macroeconomics (June 11). http://elliswinningham.net/index.php/2018/06/11

Witzling, D. (2016). Financial complexity: Accounting for fraud. Science, 352 (6283): 301

Wolin, S. (2007). Democracy Incorporated: Managed Democracy and the Specter of Inverted Totalitarianism. Princeton: The University Press.

Wray, L.R. (2009). Job guarantee. New Economic Perspectives, (August 23).

Zajac, E. (1995). The Political Economy of Fairness. Cambridge: MIT Press.